State Violence and Legal Accountability

This book pursues a critical perspective on the phenomenon of state violence and its legal unaccountability.

Focusing on the role of myths, assumptions and ghosts that surround the meaning of the state and performance of state violence, this book details a fresh perspective on that violence and its legal unaccountability. It asks: How does our understanding of the state reflect on the political demands and legal processes of accountability? To pursue this question, the book traces the political and legal aftermath of the police killing of a 14-year-old boy, Berkin Elvan, during the nationwide Gezi protests of the summer of 2013 in Turkey. Countering imaginaries of the state clash between the state officer's attempt to attribute personal responsibility to Elvan for his own death and public demands for state accountability. Meanwhile, the prolonged legal process ensures that subjects who seek accountability find themselves in a long and exhausting legal battle which dominates their lives and transforms their subjectivity. As the Elvan family continues to wait for accountability and justice, this book suggests that waiting and suspense are key elements of legal performance in trials concerning state violence. As such, and unlike the usual reading of legal violence, which focuses on judgement, the book explores how this violence – and its implications for an understanding of justice and accountability – is bound to the very act of waiting.

This critical interdisciplinary study of state violence and its legal handling will appeal to scholars and students from a wider range of disciplines including law, criminology, politics, sociology and political and legal philosophy.

Ceylan Begüm Yıldız is Lecturer in Law at School of Law and Criminology, University of Greenwich, UK.

State Violence and Legal Accountability

The Wait for Justice

Ceylan Begüm Yıldız

Routledge
Taylor & Francis Group
a GlassHouse Book

First published 2025
by Routledge
4 Park Square, Milton Park, Abingdon, Oxon OX14 4RN

and by Routledge
605 Third Avenue, New York, NY 10158

Routledge is an imprint of the Taylor & Francis Group, an informa business

A GlassHouse book

British Library Cataloguing-in-Publication Data
A catalogue record for this book is available from the British Library

Library of Congress Cataloging-in-Publication Data
Names: Begüm Yıldız, Ceylan, author.
Title: State violence and legal accountability: the wait for justice / Ceylan Begüm Yıldız.
Description: Abingdon, Oxon [UK]; New York, NY: Routledge, 2025. |
Includes bibliographical references and index.
Identifiers: LCCN 2024046287 (print) | LCCN 2024046288 (ebook) |
ISBN 9781032690018 (hardback) | ISBN 9781032690131 (paperback) |
ISBN 9781032690070 (ebook)
Subjects: LCSH: Government liability–Turkey. | Justice, Administration
of–Turkey–History–21st century. | State-sponsored terrorism–Law and
legislation–Turkey. | Protest movements–Turkey–History–21st century. |
Turkey–History–Gezi Park Protests, 2013. | Turkey–Politics and
government–21st century. | Elvan, Berkin, 1999–2014.
Classification: LCC KKX2850 .B44 2025 (print) | LCC KKX2850 (ebook) |
DDC 342.56108/8–dc23/eng/20241008
LC record available at https://lccn.loc.gov/2024046287
LC ebook record available at https://lccn.loc.gov/2024046288

ISBN: 9781032690018 (hbk)
ISBN: 9781032690131 (pbk)
ISBN: 9781032690070 (ebk)

DOI: 10.4324/9781032690070

Typeset in Sabon
by Deanta Global Publishing Services, Chennai, India

To Berkin Elvan, and to all others whose lives were cut short by the ones who kill on behalf of the state.

Contents

Acknowledgements

This book was researched and written during challenging times: countless state killings, protests, legal intimidation and the global rise of authoritarianism. It has been painful to witness the endless cycle of state violence and unaccountability. As the list of those who lost their lives at the hands of the ones who acclaim the state and its killing powers perpetually grows, it is becoming harder to pause, reflect, grieve and act for justice and accountability after each loss. At times, I felt lost and defeated against the state and its violence. This book could not have happened without the guidance and support of many colleagues, friends and comrades who deserve mentioning.

This book is a product of my PhD research at Birkbeck College, School of Law. I am grateful to my MA supervisor, Turgut Tarhanlı, for introducing me to critical legal scholarship and Costas Douzinas for welcoming me to the Birkbeck, School of Law. I am forever thankful to my supervisors, Başak Ertür and Elena Loizidou, for their endless support and continuing guidance. I thank them for their generous engagement with my work, for all the thought-provoking discussions and for allowing me to discover my own voice at my own pace. I am fortunate to work closely with such exceptional scholars whose wisdom, kindness and wit will forever be my inspiration. I am indebted to Birkbeck's commitment to critical thinking and creativity and lucky to have met with ground-breaking scholars whose work dares to dream of another future in these troubling times. I will cherish the memories of heavy debating at the reading groups organised by Peter Fitzpatrick and the memories of Drucilla Cornell; I am thankful for her generous curiosity towards my work at Birkbeck's Critical Theory Summer School. I am lucky to have the support of the critical legal community, especially when I feel out of place within the borders of black-letter law. I thank the colleagues and comrades at the Critical Legal Conference and Nomos Research Centre for constantly provoking my intellectual curiosity and creativity. I am especially indebted to Penny Green, Illan rua Wall and Tarik Kochi for encouraging me to publish my research. I am grateful to Routledge editors Collin Perrin and Naomi Round Cahalin for their meticulous editorial work. I would like to thank Carrie Hamilton for her careful reading of the earlier version of this book and for rendering my thoughts intelligible.

I extend my gratitude to the lawyers of the Elvan family, Can Atalay, Çiğdem Akbulut, Akçay Taşlı and Deniz Özen for patiently responding to every single request of mine while grappling with the legal farce. As I am writing these words, Can Atalay is still in prison with ridiculous charges against him. While his imprisonment exposes the fallacies of law, he continues to demand justice and accountability from behind bars. His stubborn persistence to expose state violence and advocate for accountability and justice illuminates this work.

While researching for this book, state violence in the form of legal violence exceeded borders and extended to more than a thousand Turkey-affiliated scholars around the globe who dared to challenge it with a petition, me included. Although the ones living outside the borders of Turkey were relatively safe and secure, the legal process and prosecutions hung over our heads like the sword of Damocles. This gave birth to a global network of resistance and solidarity, which, after some painful years, delivered everyone's acquittals. Although the legal battle to return to academic positions continutes for those within Turkey, *Academics for Peace* is one of the significant victories against state violence and legal intimidation in recent years. I am extremely fortunate to be surrounded by incredibly supportive and caring friends during this difficult time. Alexandra König, Grietje 'River' Baars, Ana Rita Tiene Grotta, Marianna Fernandes and Milo van der Maaden, whose presence and support allowed me to continue. I must thank Eirini Avramopoulou for her wisdom, Rüzgar Buski for his constant companionship and Richard Braude for being a refuge when I was not welcomed in my home country. I am forever grateful to Tar Schreiber for entering my life while concluding this book, for their brilliant contributions and for introducing joy and fantasy into my life.

I am also incredibly lucky to be haunted by the loving memories of Burak Özgüner, Ali Arıkan, Boysan Yakar and Zeliş Deniz, who taught me the art of being an unruly woman.

Above all, I thank my family, and especially my mother, Yasemin Dorken, and my grandparents, Sürreyya Dorken and Öznur Dorken, for their endless love and support.

Introduction

'We will bring justice to Berkin Elvan', said the masked face on the news. What had begun as a mundane morning evolved into a remarkable day, a day to remember with a heavy heart. I was glued to the breaking news, captivated by the sparkling eyes of the masked man who was listing his group's demands as he was holding another man at gunpoint. The news reported that there was a hostage-taking incident unfolding at the Istanbul Courthouse, that militants from the Revolutionary People's Liberation Party/Front (known by the name of People's Front) had taken Mehmet Selim Kiraz hostage – at the time he was the prosecutor in charge of Berkin Elvan's case – and that negotiations were ongoing.

It was 31 March 2015. I was haunted by the sparkling eyes of the masked man, by the young and almost joyful tone of his voice. Not only was he promising justice for Berkin Elvan, he was promising a just future for the people of Turkey. He was promising revolution. What I was seeing was an animated corpse who aligned himself with death; to defend the dead, to speak on behalf of the dead until his own death. Yet he was so alive. I wished for him to be a lousy militant and cheat his approaching death. Suddenly, I was enraged; I was enraged at him for believing his death mattered more than his life. Then I was furious at the high ranks of the People's Front and organised left in Turkey; I accused them of brainwashing him, of making him believe that only his death would bring a better future. However, I soon realised my anger was misdirected. After all, their action was a response to the police killing of Berkin Elvan and the lack of accountability over his death. If this is the case, then who was to blame for the death of the People's Front militants, the prosecutor Selim Kiraz and for the death of Berkin Elvan? Is it the police officer who shot Elvan or the government which violently oppressed the Gezi protests? What about the deeply rooted political culture of state violence in Turkey? My mind drifted away from Elvan's killing to the other countless state killings in order to identify a common perpetrator: the state? But then, who is the state? And how is it possible to hold it accountable? I realised that the more I struggled to direct my curse towards a perpetrator, the more abstract the notion of state violence appeared to be ungraspable, mythical, almost ghostly.

DOI: 10.4324/9781032690070-1

As I struggled to tell apart the beginning and the end of my train of thought, the masked man continued to list the People's Front's demands with a determined tone; perhaps these associations were more transparent to him than it was to me. Essentially, the group demanded the names of the police officers who were responsible for the killing of Berkin Elvan; they wanted the police officers to confess on public television. They promised a public tribunal; they wanted to prosecute (by which they probably meant execute) the police officers in a public square. In other words, the militants called for a public spectacle of punishment, something they were already delivering by taking the prosecutor hostage. All this could have been avoided, I thought, if the investigation over Elvan's death had not stalled for two years and if the legal processes of accountability had been implemented according to legal conventions. However, I struggled to remember a single exemplary case in which the legal processes of accountability were carried out according to legal conventions, or rather according to public expectations of accountability and justice. At that point, I realised the People's Front's violent intervention was a signifier of this failure, the failure to hold those responsible to account. The hostage-taking was exposing the violence of this failure by replacing it with another violent act. Beyond its violent manifestation, the hostage-takers were demanding the implementation of the legal conventions of accountability while at the same time exposing its repetitive failure and its impossibility in the hands of the state juridical system. Thus, on the one hand, they were demanding something that had never taken place: an expectation, an assumption, a fantasy of legal mechanisms of accountability, while, on the other hand, promising to deliver it themselves.

Christina Sharpe (2016), in her work *In the Wake*, defines her work on 'Black dead and dying' as a work to 'defend the dead' (10). Although I was captivated by the sparkling eyes of a living dead person, I do not think I am capable of making such a heroic claim, as I do not believe I can speak on behalf of the dead, on behalf of Berkin Elvan and the militants Şafak Yayla and Bahtiyar Doğruyol, but I can tell their stories. Perhaps their death tells us some things, things that we, as the citizens of the modern political and legal world, and even worse as legal scholars, do not wish to hear. Their death exposes our assumptions about the state and our expectations from the law to protect us against the state's deadly manifestations, and, when needed, we expect the law to ask for answers on behalf of the dead, to hold the state accountable. However, this expectation begs the question: who is the state? Is it something separate from the people, society, or from the ones who kill on behalf of the state? What is it, then? An illusion of our own making? A feeling, a fantasy that we all share and live accordingly? A human-like subject without a material body, a ghostly matter? If so, how to explain its ghostly existence and yet its deadly effects? And finally, how is it possible to hold it to account? Following the words of Jacques Derrida (1992), 'Let us return to the thing itself, to the ghost, for this text is a ghost story' (44).

The Gezi Protests and the Killing of Berkin Elvan

This book traces the aftermath of Berkin Elvan's killing. Elvan received a deadly head injury on 16 June 2013 during the Gezi protests. These nationwide protests in the summer of 2013 originated as an act of defence against the government's plans to demolish Gezi Park, hence the name, which quickly escalated into a nationwide protest against the decade-long authoritarian rule of the Justice and Development Party (Adalet ve Kalkınma Partisi – AKP). Some called it an 'impromptu uprising' to emphasise the spontaneous nature of the protests (Yıldırım and Navaro-Yashin 2013). In every aspect, the summer 2013 protests in Turkey resembled the others within the global wave of protests which took place between the years of 2009 and 2013,[1] although each was grounded in its own social, economic and political nuances.[2] In the case of Turkey, what began as a localised peaceful occupation to save the trees at Gezi Park was transformed into a nationwide protest almost within the space of a single day as a response to the police violence directed towards the peaceful protesters at the park.[3]

Mehmet Ayvalıtaş was the first causality related to the Gezi protests. He died on 2 June 2013 when a car drove into the protesting crowds in Istanbul. The following day, Abdullah Cömert died in Hatay: he was hit by a tear gas canister during the protests.[4] On that same day, Ali İsmail Korkmaz was battered by a mob of AKP sympathisers during the protests in Eskisehir: he lost

1 There is a vast literature on the Gezi protests, covering diverging perspectives, from political analysis to performance arts. The edited collection titled *'Everywhere Taksim': Sowing the Seeds for a New Turkey at Gezi* provides a good array of analysis from various perspectives, from political economy to performance, and locates Gezi protests within the international wave of protests (see David and Toktamış 2015).

2 Cihan Tuğal (2013), in his commentary on the Gezi protests, provides a reading from a global perspective and suggests that protests in Turkey and Brazil were, to a significant degree, against rapid neo-liberal development. According to Tuğal, although the 2009–2013 global wave of protests has a common axis that is 'against commodification and authoritarianism', the case of Turkey and Brazil diverged from the rest as they were against neo-liberal development and its authoritarian implementation rather than protesting the collapse of neo-liberal policies. Thus, Tuğal adds, unlike the others, the protests in Turkey and Brazil were 'specially urban' and that '[u]rban rights issues kicked off the protests' (162). Similarly, Bethania Assy and Başak Ertür also elaborate on the special cases of Brazil and Turkey and provide a reading of neo-liberalisation policies in relation to law and resistance (see Assy and Ertür 2014). Slavoj Žižek also emphasised the distinct nature of protests in fast-growing neo-liberal economies under the title 'Trouble in Paradise' (Žižek 2013).

3 See Constanze Letsch, 'Turkey Protests Spread After Violence in Istanbul Over Park Demolition'. *The Guardian*. 1 June 2013. Accessed 19 July 2024. www.theguardian.com/world/2013/may/31/istanbul-protesters-violent-clashes-police.

4 In March 2020, police officer Ahmet Kuş was found guilty of 'probable intent to kill'. See 'Police Officer Who Shot Abdullah Cömert During Gezi Protests Arrested'. *Bianet*. 12 March 2020. Accessed 19 July 2024. https://bianet.org/english/human-rights/221288-police-officer-who-shot-abdullah-comert-during-gezi-protests-arrested.

his life a week later.[5] On 14 June, Ethem Sarısülük was shot dead by a police officer, Ahmet Şahbaz, during the protests in Ankara.[6] Medeni Yıldırım was shot dead by soldiers on 28 June in Diyarbakır at protests against the high-security military compound.[7] On 9 September, Ahmet Atakan died in Hatay during the protests.[8] On 29 September, Hasan Ferit Gedik was shot dead during protests in Istanbul by gang members who are believed to have connections with the police. [9]

On 16 June, early in the morning, Berkin Elvan was struck down by a tear gas canister on his way to a bakery in Okmeydanı, Istanbul. Elvan stayed in a coma for almost a year. He was fourteen years old when he got injured and passed away when he was fifteen on 11 March 2014. Although, for the state officials, Elvan's death was just a tragic incident, if not an exemplary consequence of his own actions, his deadly injury was a result of excessive and arbitrary police force that was used on the protesters to suppress the protests. Tear gas canisters and rubber bullets were raining down on people randomly.[10] However, it is hard to conclude that the arbitrary violence inflicted in the Gezi protest targeted victims at random. The fact that the ones who lost their life during the protest were all young men with Alevi and Kurdish working-class backgrounds indicates that some subjects are more likely to be subjected to violence by the ones who claim to act on behalf of the state.

In that regard, it is possible to observe a colonial logic within the operation of state violence in Turkey, which appears as if it were fate. Indeed, Banu Bargu (2016) reads the distribution of fatality as a form of biopolitical power of the state (32). In this regard, it is no wonder all those who lost their lives during the Gezi protests were young men from the Alevi and Kurdish

5 By April 2017, the perpetrators received various prison sentences ranging from seven months to ten years. See 'Ali İsmail Korkmaz Davasında Cezalar Açıklandı'. *CNNTürk*. 5 April 2017. Accessed 16 July 2024. www.cnnturk.com/turkiye/ali-ismail-korkmaz-davasinda-cezalar-aciklandi.

6 The officer Ahmet Şahbaz's prison sentence was converted into a merely pecuniary fine. In response, the family of Sarısülük has appealed to the Constitutional Court: see Ayça Söylemez, 'Impunity in the Case of Ethem Sarısülük Taken to Constitutional Court'. *Bianet*. 14 May 2019. Accessed 16 July 2024. https://m.bianet.org/english/law/208466-impunity-in-the-case-of-ethem-sarisuluk-taken-to-constitutional-court.

7 The first court hearing took place in October 2015. In the final hearing, the court acquitted the accused, Adem Çiftçi, on the grounds of lack of evidence. See 'Medeni Yıldırım Davası'. n.d. *FailiBelli*. Accessed 16 September 2024. www.failibelli.org/dava/medeni-yildirim-davasi/.

8 The investigation has not yet led to a trial.

9 In February 2018, the trial ended with three perpetrators sentenced to twenty-five years of imprisonment each. See Ayça Söylemez. 'Hasan Ferit Gedik Davasında Neler Yaşandı?' *Bianet*. 30 September 2019. Accessed 16 July 2024. https://bianet.org/bianet/insan-haklari/213760-hasan-ferit-gedik-davasinda-neler-yasandi

10 For a detailed account of excessive and arbitrary use of violence and impunity for police abuses, see Amnesty International (2013).

working class. Even within the context of a national uprising, we observe that state-sponsored violence (either in the forms of police violence, paramilitary or pro-state mobs and gangs) targets certain subjects and concentrates on their space of residence. Okmeydanı, where the Elvan family resides, is one of those spaces. Okmeydanı is known as a revolutionary neighbourhood. It is a predominantly Alevi and Kurdish working-class neighbourhood situated at the heart of Istanbul, just below Taksim Square, where the Gezi Park is located and the protests originated. Deniz Yonucu's (2014, 2018, 2022) work is illuminating to understand the special regime of violence inflicted upon Turkey's racialised Alevi and Kurdish population in the working-class neighbourhoods of Istanbul. Her ethnographic work, *Police, Provocation, Politics: Counterinsurgency in Istanbul* (2022), exposes how particular counterinsurgency policing strategies operate in these neighbourhoods and design the lives of their residents. As Yonucu demonstrates, the counterinsurgency policing strategies actively create an atmosphere of constant low-intensity conflict and violence in these neighbourhoods as a governing strategy (5). These practices aim to control and reorganise violence, and, in doing so, aim 'to transform political subjectivities and practices within the targeted space' (12). These neighbourhoods are constantly under police surveillance and provocation, which shapes their residents' lives and determines their fate. On the other hand, these neighbourhoods are spaces where the semi-armed left is organised, for example in the form of the People's Front. Yonucu's work on these neighbourhoods not only guides us to understand the atmosphere of the counterinsurgency policing strategies that provoke and reproduce these groups but also, describes a mimetic relationship involving the coexistence of 'intense police surveillance and militarized special control alongside armed and masked revolutionary vigilante activities and gang activities' (4).

Policing strategies and practices are beyond the parameters of this book, as it sets up as its primary concern the question of accountability after state violence and thus focuses on the legal and political aftermath of police violence. Nonetheless, I find Yonucu's work illuminating to comprehend the specific regime of violence that transformed Elvan's task of fetching fresh bread one morning into a deadly encounter with the police. Furthermore, I find Yonucu's observations helpful in understanding the psyche and motivation of the People's Front militants in their hostage-taking action in the name of bringing justice to Berkin Elvan. It is possible to argue that the state manifests only through violence in these neighbourhoods and communicates with Alevi and Kurdish subjects only through violence. Indeed, elsewhere I explore the different facets of the Turkish state within the context of exceptional legal measures, which, on the one hand, orders the killing of some and grants amnesty to the others who do the killings (Yıldız 2020). Thus, state violence has been painfully familiar within the Alevi and Kurdish communities since the foundation of modern Turkey, and justice and accountability have been a constant demand that never arrived via the state legal system.

Police Violence and Accountability

There is a growing critical literature on police powers across the disciplines of politics, political philosophy, criminology, sociology and their intersections. Among the prominent ones, Jacques Rancière (1999) elaborates on the police to critique the politics of 'organisation of powers, distribution of places and roles, and the systems for legitimizing this distribution' (28), while Mark Neocleous (2014) offers a detailed account of police power to understand the merging of war and peace in contemporary times and understands police power as 'a set of apparatuses and technologies constituting political order in general and the law of labour in particular' (11). Furthermore, Melayna Kay Lamb (2024), in *A Philosophical History of Police Power*, presents a comprehensive study of police power. Against the common reading of police power in relation to the sovereign power that suppresses people through maintaining order, Lamb's analysis on police power leads her to conclude that 'police power is *an-archic* in character' (162), with police power 'unbounded and dislocated from sovereignty and law while simultaneously being linked to them, in the form of a mythological projection of a legitimizing, transcendent power from which its own power derives' (163).

This book is neither concerned with police as an institution nor provides an in-depth study of its origins and power. However, Lamb's conclusion on police power interests me. Although I find her conclusion convincing, Lamb's work fails to address 'the mythological projection' that associates police power with state (sovereign) power. In other words, it does not provide an explanation of how and why police violence is often understood as state violence. Instead, this book suggests shifting the focus to mythological projections on the state and police violence. It aims to disclose myths and assumptions that shape our understanding of the state and its violence. Thus, the book directs its first set of questions: *How does the state manifest through police violence?* and *How does the manifestation of the state render the police invisible?*

Similar to this book, Lamb's point of departure is Walter Benjamin's (2007) remarks on police in his essay 'Critique of Violence', which describes the police as 'formless, like its nowhere tangible all-pervasive, ghostly presence in the life of civilized states' (287). However, Lamb reads Benjamin's remarks as a guide towards displaying the *an-archic* character of police power and explains the unaccountability of police violence in relation to this formation; as she suggests, 'that police power in modernity is structurally incapable of being held to account by the law in a way analogous to, but not reducible to, sovereign power' (21). Where the ghostly presence of police in everyday life is concerned, I suggest instead it is necessary to consider Benjamin's remarks in a literal sense. Furthermore, as I demonstrate throughout the book, it is possible to observe that the ghostliness of the police, and its violence, extends to its legal address. Not only do police appear as a ghostly figure in police violence trials, but the mythical imaginary of the state haunts the legal proceedings and paralyses the legal accountability processes. Thus this book also inquires into the performance of the state in the courtroom. In that regard, diverging from Lamb's conclusion, the book suggests that the legal unaccountability of the police power, in other words violence, is indeed related to sovereign/state power; that is not sovereign power as an absolute, omnipotent and omnipresent power, but rather, as the mythical construction and performance of the state power. I argue that assumptions regarding the state and its killing powers shape expectations from the law in regard to justice and accountability on the one hand, while on the other hand impacting the operation of legal processes of accountability. Thus this book asks: *How do the myths and assumptions concerning state violence impact the political demands and legal processes of accountability?*

Indeed, currently, there is a global academic and public discussion on police violence and its unaccountability that has accelerated after the Black Lives Matter protests, which took centre stage after the police killing of George Floyd in March 2020. In the US and the UK, public and academic discussions have been inquiring how state institutions, and especially the police, generate, criminalise and target racialised subjects. Thus contemporary public and academic debates on police violence and its accountability are intertwined with the discussion on its colonial foundations and the systematic and institutional racism embedded within the state institutions. As a result, the current literature on the issue mainly offers analyses that focus on the institutions to expose the colonial legacy and its contemporary operational logic even when collective acts of resistance towards police violence are considered (i.e., Elliot-Cooper 2021; Bruce-Jones 2017). As mentioned previously, it is also possible to trace a colonial logic within Turkish institutions. The obvious example of the Kurdish issue, which, depending on the perspective, could be reformulated as the Turkish issue (see Gambetti and Jongerden 2015), and the systematic exclusion of Alevis can be explained through the perspective of the state institution's colonial operation. Although such analyses provide invaluable knowledge on how the violent performances of the state and its unaccountability are deeply rooted in colonial ideology, I argue that institution-orientated analysis can be limiting in providing openings towards a resolution as they encounter the danger of limiting the issue to the failings of modern political and legal institutions. Moreover, an institution-orientated analysis of state and police violence attributes a high value to institutions and, I argue, reproduces the power hierarchy between the state and subject. In other words, institution-orientated analysis strengthens the authority of the state, and its mythical omnipotent and omnipresent powers.

On the other hand, the political and legal aftermath of the police killings generates a discussion on the limits of institutions and institution-based processes of accountability. Even when the courts sentence the perpetrator police officers with the highest sentence possible, such as in the case of George Floyd, sentencing one police officer to imprisonment does not correspond with the public's demands for accountability. Although guilty verdicts could be considered as a step forward against the impunity of the police, they fail to address the systematic violence. Hence, the demand for accountability exceeds institutional limits. It urges us to rethink the notion of accountability as a social concept in relation to social justice. The significance of setting the question in this book as an issue of accountability rather than impunity should be understood in this regard, as impunity investigates the issue and suggests its resolution within the institutional parameters. Against this, I argue, accountability allows us a broader perspective, which enables us to consider the issue in relation to the subject. It urges us to consider the existing societal disparities when law and its performance are concerned. It dares us to think beyond the myth of the state, as well as the myth of objectivity and equality before the law.

For this purpose, this book offers a subject-orientated study of state violence and its legal unaccountability. Although the subject is at the heart of the state violence cases; as the ones who perform violence, are subjected to violence and demand accountability and justice, the subject is often left *unseen*. This book challenges the privileged position of the state and its institutions by repositioning the subject at the centre of its analysis. In so doing, it discloses the doings of the subject, as the ones who perform the state and its violence, and is able to acknowledge the agency of the ones who demand accountability and justice. From this perspective, it is possible to register the impact of the agonising wait for justice that many justice-seeking subjects endure. While asking *how the legal processes of accountability transform the subject*, the book provides an opening to comprehend the impact of the law's waiting game. This book argues that the justice-seeking subject is not a passive object; the state and its institutions do not happen on them. Waiting before the law is not a passive act. Furthermore, the meaning of the state and its institutions also transform with the subjects. By positioning the subject at its centre, the book exposes a constant movement of undoing and redoing of the subject, the state and its institutions.

This book draws its analysis from critical legal scholarship. Critical legal perspective allows us to deconstruct the law, its authority and its foundational assumptions. The law claims to bring justice and accountability. However, what we observe instead in state-violence trials is a repetition of unaccountability. It is not possible to comprehend the gap between the law's promise of justice and accountability and its repetitive and global failures in state violence trials from the institutional boundaries of the law. Critical legal scholarship considers law beyond the boundaries of what is commonly referred to as black-letter law; not only does it question the authority of law, but it also provides an insight to read the gaps in between its black letters. In that regard, critical legal scholarship, with its interdisciplinary approach, provides us a rich literature to study law's entanglement with the state and violence and its impact on the subject while focusing on the gaps that are filled with ghosts, myths and assumptions.

The State We Are In

At this point, I would like to provide a brief direction to clarify what I understand by 'the state'. While studying state violence and its unaccountability, I draw inspiration from two interpretations of the state. The first one is Judith Butler's and Gayatri Chakravorty Spivak's (2010) conversation on the nation-state, published under the title *Who Sings the Nation-State?* Undoubtedly, the notion of 'nation-state' brings another dimension to the question of the state, as it points to the issues around citizenship and belonging. However, what inspires me in this conversation is the relationship between the two meanings of the state. The first meaning is the state as a political entity that 'signifies the legal and institutional structures that delimit a certain territory (although not all of those institutional structures belong to the apparatus of the state)' (3). The second one refers to 'the "conditions in which we find ourselves"' (ibid.). Revisiting the notion of state violence in relation to the two meanings of the state – as in the state which leaves us in a certain state – allows us to separate the state (the political entity) from its effects. In that regard, it is possible to acknowledge and register the conditions and dispositions of the subject after being subjected to state violence while keeping an inquisitive lens towards the state as a political, social and legal construct. From such a perspective, the state does not appear to have a fixed meaning, but rather something that is relational to the subject. Taking into account the relationality between the state as a political entity and the state as a condition allows us to address its various meanings and manifestations. For example, meanings attributed to the state by those who are positioned against the state are different than those who align themselves with the state. In that regard, this relational approach between the two meanings of the state shines a light on the reciprocal (re)constructions of the state and the subject in the context of state violence. Regarding the case study of this book, this allows us to register and prioritise the subject's positions while focusing on their articulations of the state, their experiences of state violence and their expectations from the legal processes. Thus, rather than unpacking the issue of state violence from a state-orientated perspective, which would bring limitations to the meanings of the state, this book offers a subject-orientated perspective to study the effects of state violence and its unaccountability.

The other inspiration is Philip Abrams's (1988) essay titled 'Notes on the Difficulty of Studying the State', which addresses the limits of considering the state as a fixed, given entity. What Abrams notes as the difficulty is related to the issue of not attributing a pre-given meaning or a definition to the state while studying its effects. He suggests that the ones studying the state, including those taking Marxist approaches to the state, consider the state as a given, a distinct unified entity which frees the concept of the state from scrutiny. When the state is considered distinct from the subjects, this renders the state ungraspable. As a result, Abrams argues that the concept of the state masks the reality, as if 'there is a hidden reality in political life' (61). According to his view, taking the state as reality disables us from acknowledging the political relations that takes place in front of our eyes. His essay can be considered as a caution to the social sciences, as he concludes:

> The state comes into being as a structuration within political practice; it starts its life as an impact construct; it is then reified – as the *res publica*, the public reification, no less – and acquires an overt symbolic identity progressively divorced from practice as an illusory account of practice. The ideological function is extended to a point where conservatives and radicals alike believe that their practice is not directed at each other but at the state; the world of illusion prevails. The task of the sociologist is to demystify; and in this context that means attending to the senses in which the state does not exist rather than to those in which it does
>
> (82)

These two accounts of the state are my point of departure in studying the manifestation of state violence and its unaccountability in Berkin Elvan's case. In *Ghostly Matters*, Avery F. Gordon (2008) notes that, '[p]ower can be invisible, it can be fantastic, it can be dull and routine. It can be obvious, it can reach you by the baton of the police, it can speak the language of your thoughts and desires' (3). While focusing on the ghostly operation of state violence, the mythical constellation of the state, and the fantasies and fetishes of state power, I aim to demystify this haunting phenomenon called state violence.

Structure

This book is organised into four chapters and a conclusion. Each chapter deals with different facets of state violence while following the events which took place in the aftermath of Berkin Elvan's killing. As I introduce below, starting from Elvan's funeral ceremony to the legal process, each chapter aims to comprehend the notion of state violence and its different forms of manifestation through the reciprocal (re)construction of the state and the subject. In so doing, the book does not occupy itself with discussing remedies that modern state and legal systems provide, or fail to provide, regarding the issue of accountability. Instead, in this book, I aim to reveal the association between the repetition of state violence and its unaccountability through the myths, assumptions and expectations surrounding the notion and manifestation of state violence. To do so, the book first explores the manifestation of state violence and the meanings and assumptions that the convergence of *state* and *violence* bears. Then it analyses how countering performances on state violence construct the state and the subject, and, finally, the book inquiries into how the meanings of the state reflect onto legal processes of accountability.

At Elvan's funeral ceremony, the funeral crowd chanted, 'The murderer state will be held to account'. That serves as a point of departure for this book's investigation on the notion of state violence, as the chant called on the state rather than the police. In light of the chant, Chapter 1 introduces the story of Berkin Elvan's deadly encounter with the police to explore the manifestation of the state within this encounter. Indeed, interpreting police violence as state violence is a common articulation not unique to this example. My objective in inquiring into the manifestation of the state is not to dispute the association between police violence and state violence; however, I argue that this association bears meanings that reflect on the legal processes of accountability and contour the performance of accountability. What is often dismissed in this interchangeable usage of police violence and state violence is that the state is an imaginary construct of the modern psyche. It is a construct of modern (Western) political and legal systems. This aspect, however, is often overlooked, as modern political and legal institutions are founded upon the assumption of the material existence of the state and its powers. This is also the case regarding the notion of state violence, and perhaps the materiality of violence makes it harder to acknowledge the relativity of the state. This particular state of being, however, reflects on the issue of accountability; *is it even possible to hold the state accountable?* If so, *who is to be held to account?* Thus, the task of Chapter 1 is to provide a conceptual lens to acknowledge both the imaginary construction of the state and its deadly effects and to provide a reading of Elvan's encounter with the police from such a perspective. In doing so, I follow scholars who consider the state in terms of fetish (Taussig 1992) and fantasy (Aretxaga 2005, Navaro-Yashin 2002, Rose 1996).

While presenting a detailed analysis of Elvan's deadly encounter with the police, I address the question of *what renders police violence as state violence?* When it is the police that enacts the violence, I wonder *how the state manifests through the police*. The state appears to manifest through the totem-like body of the police (Taussig 1992), as the police enact violence on behalf of this assumed higher authority that we call the state, which in return demands recognition of this authority from the subject. In that regard, I understand Elvan's deadly encounter with the police as a scene that (re)constructs both the state and the encountering subjects, which I discuss through the limits and revisions of Louis Althusser's (2014) notion of *interpellation*. While unpacking the moment of Elvan's encounter with the police, I aim to problematise how we attribute absolute killing powers to the state, which, I argue, hides the police's actions and responsibility. In that regard, redesignating police violence as state violence leads to the police being disguised by the imaginary construction of the state, which haunts the political and legal afterlife of the violence.

Furthermore, in the police's embodiment of the state and its powers, I observe a bodily overlap between the body of the police officer and the imaginary *body politic* of the state, which I inquire into through the bodily description of Thomas Hobbes's (1991) *Leviathan*. Hobbes's bodily description of the state in *Leviathan* exposes how the modern understanding of the state is mythical and situated between Godly and worldly, a unified omnipotent and omnipresent entity that is human with a machine-like bureaucratic operation. Yet the mythical imaginary of the state is fragile and often challenged by the people. Hobbes's disapproval of public challenges in *Leviathan* provides us with a conceptual guide to comprehend how the victims of state violence are found responsible for the violence inflicted upon them, especially within the context of public revolt and protests, as incidences that perform a refusal of the authority of this mythical creature which we call the state.

Law plays a crucial role in communicating the police's command that urges the subjects to recognise the mythical constellation of the state and its authority. Law provides recognition to the subjects, since the subjects are recognised as the subjects of law; however, despite the common belief, this recognition neither brings protection from state violence nor guarantees legal accountability. The final conceptual investigation of the chapter discloses the associations between the state, myth and law through Walter Benjamin's (2007) famous essay 'Critique of Violence', which serves as a framework to explore their connections throughout the book. I continuously find myself returning to some of the points that Benjamin raises in his essay: violent foundations of law, the ghostliness of the police and the deadly fate of those who disobey. Indeed, the state official's response to Elvan's death as nothing but an expected tragic event of a disobedient boy becomes intelligible through Benjamin's remarks on fate in relation to ghostly police violence. Following Benjamin's remarks, the chapter unpacks how and why it is necessary for the law to turn a blind eye to police violence, as the law's existence depends on police violence, which consolidates the fragile mythical imaginary of the state and its authority through repetition of violence.

The following chapters expand on the conceptual framework introduced in Chapter 1 by following the chain of events that occurred in the aftermath of Elvan's death. Chapter 2 provides a detailed analysis of the mythical imaginary of the state and its operation through a close reading of now-President and then-Prime Minister R.T. Erdoğan's response to Elvan's death at a rally. Primarily, in his speech there, Erdoğan accuses Elvan of acting like a terrorist and accuses his family of his bad upbringing, which serves as a response to public demands for accountability. In other words, Erdoğan insinuates that Elvan does not deserve accountability because he is a disobedient son of the state. However, the doings of Erdoğan's rally speech are not limited to this. The conceptual framework of performative utterances (Austin 1975) – through Butler's (1997, 2003) revisions and Stanley Cavell's (2005) and Marianne Constable's (2015) contributions to the literature – present us with a lens to register how Erdoğan's rally speech (re)constructs the mythical imaginary of the Turkish state as he speaks and how this imaginary manifests onto himself, a process which I refer to in the chapter as *stately performative*. Erdoğan's *stately performative* exposes the Turkey-specific imaginary of the state, the *father-state* which is originally associated with Turkey's founding father M.K. Atatürk and was thus utilised as a founding myth for an imagined united Turkish nation. The significance of the figure of the body and its function in manifesting the state and its powers becomes apparent as Erdoğan evokes the *father-state* through his own body. The chapter expands on Erdoğan's *father-state* performance; the assumptions it bears and the ways in which he utilises the *father-state* myth to reconsolidate the troubled unity of the Turkish state after the Gezi protests and a series of political scandals. As I read Erdoğan's *stately performative* of the *father-state* as an attempt to reconsolidate both the unity of the mythical imaginary of the Turkish state and his power as the *father-state*, I argue that, despite being an authoritarian performance, Erdoğan's speech indicates the imaginary construct of the state while excluding Elvan and his family from its imagined unity.

Inquiring into the state and its violence from the perspective of its mythical construction, then, enables us to comprehend the meanings behind the violent acts of refusal. In Chapter 3, this is how I read the People's Front's hostage-taking of the then-head prosecutor of the Elvan case. The violence of the hostage-taking responds to the violence of the state and its unaccountability. The People's Front's hostage-taking action exposes the limits of the state and its juridical system, while the hostage-takers mock the state power's inability to deliver justice. Although the hostage-taking is an act that contests the state and its violence, I register appropriation of state power within the performance of this violent refusal. The hostage-taking action's refusal of the state and its violence manifests in the form of assimilation of the state's killing and punishing powers. In that regard, it is possible to recognise an interplay between the state, or rather the imaginary powers of the state, and the demands of the hostage-takers. Furthermore, what makes the hostage-taking action possible is the deadly devotion of the People's Front militants, who knew well that the action will bring their death. Their deadly devotion, which is admirable for some, troubles me. The militants who carry out the hostage-taking and Berkin Elvan come from similar backgrounds — working-class, urban-poor young men — which the state subjectifies as suspects. They are the potential disobedient sons of the *father-state*, and thus more likely to be subjected to the deadly violence of the state. What I notice in their deadly devotion to carry out the hostage-taking is the assimilation of this deadly fate attributed to them by the state. I consult the literary figure of Antigone to comprehend the meanings behind the militant's self-sacrificial devotion to bringing justice to the dead while asking, *Why must the militants die?*

Following this, in Chapter 4, I present a reading of the legal process of the Elvan case through Franz Kafka's (2007) famous parable 'Before the Law' in order to address the issue of repetitive failure of accountability in state-violence cases. I understand the prolonged legal process of the Elvan trial as a legal version of the initial violence, which exposes a common, but yet to be explored, operation of law in state-violence trials. While expanding on how police violence transforms into legal violence, I notice that, while the legal process dismisses the responsibility of the state and delivers one bad cop, it also hides the perpetrator police officer from appearing before the court. This raises the question, *Who is on trial?* Kafka's parable, and its resonances within the critical scholarship, expose this ambiguity, which manifests in terms of the Elvan family's expectation from the law and how they are kept waiting before the law in anticipation of justice. Different to the common readings of legal violence, which operate through uttering a decision in the form of a judgement, it appears that the state-violence trials instead suspend delivering the judgement and hold, waiting in anticipation, the ones who were subjected to state violence. This is how state violence trials become never-ending, life-long battles for those who demand accountability from the state. Indeed, in the specific context of enforced disappearances and legal processes of accountability in Turkey, the law's waiting game has also been observed by Özgür Sevgi Göral (2019, 2021). Drawing from existing literature on waiting in reference to the Turkish context, the chapter develops the conceptual framework of law's function as a *waiting apparatus*, which the book argues is a specific type of legal violence that operates through the legal performance of failure.

Finally, I would like to say a few words about my usage of fiction throughout the book. Although neither the methodology nor the content of this inquiry belongs to the rich scholarship of law and literature, the literary works that are mentioned in this book have led me to navigate between the borders of what is fiction and what is real and to elaborate on the transgressions between those two realms. In that regard, the literary works guided me to comprehend the passage between the mythical imaginary of the state and its concrete, deadly effects. This book is my invitation to legal scholarship to focus on the blurred space between the imaginary and deadly reality, that space between the lines, beyond the written and spoken, which belongs to the ghosts of state violence that keep haunting us. Thus, this book is a ghost story about state violence. Not only is the story haunted by the dead, but it is also haunted by the ghostly, mythical imagination of the state, its deadly manifestation and its impact on the legal processes of accountability.

References

Abrams, Philip 1988. 'Notes on the Difficulty of Studying the State'. *Journal of Historical Sociology* 1(1): 58–89.

Althusser, Louis. 2014. 'Ideology and Ideological State Apparatuses'. In *On the Reproduction of Capitalism*. London: Verso. 232–272.

Amnesty International. 2013. 'Gezi Protests: The Brutial Denial of Right to Peaceful Assembly'. 2 October. Accessed 16 July 2024. https://www.amnesty.org/en/documents/EUR44/022/2013/en

Aretxaga, Begoña. 2005. *States of Terror: Begoña Aretxaga's Essays*. Edited by Joseba Zulaika. Nevada: Center for Basque Studies.

Assy, Bethania, and Başak Ertür. 2014. 'Law and Resistance – Turkey and Brazil'. *Law and Critique* 25: 1–13.

Austin, J. L. 1975. *How to Do Things with Words*. Oxford: Oxford University Press.

Avery, F. Gordon. 2008. *Ghostly Matters Haunting and the Sociological Imagination*. Minneapolis: University of Minnesota Press.

Bargu, Banu. 2016. 'Why did Bouazizi Burn Himself? The Politics of Fate and Fatal Politics'. *Constellations* 23(1): 27–36.

Benjamin, Walter. 2007. 'Critique of Violence'. In *Reflections: Essays, Aphorisms, Authobiographical Writings*. New York: Harcourt Inc. 277–300.

Bruce-Jones, Eddie. 2017. *Race in the Shadow of Law: State Violence in Contemporary Europe*. Oxon and New York: Routledge.

Butler, Judith. 1997. *The Psychic Life of Power: Theories in Subjection*. California: Stanford University Press.

Butler, Judith. 2003. 'Afterword'. In Shoshana Felman. *The Scandal of the Speaking Body: Don Juan with J.L. Austin, or Seduction in Two Languages*, edited by Stanley Cavell.. Stanford: Stanford University Press. 113–123.

Butler, Judith, and Gayatri Chakravorty Spivak. 2010. *Who Sings the Nation-State?: Language, Politics, Belonging*. Calcutta: Seagull Books.

Cavell, Stanley. 2005. 'Performative and Passionate Utterance'. In *Philosophy the Day After Tomorrow*. Cambridge, MA: Harvard University Press. 155–191.

Constable, Marianne. 2015. *Our Word Is Our Bond: How Legal Speech Acts*. California: Stanford University Press.

David, Isabel, and Kumru F. Toktamış. 2015. *'Everywhere Taksim': Sowing the Seeds for a New Turkey at Gezi*. Amsterdam: Amsterdam University Press.

Derrida, Jacques. 1992. 'Force of Law: The "Mystical Foundation of Authority"'. In *Deconstruction and the Possibility of Justice*, edited by David Gray Carlson, Drucilla Cornell and Michel Rosenfeld. New York and London: Routledge. 3–67.

Elliot Cooper, Adam. 2021. *Black Resistance to British Policing*. Manchester: Manchester University Press.

Gambetti, Zeynep, and Joost Jongerden. 2015. *The Kurdish Issue in Turkey: A Spatial Perspective*. Oxon and New York: Routledge.

Gordon, Avery F. 2008. *Ghostly Matters: Haunting and the Sociological Imagination*. Minneapolis and London: University of Minnesota Press.

Göral, Özgür Sevgi. 2019. '"İmkansız Bir Talep" Olarak Adaleti Beklemek: Kaybedilenler ve Yakınları'. In *Beklerken: Zamanın Bilgisi ve Öznenin Dönüşümü*, edited by Zerrin Özlem Biner and Özge Biner. Istanbul: İletişim. 45–85.

Göral, Özgür Sevgi. 2021. 'Waiting for the Disappeared: Waiting as a Form of Resilience and the Limits of Legal Space in Turkey'. *Social Anthropology/ Anthropologie Sociale* 29(3): 800–815.

Hobbes, Thomas. 1991. *Leviathan*. Edited by Richard Tuck. Cambridge: Cambridge University Press.

Kafka, Franz. 2007. 'Before the Law'. In *Metamorphosis and Other Stories*, translated by Michael Hofmann. Great Britain: Penguin Books. 171–172.

Lamb, Melayna Kay. 2024. *A Philosophical History of Police Power*. London: Bloomsbury Academic.
Navaro-Yashin, Yael. 2002. *Faces of the State: Secularism and Public Life in Turkey*. Princeton and Oxford: Princeton University Press.
Neocleous, Mark. 2014. *War Power, Police Power*. Edinburgh: Edinburgh University Press.
Rancière, Jacques. 1999. *Disagreement: Politics and Philosophy*. Minneapolis and London: University of Minnesota Press.
Rose, Jacqueline. 1996. *States of Fantasy*. New York: Oxford University Press.
Sharpe, Christina. 2016. *In the Wake: On Blackness and Being*. Durham and London: Duke University Press.
Taussig, Michael. 1992. *The Nervous System*. New York and London: Routledge.
Tuğal, Cihan. 2013. '"Resistance Everywhere": The Gezi Revolt in Global Perspective'. *New Perspectives on Turkey* 49: 147–162.
Yıldırım, Umut, and Yael Navaro-Yashin. 2013. 'An Impromptu Uprising: Ethnographic Reflections on the Gezi Park Protests in Turkey'. Hot Spots, *Fieldsights*, 31 October. Accessed 16 July 2024. https://culanth.org/fieldsights/series/an-impromptu-uprising-ethnographic-reflections-on-the-gezi-park-protests-in-turkey.
Yıldız, Ceylan Begüm. 2020. 'A State in Anomie: An Analysis of Modern Turkey's States of Exception'. *States of Exception: Law, History, Theory*, edited by Cosmin Sebastian Cercel, Gian-Giacomo Fusco and Simon Lavis, London: Routledge. 167–183.
Yonucu, Deniz. 2014. 'Okmeydanı Üzerine Notlar (1)'. *Evrensel*. 1 June. Accessed16 July 2024. https://www.evrensel.net/haber/85437/okmeydani-uzerine-notlar-1.
Yonucu, Deniz. 2018. 'The Absent Present Law: An Ethnographic Study of Legal Violence in Turkey'. *Social and Legal Studies* 27(6): 716–733.
Yonucu, Deniz. 2022. *Police, Provocation, Politics: Counterinsurgency in Istanbul*. Ithaca and London: Cornell University Press.
Žižek, Slavoj. 2013. 'Trouble in Paradise'. *London Review of Books* 35(14). Accessed 28 September 2021. https://www.lrb.co.uk/the-paper/v35/n14/slavoj-zizek/trouble-in-paradise

Chapter 1

'The Murderer State Will Be Held to Account'

It is 12 March 2014. Berkin Elvan's coffin floats on the streets of Okmeydanı, Istanbul.[1] On the shoulders of the sea of people, Elvan wanders through the streets of the neighbourhood where he grew up and where he was hit by a police tear gas canister on 16 June 2013 during the Gezi protests. Elvan's coffin was draped in a red flag and covered with carnations. The red flag, without the crescent moon and star of the Turkish flag, is a symbol of leftist politics. For those who attended, the ceremony served as an indication, a location and a disposition of a political stance under the sacredness of a funeral.

Once he was announced dead, Berkin Elvan joined the ranks of 'Gezi martyrs' who were killed either by the police or by government supporters during the protests.[2] Consequently, Elvan's funeral rekindled the anti-governmental and anti-state disposition of the Gezi protests. The main arteries of Istanbul were shut down by protesters marching towards the funeral while, simultaneously, protests took place across Turkey. Chants filled the air: 'Berkin's murderers are the AKP police', 'Erdoğan, killer', 'The murderer state will be held to account' and 'Berkin Elvan is immortal'.[3] Shops were closed, and thousands escorted the funeral procession through the streets of Istanbul from Okmeydanı Cemevi to Şişli mosque and concluded at the Feriköy cemetery.[4] The picture of Berkin Elvan, which was placed in front of the coffin, gazed at the crowd from above, from the heavens, as he is often illustrated

1 'Thousands Bid Farewell to Berkin Elvan'. *Bianet*, 12 March 2014. Accessed 16 July 2024. http://bianet.org/english/human-rights/154119-thousands-bid-farewell-to-berkin-elvan.

2 Those referred to as Gezi martyrs are Mehmet Ayvalıtaş, Abdullah Cömert, Ali İsmail Korkmaz, Ethem Sarısülük, Medeni Yıldırım, Ahmet Atakan, Hasan Ferit Gedik and Berkin Elvan.

3 'Berkin'in katili AKP'nin polisi', 'Erdoğan katil', 'Katil devlet hesap verecek' and 'Berkin Elvan ölümsüzdür'.

4 'Funeral of Turkish Boy Berkin Elvan Brings Thousands to Istanbul Streets'. *The Guardian*, 12 March 2014. Accessed 16 July 2024. www.theguardian.com/world/2014/mar/12/funeral-turkish-boy-berkin-elvan-thousands-istanbul-streets-protests-tear-gas-canister.

DOI: 10.4324/9781032690070-2

among other Gezi martyrs. On top of his picture was written: 'Berkin Elvan is immortal!'; and, below: 'We will call to account!'. Both statements end with exclamation marks. They are not only signs of emotional states of despair, or anger, but rather they are signs of warning: 'We *will* call to account!' (emphasis mine).

I consider this claim, 'We will call to account', within the context of the cross-generational leftist chant, 'The murderer state will be held to account', that communicates the public response in Turkey after each act of state killing. It is an oath that is passed from generation to generation among Turkey's political dissidents, like the passing of a torch from the old to the young: 'The murderer state will be held to account'. It is a timeless chant which connects its past and future utterers within the present. As the chant travels through time, it locates Berkin Elvan's death within the history of state killings in Turkey. On the other hand, this history is also the history of resistance, which often takes the form of demanding accountability, as the chant, 'The murderer state will be held to account', suggests. In that regard, the chant indicates a continuity, not only signifying a continuity of state killings but also of contestation over the state's accountability. As the double-folded history of state violence and demands for accountability intertwine on the subject-bodies, it transforms the subjects into a site of contestation. As I discuss throughout the book, Elvan's name acquires many meanings – from an ill-fated child to a terrorist, from a terrorist to a revolutionary martyr – all of which signify different forms of contestation over his killing and the processes of accountability, as well as associating him with others whose names bear the same meanings, recalling their memories and rekindling past unresolved demands for accountability.

Elvan's young age summons the memories of past young revolutionaries both within and outside the borders of Turkey. Chants shouted during Elvan's funeral associate his killing with past state killings in Turkey and locate him as a figure in a leftist mythology, such as the chant, 'Fifteen-year-old sapling, Berkin Elvan', which recalls the underaged revolutionaries of the 1980s who were hanged by the military coup regime of the time and are commonly referred as 'saplings' in Turkey's political culture. Internationally, Elvan's killing brought back the killing of 15-year-old Alexis Grigoropoulos by police during 2008 protests in Athens. Elvan and Grigoropoulos are often illustrated together in the streets of Athens and Istanbul under the caption of, 'You are my brother, Alexis; you are my brother, Berkin'. These illustrations do more than challenge the so-called historic hostility between the Turkish and Greek states. They challenge the general official response that singularises the police killings of Elvan and Grigoropoulos. With only a sea separating them, the illustrations could be understood as an international call for accountability after police killings.

As the call for accountability after Elvan's killing bears memories of the past, it is heavy with anticipation of bringing justice by holding the state accountable, not only for Elvan but for all the past state killings. In that regard, accountability for Elvan's killing, in terms of its demand and its performance, gains a historical significance as it conveys the possibility of rupturing the continuity of state violence and its unaccountability. This exposes something about the notion of state violence: it never refers to a single incident, and it recalls the past and carries a bitter hope for the future, which materialises through demands of accountability for that particular incident. The chant, 'The murderer state will be held to account', communicates this hope while indicating a historic perpetrator, the state. At this point, the chant, 'The murderer state will be held to account', reveals a dilemma that demands accountability from the perpetrator. In that formulation, the state appears not only as the historic murderer but is also expected to carry out a historic prosecution that would rupture the doings of its murderous self.

Before elaborating on the demands of accountability, this chapter offers a reading of the killing of Berkin Elvan by focusing on the state imaginary that surrounds his killing. The chant, 'The murderer state will be held to account', bears a significant claim that the police violence which had led to Elvan's death is indeed an act of state violence; it signifies the state as the murderer. Although it can be argued that the chant aims to display the linkage between police and the state through the act of violence, I suggest it instead insinuates a murderous subject beyond the police officer, a state-subject that acts similarly to a human subject; a 'murderer state' which I read as the omnipotent and omnipresent imaginary of the state. With the aim of disclosing the state imaginary surrounding the notion of state violence, I first explore the manifestation of the state by elaborating on the moment of Elvan's encounter with the police. In doing so, I disclose the significance of the body as a medium that merges the police and the state. Following this, I present a conceptual discussion on the bodily imaginary of the state to unpack the assumptions it bears, especially regarding state violence. Finally, I return to police violence once again, this time through the lens of Walter Benjamin, to present the conceptual framework to comprehend the violent manifestation of the state imaginary through police violence.

Encountering the Police, Encountering the State

Elvan's deadly encounter with the police is a significant moment, as it is when police violence becomes synonymous with state violence. It is the moment of the manifestation of the state. In reference to the chant, 'The murderer state will be held to account', it is when the state becomes murderous. Through the encounter, this section explores the question, *what renders police violence as state violence?* To clarify, by posing this question, I neither object to registering police violence within the notion of state violence nor aim to propose a framework for their distinction. My objective here, and throughout the book, is to expose myths and assumptions that encircle the notion of state violence, which not only set the limits of its conceptualisation but also reflect on the demands and practices of its accountability, or rather the lack thereof. Thus, this section begins with unpacking the initial moment when the state is materialised through violence. At this moment, the state and its violence become intelligible, and it is possible to begin disclosing the myths and assumptions surrounding their association.

State violence always manifests through the actions of a human subject. Furthermore, there is not a single action within the vast repertoire of state violence that is independent from other forms of violence. This is exactly the reason for the multitude of forms and facets of state violence. This is also the case in the killing of Berkin Elvan, in which state violence manifests in the form of police violence. There is always someone, a material person, or a subject-body, who executes these actions, as I read them, the one who claims and acclaims the state and acts on its behalf. This book's inquiry is particularly concerned with this claim; the myths and assumptions this claim bears while enacting the state and its violence. Additionally, this book is concerned with how such manifestations reflect on the demands and processes of accountability, as the notion of accountability is then understood and positioned in proximity to such claims of the state and its violent manifestations. To begin my inquiry, this section introduces Elvan's encounter with the police to unpack aspects that render this violent encounter a state encounter.

Berkin Elvan was hit by a gas canister in the early morning of 16 June 2013 during the nationwide protests. According to the witness testimonies, the riot police were located on the main street just a few metres away from the side street from where Elvan intended to cross to reach the bakery.[5] We also learn from the witness testimonies that the police had been teasing a small group of protesters by shooting gas canisters horizontally throughout the night, due to which the protesters ended up sheltering on the corner of a side street, where Elvan attempted to cross. As soon as he attempted to cross the street, he was hit in the head with a tear gas canister. Eyewitnesses carried him to the nearest hospital, where he stayed in a coma for almost a year before losing his life on 14 March 2014. Despite the claims of high state officials, Elvan was not participating in the protests at the time he was injured, but neither did it matter. In the context of nationwide protests, the riot police targeted anyone in the streets with tear gas, water cannons and rubber bullets. According to Amnesty International's report on the Gezi Park Protests (2014), 'by July 10 there had been more than 8,000 injuries at the scene of demonstrations' (6), injuries caused by excessive use of force by the police. The report also mentions the excessive use of tear gas: 'The government announced that 130,000 gas canisters had been used during the first 20 days of the protests alone,

5 Berkin Elvan Indictment: Republic of Turkey, Istanbul Office of the Chief Public Prosecutor, Investigation no: 2013/155787, Case no: 2016/42124, Indictment no: 2016/4484.

equivalent to a year's supply' (19) and notes that not only was tear gas used, 'against protestors fleeing police and apparently randomly against potential demonstrators and bystanders alike at the scene or close to demonstrations', but also that, 'police officers were repeatedly seen firing tear gas canisters horizontally at suspected demonstrators as a weapon. A significant proportion of persons injured at the scene of demonstrations received injuries through being struck by gas canisters, many of them fired at close range' (20).

In addition to this general atmosphere of violence, there is something particular in the violent scenario which struck Berkin Elvan, which is related to the location of this encounter and the labelling of its residents. Elvan's encounter with the police took place in Okmeydanı, a working-class neighbourhood that is located just below Taksim Square and Gezi Park, where the protests originated. At the time, the police violence was intensified around the periphery of the park, which was occupied by the protesters. Moreover, due to Okmeydanı's reputation as an urban poor, leftist neighbourhood with Alevi and Kurdish identity, its residents had always been subjected to a particular regime of violence. Deniz Yonucu explains this specific regime of violence in a commentary published after the death of another Okmeydanı resident, Uğur Kurt, who died due to the clashes between the riot police and the protesters in Okmeydanı just a few months after the death of Elvan. In her commentary, Yonucu (2014) reads Okmeydanı as a space of exception where the regime of violence and suppression that normalises the capitalist state is visible and intelligible. In relation to this, in an earlier work with Zeynep Gönen, Yonucu presents an analysis of the urban poor neighbourhoods and their systematic criminalisation in relation to the neoliberal policies in Turkey (Gönen and Yonucu 2012). In her recent book, *Police, Provocation, Politics: Counterinsurgency in Istanbul* (2022), Yonucu offers a detailed ethnographic analysis of these neighbourhoods and reveals the systematic use of counterinsurgency policing tactics as a way of governing these neighbourhoods that 'maintain order by generating and managing disorder' (27), which systematically criminalise their residents. In that regard, Okmeydanı's regime of violence can be understood through this double-bind: as a space where physical state violence is intensified and as a space which automatically marks its residents as criminals. Regarding the Gezi protests, if, according to the police, all protesters were potential suspects, in Okmeydanı everyone in the streets was potential protesters. In the following chapters, I expand on how Okmeydanı's reputation plays a role in the interplay between accountability demands and political and legal responses to such demands. At this point, however, it is necessary to note that Okmeydanı as a site indicates intensified police violence, due to which, I suggest, Elvan's mundane task of fetching fresh bread from a bakery was transformed into a deadly police encounter.

To begin with, unpacking the meanings behind this regime of violence, Louis Althusser's famous hailing scenario can be illuminating. In an essay titled 'Ideology and Ideological State Apparatus', Althusser (2014) presents a hypothetical scene in which the police officer hails; 'Hey, you there!' (264). According to Althusser's scenario, as the hailed individual turns around, and thus as the hailed recognises the hailing, 'he becomes a subject' (ibid.). Althusser calls this process *interpellation*, and it plays an important function in his grand analysis of ideology and its operation through state institutions as he concludes that 'all ideology hails or interpellates concrete individuals as concrete subjects' (ibid.). Surely, Elvan's encounter with the police is significantly different from Althusser's somewhat naïve hailing scenario; nonetheless, I suggest that it allows us to comprehend the dynamic between the police and Elvan, as a resident of Okmeydanı. However, to clarify my position here, rather than suggesting a successful process of *interpellation*, I approach Althusser's hailing scenario from its cracks to conceptualise how the state is conjured through the process of *interpellation*, in other words, through an expectation of successfully *interpellating* the subject, which I refer to as the state's expectation of *interpellation*. Below, I disclose the operation of this expectation by following the critiques posed by Butler (1997, 2011) and Žižek (2008) to expose the assumptions that the process of interpellation bears.

To return to the scenario, after presenting his notion of *interpellation* in one simple gesture – 'Hey, you there!' – Althusser (2014) adds in the footnotes that '[h]ailing as an everyday practice subject to a precise ritual takes a quite "special" form in the policeman's practice of "hailing" which concerns the hailing of "suspects"' (264 n.18). Following this, Althusser not only suggests that 'ideology hails or interpellates individuals as subjects' but also suggests that 'individuals are always-already subjects' (265). Rather than discussing this within the specific scenario of a police officer's hailing, Althusser provides a Freudian explanation to exhibit how individuals are already marked by a 'familial ideological configuration' even before birth (ibid.). In *The Sublime Object of Ideology* (2008), Slavoj Žižek humorously criticises Althusser's tautological proposition, as he writes in reference to Michel Pêcheux;

> the subject as such is constituted through a certain misrecognition: the process of ideological interpellation through which the subject 'recognizes' itself as the addressee in the calling up for the ideological cause implies necessarily a certain short circuit, an illusion of the type 'I was already there' [...] the short circuit of 'no wonder you were interpellated as proletarian, when you are a proletarian'.
>
> (xxv)

Interestingly, if we cross-read Althusser's tautological position with his former remark on the hailing of suspects, we reach an argument which roughly suggests that the police hail the suspects who are already suspects. This may explain the police's behaviour during the Gezi protests in general, and in Okmeydanı specifically. It is possible to argue that, according to the police, its residents were already suspects, which perhaps explains the police's already violent presence in the early morning the day Elvan was injured. It is possible to suggest that, for the police, Elvan was already a suspect once he stepped outside, an act that unconsciously resists the police's violent regime. This reading reveals that police violence, or any violence issued in the name of the state, simultaneously aims to *interpellate* subjects. Then, echoing Žižek (or rather Pêcheux) with a nuance particular to this situation: no wonder Elvan was portrayed as a suspect after his death by high state officials and state institutions, when he was already a suspect. However, it is important to stress that the efforts to *interpellate* Elvan as a suspect by the various state officials and institutions, as a terrorist-like boy who was born to be a terrorist, do not necessarily indicate a successful process. Rather, theories on interpellation allow us to conceptualise the events following Elvan's death as a contestation between the state's attempt to *interpellate* Elvan and the countering political and legal attempts of its refusal.

Another aspect I would like to disclose through Althusser's hailing scenario is the role of law. Although law appears to have a significant role within Althusser's hailing scenario, he fails to provide a reading on this matter. In *Bodies That Matter* (2011), Judith Butler associates the process of *interpellation* with law – '[t]here is the policeman, the one who not only represents the law but whose address "Hey you!" has the effect of binding the law to the one who is hailed' (81) – and exposes its one-sidedness: 'Althusser conjectures this "hailing" or "interpellation" as a unilateral act, as the power and force of law to compel fear at the same time that it offers recognition at an expense' (82). Elsewhere, in *The Psychic Life of Power* (1997), Butler reads the hailing as 'a demand to align oneself with the law' (107). Moreover, Butler asks why the subject would betray themself and allow themself to be reduced by the gesture of turning 'toward the law, against the self' (108). In that regard, turning to the police's hailing is a gesture which does not only result in misrecognition of the self, as Žižek puts it, but also, as Butler observes accurately, it is the 'scene both punitive and reduced' (106). This is something I discuss further in Chapter 4 through a detailed analysis of the trial concerning Berkin Elvan's killing. However, here, I would like to note that what I refer to as the state's expectation of *interpellation* is also a legal claim that is enacted by police violence. In that regard, the law becomes one of the main sites of contestation, especially when state violence is considered, and this association becomes intelligible during the legal processes of accountability.

According to Althusser, however, *interpellation* is the only, and somewhat inevitable, outcome of the hailing scenario, in which the addressee gets *interpellated*, or subjectified, as they turn. Althusser does not elaborate on other alternatives and possible outcomes for the sake of illustrating how ideology *interpellates* the subject. As a result, he conditions the subjects to internalise their subjection, which Žižek refers to as misrecognition. In addition to the points discussed above, however, the inevitability of this scenario reveals a curious assumption. Althusser gives an unusual explanation for the inevitability of *interpellation*. For him, the act of turning to the hailer is not only automatic but almost a telepathic response in which hailing always finds its right addressee and makes the addressee turn. As he writes, '[e]xperience shows that the practical telecommunication of hailings is such that they hardly ever miss their man: verbal call or whistle, the one hailed always recognises that it is really him who is being hailed' (264). Although Althusser adds that this 'cannot be explained solely by "guilt feelings"' (ibid.), as he fails to provide any other explanation to this phenomenon, Butler (1997) asks: 'How and why does the subject turn, anticipating the conferral of identity through the self-ascription of guilt?' (107).

If Althusser's hypothetical scenario attributes a limited agency to the hailer, as someone enacting the ideology and instigating the process of *interpellation*, it completely pacifies the addressee. Butler's persistence in using the notion of guilt, despite Althusser's note against it, can be comprehended in this regard as they criticise Althusser's erasure of agency. Butler points towards the disobedient subjects who defy the legal command in various forms. As they put it, 'the law might not only be refused, but it might also be ruptured, forced into a rearticulation that calls into question the monotheistic force of its own unilateral operation (2011, 82). In *Bodies That Matter*, by presenting an analysis through gender subversive practices of drag, Butler indicates the parodic responses to the law's command, which 'calls into question the legitimacy of the command' (ibid.) Such parodic responses occur through a repetition that is, as Butler puts it, 'a repetition of the law into hyperbole, a rearticulation of the law against the authority of the one who delivers it' (ibid.). However, if we return to the hailing scenario, then Butler's criticisms expose what I refer to as the state's expectation of *interpellation*, which indicates the police's expectation from the addressee to obey and turn to the law. This, as Butler indicates, also requires the addressee to accept their own guilt and recognise the self as a suspect. However, it is necessary to direct a question here: if the inevitability of *interpellation*, in the form of a call and answer, is not something emerging out of guilt for Althusser, is it due to the supernatural merits of ideology that the hail, or the hailer, always finds its target and successfully subjugates them? As Althusser's *interpellation* operates in mysterious ways, it assumes a mysterious force which not only always finds its right addressee but also to which the subjects always respond in submission.

As Althusser's hailing scenario does not provide further guidance on its mysterious operation, to unpack this, I consult Jean Genet's encounter with the police: 'A man stumbled against me [...] It was a coast-guard of about thirty. Armed with his rifle [....] In submitting to the whims of the coast-guard

I was obeying a dominating order which it was impossible not to serve, namely, the Police' (Genet 2019, 152). In *The Thief's Journal*, Genet (2019) describes his encounter with a coast-guard in these words. I consider Genet's – the thief's – encounter as a guide to exposing what I referred to above as the mysterious force that, as Althusser proposes, always finds its addressee and successfully subjugates the subject. I read the mysterious operation of *interpellation* as something related to the dominating order that Genet's thief recognises through the coast-guard, which makes him submit. It is possible to register Genet's encounter as a supporting example for Althusser's *interpellation*, in which Genet, the thief, cannot resist obeying. On the other hand, Michael Taussig, in *The Nervous System* (1992), reads Genet's encounter with the police as something exposing the state fetish (134–136). In one sentence Taussig summarises *state fetishism* as '[t]his peculiar sacred and erotic attraction, even thralldom, combined with disgust, which the State holds for its subjects' (111). Taussig argues that state fetish is 'so studiously, so dangerously, ignored by the great theorists of the poetics of the commodity-fetish' (ibid.) – and lists Walter Benjamin among others. However, Taussig suggests that Genet's encounter brings 'the fetish character of the modern State into a clear and sensual focus' (133).

It is necessary to note that Taussig's notion of state fetish has to do with the homoerotic aspect of Genet's encounter, which almost suggests that it is the thief's submissive desire that manifests the state.[6] In that regard, in his own words, 'what the notion of State fetishism directs us to is precisely the existence and reality of the political power of this fiction' that is 'the fiction of the State – the big S' (113). Moreover, Taussig not only reads the state as fiction, but, as he cross-reads sociology in reference to Durkheim with sorcery, Taussig suggests that the state is an impure sacred (114), a bad fetish: the *maleficium* (118–119).

Although Genet's encounter with the police differs significantly from Elvan's, nonetheless I consider it as an encounter that illuminates the question, *what renders police violence as state violence?* As Genet the thief's encounter surpasses the two encountering material bodies, namely the thief's (Genet's) and the police officer's, it is an encounter through which, in Genet's words, 'a dominating order' manifests. In Taussig's reading, the figure of the body plays a significant role in recognising, and fetishising, the state through the body of the police officer. Taussig points out to the gears and emblems that are embellished on the uniform of the police and suggests that they

6 Following the encounter, the thief performs a sexual act with the police officer. Although it is not clear whether it is a direct order from the officer, nonetheless, the thief feels the pressure of the dominating order to 'serve'. It is possible to read the fetishisation of an omnipotent and omnipresent power in Genet's writings, which often translates into sexual desire and manifests through obscene sexual acts.

signify a higher power from which the police extract authority. In reference to Durkheim, Taussig concludes that the policeman stands in front of the thief as a totem, a sacred power (139). As a result, Taussig explains, the thief recognises the police officer not as an individual, but in an institutional form:

> but there's something else, more metonymic, more carnal, tactile and sensuously material, which is central here – and this is the issue of fetish, of the State with its big S rearing, of the Dominating Order as that which oscillates, like Durkheim's 'society,' between *res* and *deus*, between thing and God, with a carnal and ritualised relation to objects, as with the totems. Here the policeman and his gear are precisely that.
>
> (135)

In the quote above, Taussig proposes that the state gains a material body through the symbolic function of gears and emblems on the police uniform, which transform the police officer into a totem. At this point, if we return to Elvan's encounter as it took place during the Gezi protests and consider the gear of the Turkish riot police – with a helmet and full body armour, armed with batons and weapons, shooting tear gas and rubber bullets – it becomes evident that this totem conveys a certain message. At the encounter with Elvan, the police directly communicate violence. Although violence is not what Genet the thief highlights in his encounter, nonetheless he recognises it almost immediately: 'It was a coast-guard of about thirty. Armed with his rifle' (152). If by guessing the police officer's age, the thief first acknowledges him in a material form, as a human and a mortal being, by noticing his rifle, the thief recognises the possibility of violence which the police officer carries on himself, as if it is an embellishment. In that regard, I suggest, what Genet recognises as 'a dominating order' through the police officer's material body is also the potential of violence. At first glance, such a reading may appear as a shift from Taussig's notion of state fetishism due to the lack of the carnal, homoerotic aspect which is the highlight of Genet the thief's encounter. On the contrary, however, Taussig notes that violence, combined with reason, are elements of state fetishism; he writes, '*it is precisely the coming together of reason-and-violence in the State that creates, in a secular and modern world, the bigness of the big S*' (116). I read Taussig's emphasis on the combination of reason and violence in relation to the chant 'The murderer state will be held to account', which, as mentioned before, attributes omnipotent and omnipresent powers to the state and signifies an evil mastermind.

If Taussig, through Genet, presents an account of a police encounter from the perspective of the thief, Althusser's hailing analogy presents the encounter from the perspective of the police officer who carries out the violence of *interpellation* in the name of the law and, in return, demands obedience and submission from the addressee. Hence, when Genet the thief's encounter is cross-read with Althusser's hailing scenario, it becomes apparent that any form of police hailing carries a legal claim and demands a twofold recognition from the addressee. This twofold recognition is intelligible in Genet the thief's encounter in which the thief first recognises the dominating order, in other words *the State*, and this is followed by his own self-recognition as the suspect, in other words, as the thief. However, as argued above, this scenario rather indicates the state's expectation and, furthermore, Taussig's reading of the state as a fetish allows us to recognise the imaginary construction of this scenario, which manifests through the material body of the police officer. I suggest that this is also the case regarding Elvan's encounter: the state manifests through the material body of the police, and, thus, what renders police violence as state violence is founded upon their bodily overlap, when the imaginary body of the state manifests through the material body of the police officer.

Moreover, this cross-reading exposes the imaginary construction of the state but also reveals that the imaginary construct of the state does not only depend on the fetishes of the thief, or the hailed. The imaginary construct of the state also manifests through the hailer, through the enactment of the ones who claim to act and speak on behalf of the state. Jacqueline Rose (1996), in *States of Fantasy*, provides a psychoanalytic explanation for this phenomenon:

> If the state has meaning only 'partly as something existing', if it rests on the belief of individuals that it 'exists or should exist', then it starts to look uncannily like what psychoanalysis would call an 'as if' phenomenon. You mould your acts and gestures to a persona that deep down you know isn't really there [...] The modern state enacts its authority as ghostly, fantasmatic, authority.
>
> (8–9)

Following this, Begoña Aretxaga (2005), in a collection of essays on the fantasy of the state and terror, highlights that, '[t]o look for state effects is also to follow the ways in which those identified as the state enact their fantasy vis-à-vis those others it considers its enemies' (263). If the state is an imaginary construct, a product of a collection of fetishes and fantasies, then how to understand its dominance in every aspect of our lives? Yael Navaro-Yashin in *Faces of the State* (2002), whom Aretxaga references throughout her work, presents a Turkey-specific analysis of the manifestation of the state imaginary. Navaro-Yashin agrees with Taussig's conceptualisation of state fetishism, and she presents some everyday practices as practices of state fetishism, which she refers to as 'everyday practices of ritualistic exaltation of the Turkish state' (158). Although, according to Navaro-Yashin, state fetishism is shared among many in Turkey – 'pan-Turkists, secularists, Islamists as well as leftists' – she concludes that state fetishism fails to explain 'mundane everyday criticism of statespeople and ridicule of the state' (ibid.). By bringing Slavoj Žižek's interpretation of Lacanian *fantasy* to understand this phenomenon, Navaro-Yashin proposes that although people are aware of the state's nonexistence, they still live as if it exists. She writes: 'The state remains as long as ordinary people are able to pretend that it exists in their everyday practices of life [....] As long as what I call *the everyday life of statecraft* is maintained, the state is reproduced' (179). Navaro-Yashin reaches the conclusion that 'the signifier "state" can remain intact despite public consciousness against it, because a material and tangible world has been organised around it' (171). It is possible to recognise something similar happening in the context of state violence, that the interplay between demands of accountability and political and legal responses to such demands contribute to the making of the murderous subject of the state.

In the chapter in which Taussig introduces the notion of state fetishism, he gives Thomas Hobbes's *Leviathan* as an example. '[A]nd what do I mean by State fetishism?' he asks and responds, 'I mean a certain aura of might as figured by the Leviathan in Hobbes' rendering as that "mortal god"' (111). Following this lead, in the next section, I present a reading of Hobbes's *Leviathan* to disclose the meanings and assumptions attributed to the bodily imaginary of the state which enables this manifestation. An analysis of the *Leviathan* provides the conceptual lens to comprehend how the bodily overlap between the police officer and the state is possible with reference to modern political and legal constructions and helps us with unpacking the claims such constructions bear in relation to state violence and unaccountability.

Leviathan's Body Politic

The discussion above on Elvan's encounter with the police discloses the significance of the figure of the body in attributing certain forms of violence to the state. Its significance is not only limited to the body of the police officer, as the actor or enactor of state violence, but also, and perhaps more significantly, the material body appears as a medium through which the state manifests itself. As Taussig discloses through his totem-like reading of the police officer, it becomes evident that what enables this manifestation is the police's embodiment of the state. In this section, as I inquire into what makes this embodiment possible, I suggest the bodily imaginary of the state, which is commonly referred to as the *body politic*, enables this embodiment and manifestation of the state through an overlap of bodies: the material body of the police and the *body politic* of the state. To unpack this overlap further, in this section I diverge my focus from the material body of the police towards the bodily image of the state.

The literature on the *body politic* dates back to Ancient Greece. Claire Richter Sherman (1995) suggests that the analogy of the *body politic* was first coined by Plato in the *Republic* and in the *Laws* and developed further by Aristotle in the *Politics* (217). Furthermore, medieval political theorists

Kate Langdon Forhan and Cary Joseph Nederman (1993) demonstrate the political interest in defining a *body politic* during medieval times, including Christine de Pizan's *The Book of the Body Politic* (1994), which was written between 1404 and 1407 during the Hundred Years War between France and Britain and remarkably carries the matter to its title. In a nutshell, the common formulation of the *body politic* signifies an overlap between the political entity, whether it is the polis or the state, and the sovereign. Regarding this overlap, in *The King's Two Bodies*, the medieval historian Ernst Kantorowicz (1997) presents a detailed account of the theological foundations of the *body politic* analogy through the two bodies of the king: the fictitious body of the king as an office, in other words, his public persona, and the material one of the king as a private person. To clarify, my aim here is neither to present a discussion on the notion of *body politic* per se nor to investigate its theological foundations. Instead, I am interested in exposing what the mythical bodily imaginary of the state conveys to us when it is embodied by police and performed through police violence. To do so, and following Taussig's lead, in this section I present an analysis of Thomas Hobbes's *Leviathan* (1991), which is undeniably one of the most impactful works on state theory as it presents a model for the ideal modern (Western) state while replacing its theological imaginary power with a secular one.

The cover of the 1651 edition of Hobbes's *Leviathan* shows a man holding a sword in one hand and a sceptre in the other; his body consists of a multitude of people (lxxiv). Melayna Kay Lamb's *A Philosophical History of Police Power* (2024) presents a detailed analysis of police power in relation to the construction of sovereignty and offers a reading of *Leviathan*'s frontispiece. Lamb directs our attention to the placement of the figure of the *Leviathan* and the emptiness that surrounds him; '[t]he frontispiece depicts a huge sovereign standing *outside* and behind an almost empty city' (62). In reference to Giorgio Agamben, Lamb argues that '[o]nce the sovereign is instituted the sovereign power of "the people" is vanished into sovereign' (64). For Lamb, this explains the almost empty city; almost, however, as she observes armed guards and doctors as the only figures represented in the frontispiece. By juxtaposing the vanishing of the people with the only two representations of armed guards and doctors, Lamb suggests a splitting of power: 'Leviathan, who sits outside of the city, is manifestly distinguished from the doctor and guard who dwell within the empty city. While they may be said to exercise sovereign power, they are nevertheless distinguished from the realm of sovereignty which is where the (vanished) people are to be found' (66). Lamb's reading of the frontispiece suggests that, in *Leviathan,* sovereignty is singular and unified, whereas the doctor and the police are situated externally within the people and 'represent the praxis of government which does not threaten the unity of the essence of sovereignty' (ibid.).

Lamb's book offers an excellent analysis on the exceptional character of police power, something that derives from the exceptional powers of the sovereignty, which, as she puts it, 'is not secondary and derivative, but rather a founding power [...], an-archic condition of possibility for sovereignty itself' (4). However, I argue that such a reading of police/sovereign power attributes a reality to the mythical construction of the state. Instead, I offer a focus on the almost ghostly representation of the *Leviathan* in the frontispiece. The man representing the sovereign is a giant translucent figure, made of people, who towers over the city from the mountains. The figure is both ghostly and God-like, but at the same time composed of human subjects. Furthermore, where the bodily description of the *Levithan* is concerned, it is possible to observe a more complex structure that fluctuates between fictitious and material formulations of the state and its sovereign power. The English edition of *Leviathan* (1991) begins with its bodily description:

> For by Art is created that great LEVIATHAN called a COMMON-WEALTH, or STATE, (in latine CIVITAS) which is but an Artificiall Man; through of greater stature and strength than the Naturall, for whose protection and defence it was intended: and in which, the Soveraignty is an Artificiall Soul, as giving life and motion to the whole body: The Magistrates, and other Officers of Judicature and Execution, artificall Joynts; *Reward* and *Punishment* (by which fastned to the seate of the Soveraignty, every joynt and member is moved to performe his duty) are the *Nerves*, that do the same in the Body Naturall; The *Wealth* and *Riches* of all the particular members, are the *Strength*; *Salus Populi* (the peoples safety) its *Businesse*; *Counsellors*, by whom all things needful for it to know, are suggested unto it, are the *Memory*, *Equity* and *Lawes*, an artificiall *Reason* and *Will*; *Concord*, *Health*; *Sedition*, *Sicknesse*; and *Civill war*, *Death*. Lastly, the *Pacts* and *Covenants*, by which the parts of this Body Poltique were at first made, set together, and united resemble that Fiat, or the *Let us make man*, Pronounced by God in the Creation.
>
> (9–10)

What is striking in Hobbes's bodily description of *Leviathan* is that it does not directly overlap with the sovereign, but rather, other state institutions and functions do play important roles in its existence and operation – although, as the quote above suggests, sovereignty plays the main crucial role to animate it. However, the importance Hobbes attributes to the sovereign complicates the picture, which can also be traced in his differentiation between the fictitious (*Artificiall*) and material (*Naturall*) bodies. In his own words, Hobbes aims to describe the 'Nature of this Artificiall man' (10); however, the nature of this fictional body is not always clear. Hobbes establishes the relationship between the *Artificiall* (fictitious) and *Naturall* (material) bodies with a definition: 'When they [words and actions] are considered as is owne, then is he called a *Naturall Person*: And when they are considered as representing the words and actions of an other, then is he a *Feigned* or *Artificiall person*' (111).

In *From Humanism to Hobbes*, Quentin Skinner (2018) provides an insight into Hobbes's personification of the state by presenting a theoretical background on the matter.[7] Skinner suggests that Hobbes's formulation of a natural and artificial person and the issue of representation is grounded in a Ciceronian understanding of *persona civitatis* (12-440).[8] Skinner presents as evidence that, in *De officiis*, Cicero suggests that the magistrate bears the person of the *civitas* or the state (14). Skinner reads Hobbes's formulation of an artificial and natural person as 'his theory about the sovereignty of the *civitas* or state' (12). Furthermore, in reference to Quintilian's *Institutio oratoria*, Skinner discloses a performative logic behind the relationship between the artificial and natural person. According to Skinner, Quintilian suggests the personification of things by 'inventing fictitious speeches and ascribing them to *personæ* other than ourselves [....] By means of this way of speaking the dead are raised, and cities and even peoples acquire a voice' (15). Skinner suggests that Hobbes adopts a similar formulation in *Leviathan* when someone's words and actions can be considered as words and actions of another, 'a Feigned or Artificiall person' (Hobbes 1991, 111). Through his cross-reading of Hobbes and Quintilian, Skinner concludes that neither of the thinkers consider it necessary to have a material body to be a person: 'to count as a person, both he [Hobbes] and Quintilian end by suggesting, it is not necessary to have a bodily substance; it may be sufficient that some natural person has been accredited to play your part' (16).

What is interesting in Skinner's elaboration is that it reveals that the artificial person does not have a substance of its own, but rather is an 'invented fiction', a *persona* created by the natural person. This reading of the artificial person corresponds with the discussion in the previous section regarding the imaginary construction of the state. Furthermore, Skinner exposes that this imaginary construct is then embodied and enacted, 'played', by the natural person. This is what I mean by the 'performative logic' that operates between the artificial and material persons, which I discuss in detail in the following chapter. However, here I would like to highlight the almost theatrical manifestation of the state in which the material, or the natural, person invents fiction and animates it through acting and speaking on its behalf. In doing so, not only does the fiction manifest through the material person, but also, in a cyclical fashion, the material person ends up submitting to their own fictitious creation through its enactment.

7 Skinner also repeats a similar version of his analysis in Skinner 2007.

8 In support of this argument, Richard Tuck, in the 1991 edition of the *Leviathan*, mentions that Hobbes used *civitas* in his Latin works as a synonym for 'commonwealth' (Hobbes 1991, xviii).

Regarding the imaginary construction of the state in the Turkey-specific context, Yael Navaro-Yashin, in her study on secularism and public life titled *Faces of the State* (2002), explores an interesting expansion of the bodily imaginary of the state from sovereign to every state official. To summarise, in her study Navaro-Yashin proposes that the fantasy of the state lives through everyday practices: 'The state remains as long as ordinary people are able to pretend that it exists in their everyday practices of life [...] as long as what I call the everyday life of statecraft is maintained, the state is reproduced' (179). To explain this reproduction of state fantasy, Navaro-Yashin gives an example of a woman called Saniye from a shantytown of Istanbul who regularly goes to the municipality to file complaints in her attempt to have a better service from the state: 'Saniye approached the mayor as if he were the state personified. She had gone to the state to complain about the state.' (167). To complement Navaro-Yashin's observations, in the modern context of the state and everyday life of statecraft, as she puts it, even some objects, such as official documents and state buildings, gain a stately character.

Carl Schmitt's reading of Hobbes's *Leviathan* can be illuminating to understand this expansion. In *The Leviathan in the State Theory of Thomas Hobbes: Meaning and Failure of a Political Symbol* (1996), Schmitt offers a rather interesting reading of the fictitious body of Hobbes's *Leviathan* when he writes, '[w]hat appears to have attained is a mythical totality composed of god, man, animal, and machine' (19). Schmitt dissects Hobbes's *Leviathan* as a political myth of the modern secular state that is ruled by parliamentary democracy to expose it's contradictory and unconvincing mythical foundations. To put it briefly, Schmitt's objection to the *Leviathan* is twofold: on the one hand Schmitt suggests that, due to what he refers to as the 'mythical totality' of *Leviathan*, Hobbes's state formula demands a complete obedience; however, on the other hand, Schmitt argues that, due to its contract-based foundations and the plurality of parliamentary democracy, Hobbes's model cannot provide this form of governing.

Schmitt's description of *Leviathan* is concerned with the interchangeability of the man and the machine, which he interprets as a reflection of 'the Cartesian conception of man as a mechanism with a soul onto the "huge man", the state, made by him into a machine animated by the sovereign-representative person' (32). And, he continues, '[a]s a totality, the state is body and soul, *a homo artificialis*, and, as such, a machine. It is a manmade product. Its material and maker, *materia et artifex*, machine and engineer, are one and the same, namely, men' (34). Indeed, it is possible to read a machine-like function and motion of a body in *Leviathan*'s opening description as quoted above. This allows the fictitious body of the *Leviathan* to transcend the material body of a sovereign. Its machine-like operation, reminiscent of Navaro-Yashin's notion of statecraft, expands to all state officers and even to unanimated objects alike.

Furthermore, the fact that it is a 'manmade product' secularises the theological sacredness of the state. However, this expansion does not signify a diffused organisation; on the contrary, it is a mythical totality, that suggests a unified constellation of state institutions. This totality results in the adapting a secular version of a sacred state power. Overall, what the analogy of *Leviathan* establishes within the psyche of the modern political and legal systems is this fictitious, unified, omnipotent and omnipresent bodily image of the state that operates like a machine through its institutions and is, at the same time, a human-like subject. Thus, it results in such curious incidents as going 'to the state to complain about the state' as Navaro-Yashin puts it, which can also very well describe the police's embodiment of the state and the processes in the aftermath of police/state violence – such as filing a criminal complaint to the state against the state, as the Elvan family did.[9]

Despite *Leviathan*'s complex constellation, at times it becomes synonymous with the sovereign, as Hobbes does not consider sovereignty, the artificial soul which unites *Leviathan*, separately from the *Naturall* person of the sovereign: '[a]nd he that carryeth this Person, is called SOVERAIGNE, and said to have *Soveraigne Power*; and every one besides, his SUBJECT' (121). By this move, sovereignty, the artificial soul which, according to Hobbes, unites the state, is bound to the material person of the sovereign – whether it is one person or a group of people acting as the representative of this the sovereign power. This can be explained by Hobbes's royalist stance, as, in response to the English Civil War, he aims to protect the sovereign power against the destruction of people.[10] It is possible to suggest that Hobbes's remarks on the form of political unity lead to such a conclusion as he claims political unity does not come from the unity of the represented but from the representer: 'For it is the Unity of the Representer, not the Unity of the Represented, that maketh the Person One' (114). According to Hobbes, the masses can form a political unity only through the singularity of the representer as he rejects the idea that the masses can be a political group, the people, without a sovereign (157–180). Although the representer can either indicate one sovereign or a sovereign assembly, nonetheless, for Hobbes, *Leviathan* only refers to the *body politic* of the representer, of the state institutions and officers, which exclude the represented within the unified imaginary of the state. In

9 The Elvan family filed a criminal complaint to the Istanbul Prosecutor in June 2013, right after Berkin Elvan was hit by the tear gas canister. I discuss the legal proceedings in detail in Chapter 4.

10 In the introduction to *Leviathan*'s 1991 edition, Richard Tuck mentions a letter exchange between Hobbes and a royalist friend right after Charles I's execution. The friend suggests Hobbes translate one of his earlier works to 'influence on the current English political scene' to which Hobbes responds with 'he hath another trifle on hand', that is, *Leviathan* (ix). Once it was done, as Tuck notes, Hobbes 'attempted to persuade Charles II of the merits of the book' (xxv). In that regard, it would not be wrong to suggest that Hobbes aimed to influence the constellation of post-Civil War English politics with his moderate royalist approach in the *Leviathan*.

the contemporary literature this is discussed in terms of the state and society divide that results from state-centric theories in which the state 'is often portrayed as a unitary and autonomous actor that possesses the supreme authority to regulate populations within its territory' (Sharma and Gupta 2006, 8). Hobbes' construction of *Leviathan*'s *body politic* not only signals such a divide, which excludes the people from the imagined unity of the state, but also Hobbes's objective to protect the sovereign locates the fictitious body of the state against the people.

Regarding violence, Hobbes touches upon the state's use of violence in 'The Rights of Soveraignes by Institution', under three scenarios, all of which are related to securing the sovereign power (121–129). The first one is the sovereign's right to wage war, and the second one is about the sovereign's right to punish offenders either according to an existing law or in the absence of law (126). In the third scenario, the sovereign's right to use violence comes up as a legitimate response to the people's revolt against the sovereign. It is necessary to note that, in all cases, Hobbes places the sovereign in a higher rank than the appointed army generals, officers and judges. In keeping with his royalist stance, as mentioned above, Hobbes states that people do not have the right to change the form of government, and he writes: 'if he that attempteth to depose his Soveraign, be killed, or punished by him for such attempt, he is author of his own punishment' (122). This scenario of the sovereign's right to violence consists of matters commonly referred to as crimes against the state in modern legal and political systems, which refers to some form of treason and rebellion against the state or the government.

Hobbes does not provide any accountability measures except his broad proposition that the sovereign should respect the covenant. As mentioned above, Hobbes is rather concerned about establishing political unity based on loyalty to sovereign power. In order to establish the people's loyalty to the sovereign power, he comes up with a rather interesting formula of separating the act from the author: 'Of Persons Artificiall, some have their words and actions Owned by those whom they represent. And then the Person is the Actor; and he that owneth his words and actions, is the AUTHOR: In which case the Actor acteth by Authority' (112). In other words, Hobbes suggests here that, while the people are the author, the sovereign is the person who represents this authority and, as the representer, the sovereign is the actor who enacts that authority. This separation between the author and the act reflects Hobbes's position on the authorship of violence. Following this train of thought, anyone who challenges the sovereign not only goes against the contract they authored but, strikingly, as Hobbes argues, they are the very authors of the sovereign violence inflicted upon them.

At this point, I observe striking similarities between the Hobbesian rationale on the authorship of state violence and Erdoğan's response to Elvan's killing, which I discuss in detail in Chapter 3. However, it is also possible to drive parallels between Hobbes's royalist response to parliamentarian demands during the English Civil War and the Turkish authorities' response to the 2013 Gezi protests. Following the protests, many protesters had been charged with 'attempting to overthrow the government by force', among other counter-terror charges such as 'membership of an illegal organisation'.[11] Furthermore, in 2015, Turkish authorities carried out a criminal investigation and prosecuted Taksim Solidarity Platform activists with similar charges.[12] Following their acquittal, Turkish authorities carried out yet another criminal investigation in 2019 and accused nine human rights defenders of, among other counter-terror charges, financing and organising an 'attempt to overthrow the government of the Turkish republic or to prevent it from performing its duties'.[13] The case is known as the Gezi trial. It is necessary to note that the Elvan family's previous lawyer, Can Atalay, is among the accused and currently sentenced to 18 years in prison. The trial should be understood as a retaliation not only against the Gezi protests but also a vengeance against the ones who actively demanded justice for the police killings during the protests. It is possible to trace a Hobbesian rationale behind the Turkish authorities' persistent attempts at criminalising protesters and the protests. The Hobbesian refusal of the people's right to resist against the sovereign is reflected in today's modern political and legal systems as the criminalisation of protests and prosecution of the protesters with accusations of violating the constitutional order.

The aspect that concerns this research is the final Hobbesian notion regarding the use of violence, which accuses the protesters themselves of the violence inflicted upon them. At first glance, this argument may seem old-fashioned and irrelevant to today's modern political and legal systems; however, I believe it requires our attention to grasp the underlying rationale behind the use of state violence during protests and the ineffectiveness of legal accountability processes in its aftermath. Perhaps, then, it would not be wrong to conclude that Hobbes's exclusion of accountability was not accidental, but rather unaccountability appears as a condition for the survival of the *Leviathan*.

Even so, it is possible to note the absence of accountability in modern political and legal considerations of the state and its violent acts. For example, the legal philosopher Alf Ross (1961) presents a detailed elaboration of acts of the state in which he argues for the necessity to constitutionally

11 The number of people who are charged with such offences is not known. However, detailed accounts of the prosecutions between 2013 and 2014 can be found at Amnesty International's Gezi Park reports. See, Amnesty International (2013, 2014).

12 See: 'Gezi Park Protest Trial: Turkish Court Acquits All 26 Defendants'. *The Guardian*, 29 April 2015. Accessed 16 July 2024. www.theguardian.com/world/2015/apr/29/gezi-park-protest-trial-turkish-court-acquits-all-26-defendants.

13 See: Gezi Trial Indictment: Republic of Turkey, Istanbul Office of the Chief Public Prosecutor, Investigation no: 2018/210299, Case no: 2019/9183, Indictment no: 2019/1811.

define state acts, including the use of violence, to bring clarity on the rights, liabilities and responsibilities to what he refers to as the 'organs of the state'. Although he does not explicitly refer to Hobbes, Ross's understanding of state acts is reminiscent of Hobbes's construction of *Leviathan*. Ross classifies state acts into two forms, *acts-in-law* being when an actor who possesses public authority exercises a legally granted power and *factual acts* being acts of physical force (116–121).[14] According to Ross, while the former is 'a power granted to the actor through a rule of competence' (116), the actors of the latter 'possess a qualified freedom of action [....] [T]hey are *privileged* to perform certain acts which are forbidden for people in general' (120). In other words, Ross refers to the state monopoly on violence exercised by some state actors, such as the police. What is worth noting is that Ross conceptualises the granted use of violence in terms of freedom rather than an act relying on or requiring competence like the former category, *acts-in-law*. As a result, Ross considers the issue of personal liability only in relation to the *acts-in-law*. While he concludes that one who violates their duty under *acts-in-law* 'incurs personal liability, but the validity of the act is not affected by this violation' (116), Ross does not consider liability issues regarding violations of *factual acts*. On the contrary, he suggests that 'physical power of compulsion and not a competence – does not seem to be derived from themselves [the actors] in their capacity of individuals, but is attributed to "the State"' (121).

In other words, when a state official causes a violation due to their use of violence, according to Ross, it is not the official who is responsible for this violation, it is the state. If enacting violence on behalf of the state is not an act of individual capacity, then who should be held to account? Ross does not seem to be interested in providing an answer to the issue of accountability that arises from the most critical act of the state, that is, its violence. At this point, it becomes apparent that Ross uses the term 'freedom', regarding the state's privilege to use violence, aptly, as it frees the actor from personal liability. In relation to Berkin Elvan's case, then, if it is not the police officer but the state who is responsible for his death, how is it possible to hold the state to account? In this case, if the police officer is not the person enacting, representing, the state, then who is the state? What I argue here is that the bodily fictitious imaginary of the state not only contributes to the justification of state violence for the objective of protecting its unity and integrity but is also associated with the unaccountability of state violence. On the one hand, it masks the responsibility of those who enact violence on behalf of

14 Ross also considers some non-violent acts under factual acts which are attributed to the state due to them being paid out of public funds, such as building schools and hospitals. However, Ross excludes the actors of such acts as they neither exercise public authority nor pose a public power of coercion. As a result, Ross concludes that 'there is no cause to regard the employees, whether they have the rank of civil servants or not, as "State organs"' (123).

the state, and, on the other, it cannot be held to account due to its fictious, imaginary construct.

In secular and modern legal and political constellations, this fictitious, mystical element of the state is often dismissed. For example, H.L.A. Hart (2012), in *The Concept of Law,* considers a similar unity, which, according to him, provides the foundation for a legal system. Rejecting the ultimate sovereign ruler as the source of unity, one whose command is the law and who accepts obedience in return, Hart argues that it is the community's acceptance of what he calls 'the rule of recognition' that lies at the foundation of a legal order (100–110). The fundamental difference between Hobbes and Hart is that, when the former suggests that it is the unity of the representer, the latter argues that it is the unity of the represented from which law derives its foundation and, in return, brings an order to secure the unity (ibid.). Following this, in *Law's Empire*, Ronald Dworkin (1986) elaborates further on Hart's foundational claim of a united community in respect to the personification of the state. After stating that '[p]olitical integrity assumes a particular deep personification of the community or state', Dworkin clarifies his position: 'I do not intend now to resurrect the metaphysical theory' (167–168). By metaphysical theory, he means theories such as those of Hobbes, who suggest that there is a higher subject that is 'more real than flesh-and-blood people' (ibid.). Instead, Dworkin deliberates on personification by stating that such a construction of a community results in an assumption of a shared morality. Through a short deliberation on communities feeling a 'collective guilt', based on examples such as German society after Nazi rule, Dworkin concludes that the personification of a community is an integral step in constructing political unity, or, in his choice of words, integrity. He concludes, '[o]nce we accept that our officials act in the name of a community of which we are all members, bearing a responsibility we therefore share, then this reinforces and sustains the character of collective guilt, or sense that we must feel shame as well as outrage when they act unjustly' (175). Although he does not aim to resurrect metaphysical theories in his own words, Dworkin kindles yet another, one that not only suggests an imagined united community but also assumes that they share a common belief regarding the state and its institutions. Dworkin's objective to conceptualise a unified community in turn results in his indifference to the hierarchies and cracks within communities, hence resulting in his argument being nothing more than a modern version of the *body politic.* Considering Berkin Elvan's case, the following questions can be posed: What happens then when a group of people within the community do not share the belief that the officials, and hence the state, act on their behalf or in their interest? Or what happens when only a group of the community feels the guilt over the acts of the officials, while others defend the same act? If shared morality is nothing but an assumption, as Dworkin also admits, is it still possible to talk about a united community which constitutes political integrity? When the course of global political history demonstrates that political unifications are always violent events, is it even possible to conceptualise a peaceful unification or set it as an objective in the first place?

To conclude, any modern political and legal conceptualisation of unity and integrity inevitably fails to address the inequalities, hierarchies and cracks for the sake of its defence. This leads to a dismissal of state violence, which occurs as a result of the inequalities and hierarchies present within the imagined unity. In the end, such modern political and legal projections exceptionalise state violence and conceptualise a democratic political and legal system of its unaccountability. What is quite remarkable in the examples presented above is that, although political and legal conceptualisations differ, there is always an imagined unity or integrity. Although it takes different names – subjectification of the state or personification of a community – the unity is a constant insinuation of a unified body, a *body politic*. Yet there is a constant struggle not to fall into mythical terrains. Despite all the attempts to rationalise political and legal myths, they appear time and again at the core of the legal and political constellations. Thus, rather than dismissing the role of myths, I propose that this is exactly what needs to be addressed here. The discussion above exposes a relation between the mythical construction of political unity, law and violence. The mythical, bodily imaginary of the state is the terrain where state and violence become the condition for one another, and in defence of which state violence is excused. Respectively, this book proposes that the convergence of state and violence should be revisited in relation to this mythical terrain.

Mythical (Police) Violence

Walter Benjamin's famous essay 'Critique of Violence' (2007) is a fundamental reference in studying the relationship between the state, law and violence. Benjamin sets out the objectives of this essay in the first sentence: 'the task of a critique of violence can be summarized as that of expounding its relation to law and justice' (277). However, what makes Benjamin's investigation unique within the scholarship is his use of myth in relation to violence and law. Hence, Benjamin's mythical lens serves as a guide throughout this book's investigation of state violence in disclosing the mythical constellation of state, law and violence. In his critique, Benjamin first exposes the mythical operation of state violence to then dismantle this mythical core by juxtaposing it with the divine, what he considers as the pure eternal order. Rather than the theological discussion between the myth and the divine,[15] what interests me in Benjamin's critique regards the role of myth and his

15 On this topic, James R. Martel's *Divine Violence* (2012) focuses on the theological aspect of Benjamin's work and presents a detailed account on his notion of divine violence in relation to sovereignty.

notion of mythical violence, as my objective is to disclose the mythical character of state violence that is performed through the police and its relation to the law. Benjamin's critique exposes the historical function that mythical violence plays in making and preserving legal ends: 'We see here that mythical violence is very much connected with the human project; it creates laws, it establishes boundaries' (Martel 2012, 51). In that regard, it provides us with an invaluable point of departure to address the mythical within the convergence of the state and violence.

Before discussing Benjamin's critique, however, I open a parenthesis here on his usage of myth. In *Myth and Metropolis*, Graeme Gilloch (1997) analyses Benjamin's varying use of myth in his works, uses which are often left unexplained by Benjamin. Gilloch suggests that '"myth" appears to have at least a fourfold significance for him: as fallacious thought, as compulsion, as tyranny, and as a metaphorical device' (9). The first one, myth as a fallacious thought, Gilloch notes, is related to 'illusions and fantasies' (ibid.). He relates the second one, myth as a compulsion, to nature's limitation on human beings: 'In myth, human life is not self-determined or self-governed, but rather is subject to fate and the whim of the gods.' (10). And, he adds, 'myth is the unchanging, a state of apparent "timelessness"' (ibid.). The third aspect, myth as tyranny, follows the second, which 'denote[s] the reversal or inversion of this human submission to nature in the modern period', and, he adds, 'Modernity presents itself as the end of myth' (ibid.). Finally, the fourth use of myth in Benjamin's work, according to Gilloch, is myth 'as a trope or metaphor', which he suggests 'offer clues to those who seek to defeat monstrous powers and facilitate overcoming of myth' (12). In that regard, Gilloch concludes, 'for Benjamin, myth is not simply to be equated with delusion and misrecognition. Myth contains within it positive elements and potentialities which must be preserved and utilized' (ibid.). It is also possible to note such a use of myth in the 'Critique of Violence'. On the one hand myth, and mythical violence, appear as a fallacious thought, something related to 'illusions and fantasies' of the divine and, in that regard, appear timeless, omnipotent and omnipresent; it is something resembling fate but, on the other hand, it presents an opening for us to dismantle itself. In that regard, following this explanation, I understand Benjamin's notion of myth in the *Critique* as twofold: myth signifying a fallacy of the positive law and a fantasy of state violence which, at the same time, bears the potential to undo itself, which I discuss further in the following chapters.

To begin unpacking this, it is necessary to briefly mention Benjamin's separation between mythical and divine, in which the former appears as a mortal imitation of the eternal form of the latter, as he writes: '[a]ll the eternal forms are open to pure divine violence, which myth bastardized with law' (300). As this quote displays, according to Benjamin, the law plays a significant role in the making of mythical violence and, hence, he begins his investigation by discussing the natural and positive law in relation to violence. According to

Benjamin, natural law 'regards violence as a natural datum', and positive law 'sees violence as a product of history' (278). Hence, he suggests that, when natural law justifies violence as a means, the positive law justifies it in terms of just ends (ibid.). Although this may appear as two opposites at first, Benjamin suggests that this leads to a common maxim in justifying violence: 'just ends can be attained by justified means, justified means used for just ends' (ibid.). Benjamin does not address the question of justness *per se*, but, rather, his critique circles around the means/ends relation of violence, which finds its legitimation through its historical acknowledgement. Indeed, although Benjamin does not discuss it at great length, he attributes a pivotal role to history.[16] In the 'Critique of Violence', history appears to offer a grand narrative to argue the necessity of positive law and to legitimise its end; as he writes, 'positive law demands of all violence a proof of its historical origin, which under certain conditions is declared legal, sanctioned' (280). Furthermore, for Benjamin, history appears to establish a separation between unsanctioned and sanctioned, violence: 'The distinction is between historically acknowledged, so-called sanctioned violence, and unsanctioned violence' (279).

Although Benjamin does not explicitly refer to Hobbes, I read his remarks in relation to Hobbes's *Leviathan*. By doing so, it is possible to acknowledge *Leviathan*'s historical claim, on which Hobbes builds his social contract theory, in relation to violence. To recall briefly, in *Leviathan*, Hobbes claims to provide a reading of history which begins with an all-violent state of nature – 'this warre of every man against every man' (1991, 90). For Hobbes, this is the result of equality among 'men' as he writes, 'from this equality of ability, ariseth equality of hope in the attaining of our Ends' (87–88). Similar to Benjamin's analysis on natural law, which I mentioned above, Hobbes considers violence as a natural right, *Jus Naturale*, in this state of nature; and hence, for him, violence is a legitimate means to attain ends and also to secure them (91). Hobbes' fictitious portrayal of man's state of nature serves as a legitimate ground for the necessity of his social contract theory: 'And therefore, as long as this natural Right of every man to every thing endureth, there can be no security to any man' (ibid.), and, as a result, Hobbes suggests, in the name of peace, everyone should enter into a contract through which they would exchange their limitless liberty for security by giving up their right to violence to the sovereign or, in its contemporary form, to the monopoly of the state (92).[17] While arguing so, however, Hobbes presents *Leviathan*'s fictional account of the state of nature in combination with an actual historical

16 Benjamin's detailed account of history can be found in 'Theses on the Philosophy of History', where Benjamin begins his investigation on history with a puppet analogy. In an interesting coincidence, Benjamin likens this puppet dressed 'in Turkish attire' to 'historical materialism' (Benjamin 2007, 253).

17 'That a man be willing, when others are so too, as farre-forth, as for Peace, and defence of himself he shall think it necessary, to lay down this right to all things; and be contented with so much liberty against other men, as he would allow other men against himselfe' (92).

event, the English Civil War.[18] By doing so, I suggest, Hobbes' fiction of the state of nature gains a historicity, a sense of realness and a lived experience. In that regard, to add to Benjamin's remarks on history, the example of Hobbes's *Levitahan* exposes that the historical origins of positive law are already mythical, almost like a fairy tale everyone knows but of which no one knows the origin. Additionally, to avoid another civil war, as discussed in the section above, Hobbes grants sanctioned violence only to the sovereign to protect itself against the people, and, hence, to protect the social contract. To put it in a Benjaminian context, then, while the state's use of violence gets a historical acknowledgement for the protection of the social contract, in other words, to establish and sustain the positive law, all other forms of violence, and especially the ones against the state, are unsanctioned for the same end. In other words, the peaceful premise of Hobbes' social contract is based on and secured through the state's monopoly of violence. As Benjamin also discloses, even though all parties peacefully enter into the contract, every contract contains the possibility of violence as '[i]t confers on both parties the right to take recourse to violence in some form against the other, should he break the agreement' (2007, 288). And, he adds, '[n]ot only that; like the outcome, the origin of every contract also points toward violence' (ibid.). In that regard, considering Hobbes's half-fictional, half-historical narrative through the lens of Benjamin exposes how history, or rather the state's claim on history, justifies the state's monopoly on violence as a means to the end that is positive law.

As becomes apparent through the example of Hobbes' *Leviathan*, violence as the means to the end of positive law has two functions: one that establishes the legal order and the other one that sustains it. Benjamin refers to the former as *lawmaking* and the latter as *law-preserving* violence. According to Benjamin, the *lawmaking* function is inherent to violence, whether it is issued individually or as a group: Benjamin gives the example of the labour movement and the right to strike (281–283). Contrary to the *lawmaking* function, however, Benjamin reads the *law-preserving* function as something specific to the state's use of violence 'for the subordination of citizens to laws' (284). Furthermore, Benjamin notes, 'law-preserving violence is a threatening violence' (285). For him, this resembles fate, and he adds, 'The deepest purpose of the uncertainty of the legal threat will emerge from the later consideration of the sphere of fate in which it originates' (285).

Before discussing its relation to fate, however, I first would like to consider what Benjamin refers to as violence and to then analyse his remarks on police violence. The 'Critique of Violence' was originally written in German. As

18 As Richard Tuck explains in the introduction to the *Leviathan*'s Cambridge edition, Hobbes wrote *Leviathan* in response to the English Civil War, and he wished the *Leviathan* to serve as a guide in its aftermath, so that, as Tuck notes, 'he attempted to persuade Charles II of the merits of the book' (xxv).

each linguistic form is a manifestation of contexts, concepts and meanings that merge in a unique constellation, the English translation is conditioned to present Benjamin's thoughts within its own form.[19] In that sense, to discuss Benjamin's critique further, it is necessary to register what he means by violence, or rather, by *Gewalt*. Peter Fenves (2019), in his article in the special issue of *Critical Times* on the recent translation of Benjamin's *Zur Kritik der Gewalt*,[20] reminds us that '*Gewalt* means not only "violence" but also "power," "control," "dominion," "force," "supremacy,"' (210). In that regard, the double function of *lawmaking* and *law-preserving* violence operates within the broad framework of *Gewalt*, which Fenves registers as an ambiguity of the German language.

On the other hand, Jacques Derrida, in his famous text, 'Force of Law: The "Mystical Foundation of Authority"' (1992) also touches upon the German-specific meaning of *Gewalt* and suggests that neither its English nor French translation do justice to its authentic meaning: 'These two translations [...] are very active interpretations that don't do justice to the fact that *Gewalt* also signifies, for Germans, legitimate power, authority or power of the state' (6). In that regard, unlike Fenves, I consider the broad meaning of *Gewalt* as something bearing all aspects of violence in both active and passive forms, which, through Derrida's reading, indicate both active forms of state violence and passive forms of violence of state institutions.[21]

From this point forward, Benjamin's remarks on police violence become even more intelligible as he notes that police violence contains both functions of violence. He writes, 'Police violence is emancipated from both conditions. It is lawmaking, for its characteristic function is not the promulgation of laws but the assertion of legal claims for any decree, and law-preserving, because

19 As Benjamin reminds us in *The Task of the Translator* (2009), 'Clearly a translation, no matter how good it is, can never mean anything so far as the original is concerned' (31).

20 The new translation is titled 'Toward the Critique of Violence', see: Walter Benjamin. 2021. *Toward the Critique of Violence: A Critical Edition*. Eds. Peter Fenves and Julia Ng. California: Stanford University Press.

21 Benjamin does not oppose violence per se, and he does not advocate non-violence. Hence, it is possible to advance the argument that what Benjamin critiques is state violence or, to put it in Benjaminian terms, the use of violence in relation to means/ends. He discusses his position through the commandment of 'thou shalt not kill', which he does not read as a strict restriction but rather as guidance and leaves, or rather frees, the issue of self-defence as an open-ended deliberation which is to be handled singularly on a case-by-case basis. He suggests that the commandment 'Thou shalt not kill' is rather 'a guideline for the actions for persons or communities who have to wrestle with it in solitude and in exceptional cases, to take on themselves the responsibility of ignoring it' (298). Başak Ertür reads Benjamin's handling of self-defence as a move that frees self-defence from the dialectics between natural and positive laws and instead presents it as 'an ethical option' (Ertür 2019, 274). Slavoj Žižek not only reads it as an ethical option but also as a move to oppose 'the "totalitarian" justification of killing done by those who act as instruments of the big Other' (Žižek 2008, 200). In that sense, it can be argued that, with this unexpected ethical move, Benjamin aims to free violence from the monopoly of the state which either claims to act on behalf of or drives its power from the divine.

it is at the disposal of these ends' (2007, 286–287). Through a Derridean lens, then, police violence operates in both the active and passive meanings of *Gewalt*. In reference to the discussion above on the police encounter, then, police violence is both active, in terms of its enactment of physical violence, but at the same time passive, as it aims to *interpellate*, in other words, to subjectify the other. To put this in Butlerian terms, it 'has the effect of binding the law to the one who is hailed' (2011, 81). Furthermore, Benjamin observes this peculiar double function of police violence makes the police violence formless and arbitrary, almost ghostly: 'its power is formless, like its nowhere tangible, all-pervasive, ghostly presence in the life of civilized states' (287).

Derrida (1992) picks up Benjamin's brief remark on the ghostly presence of police violence and elaborates it further. Reiterating Benjamin's account of police violence, Derrida notes the reason behind the 'phantom-like' character of police violence is 'because it mixes foundation with conservation and becomes all the more violent for this' (44). What Derrida highlights in Benjamin's remarks on police violence is the peculiar merging of *lawmaking* and *law-preserving* functions of violence, which enacts a specific terror and makes them a ghostly figure: 'that they are a faceless figure, a violence without a form', which makes police violence 'ungraspable in every way' (ibid.). On this note, Berkin Elvan's killing and its aftermath expose that the ghostliness of police violence expands beyond the act of violence to the processes of accountability. As I discuss in detail in Chapter 4, despite an investigation lasting for two years, which brought charges to one police officer, Fatih Dalgalı, covering and uncovering the identity of the police officer who is responsible for Elvan's death was the main occupation of the court hearings. In a Benjaminian vein, it is possible to argue that the reason for the failure of the legal processes of accountability, especially after the ghostly police violence, has something to do with their ticsdue to the means/ends structure.

In addition, throughout his critique, Benjamin mentions fate. Although Benjamin does not provide a clear direction on his usage of fate, it appears as something belonging to the origins of the positive law: 'It [positive law] sees this interest in the representation and preservation of an order imposed by fate' (2007, 285). Furthermore, he argues that positive law operates 'in the name of a formless "freedom" [...] which resides in the fact that there is only one fate and that what exists, and in particular what threatens, belongs inviolably to its order. For law-preserving violence is a threatening violence' (ibid.). There are a few things I would like to raise in relation to this quote. To begin with, as Benjamin clearly expresses afterwards, for him, 'violence crowned by fate, is the origin of law' (286). I read 'violence crowned by fate' as the *lawmaking* violence establishing a legal order. If this is the case, then positive law becomes essentially dependent on the existence of that fate in order to sustain itself. With this move, Benjamin discloses the arbitrary, formless freedom that lies in the basis of positive law, which erupts during its preservation. Hence, formless freedom of fate is what makes *law-preserving* violence threatening; it is the threat of reacting arbitrarily, of the formless freedom of fate to sustain the legal end: 'The deepest purpose of the uncertainty of the legal threat will emerge from the later consideration of the sphere of fate in which it originates' (ibid.). Through a Benjaminian lens, it is possible to consider Hobbes's social contract theory as a fate of the modern political systems, which establishes a legal order that presents this fate as the only fate to sustain itself. Hence, I suggest that both positive law and police violence operate within the sphere of fate as they are committed to sustaining the legal order originated by the 'violence crowned by fate' (ibid.).

This is what Benjamin refers to as the mythical violence that is 'fate-imposed violence' (294). At this point, Benjamin refers to the myth of Niobe to explain the operation of mythical violence. To reiterate Benjamin's presentation of the myth, the mortal Niobe angers the fertility goddess, Leto, by boasting that she is more fertile than her. In return, Leto orders her two children, Apollo and Artemis, to kill all of Niobe's fourteen children but to spare her. In the end, Niobe's guilty suffering turns her to stone (294–295). Benjamin calls upon this myth to argue the differences between mythical and divine violence and to demonstrate how the former imitates the latter. He concludes that 'Niobe's arrogance calls down fate upon itself not because her arrogance offends against the law but because it challenges fate – to a fight in which fate must triumph, and can bring to light a law only in its triumph' (294). I suggest reading Benjamin's remarks on the myth of Niobe with the discussion above on fate, in which Niobe challenges the only fate that sustains the mythical order of the Greek mythical world.[22] As a result, the myth has to end with the triumph of that one fate which brings death to Niobe's children and traps her in an eternal guilt. This guilt resembles the guilty feeling that makes the hailed one turn to the police's hailing, which is an internalisation of the law and accepting and submitting to its binding force. In *Parting Ways* (2014) Butler reads Benjamin's critique as 'the desire to release life from a guilt secured through legal contract with the state – this would be a desire that gives rise to a violence against violence, one that seeks to release life from a death contract with the law, a death of the living soul by the hardening force of guilt' (82). Furthermore, Derrida points out another aspect in Benjamin's reading of the myth of Niobe when he writes, 'the violence that falls upon Niobe comes from fate; and this fate can only be uncertain and ambiguous' (1992, 52) after Derrida refers to it as '"demonic" ambiguity of this mythical positioning of *droit*' (ibid.).

22 Based on Benjamin's essay 'Fate and Character', Andrew Benjamin highlights that fate has a specific Ancient Greek association in Walter Benjamin's work (Benjamin 2012, 69–93). In a similar vein, Derrida highlights in *Force of Law* that Benjamin associates mythical violence with the Greek world and divine violence with Judaism (1992, 52).

Following the discussion above, I suggest that the law and police violence both operate through this 'demonic ambiguity' which disguises itself as fate. In that regard, I read Elvan's deadly encounter with the police in terms of this disguise. When he was shot by a gas canister that morning, Elvan was on his way to the bakery to buy bread. It is possible to say that the work of fate begins here; however, what transforms this mundane task into a deadly fate is the presence of police violence on his path to the bakery, which was situated on his path to sustain the fate of the positive law during the Gezi protests. This echoes the Hobbesian position which justifies the sovereign's right to kill those who revolt. To put it in Benjaminian terms, when violence becomes the means for re-asserting and preserving the legal ends, it mimics the arbitrary, formless freedom of fate.

As I discuss in detail in the following chapter, this is the reason behind the then-Prime Minister Erdoğan's interpretation of Elvan's death as the tragic fate of a boy who has done something he should not. Fate, the only fate, is the one that confirms the legal order, which is based on the state's monopoly on violence. That is the mythical violence in which the police violence inflicted on Berkin Elvan appeared as if it was his fate, and also ambiguous, as if tear gas canisters casually rain from the skies, which at the same time erased its actor, as the police became a ghostly figure.

Graeme Gilloh writes that, for Benjamin, '[t]he mythic is not to be celebrated, but rather must be ruined, reduced to rubble to free its positive potential. To do this, however, one must find the destructive, or rather self-destructive moment hidden within the myths of modernity' and, he concludes, 'the mythic paradoxically contains the seeds of its own overcoming, the end of myth' (1997, 176). Elvan died as a result of this encounter after staying in a coma for almost one year in the passage of death. During this time, Elvan was commonly referred to as *umudun çocuğu*, 'child of hope'. The hope that manifested through Elvan does not only signify a hope for his survival but also a hope for holding the state to account, suggesting that his innocence as a child would have exposed the excessive, arbitrary police violence. It did not. On the contrary, Elvan and his family were compared to terrorists by state officials and felt as if they were the ones on trial during the court process, which I discuss in the following chapters. Nevertheless, following Benjamin's 'Critique of Violence', I do not consider Elvan's deadly encounter, and its aftermath, as a confirmation of the omnipotent and omnipresent power of the state. On the contrary, I read it in a similar vein to James R. Martel's (2018) reading of the unburied dead bodies as 'defying state projections of power and authority' (11).

Throughout this book, I consider Elvan's killing and its aftermath as a chain of interconnected events which expose various facets of myths and assumptions that surround the notion of state violence and its accountability. In this chapter, I have laid out the theoretical foundations of my investigation while inquiring into the moment when the state manifests through police violence. In so doing, through the works of Benjamin and Derrida, I disclosed the ghostliness of the police and the fateful arbitrariness of police violence. The phantom-like character of the police also signifies a lack of personal agency, as the police do not act on their behalf but on behalf of a higher subject, *the State*. As a result, as we have seen through Alf Ross's elaboration, the police are freed from being personally responsible for their actions. Perhaps it is possible to argue that the state manifests regarding the question of responsibility. It is interesting, in that regard, that although both Ross and Elvan's funeral crowd attribute responsibility to the state, rather than to the police, state accountability is not considered within modern political and legal constructions however. What we have, rather, is a phantasmatic subject, a unified political and legal entity with omnipotent and omnipresent powers. In that regard, it is significant how police violence, on the one hand, renders the material subject, the police officer, ghostly, while, on the other hand, materialising the mythical imaginary of the state. For that reason, I argue that the question of accountability requires us to analyse the mythical imaginary of the state, since this imaginary is not only unaccountable according to the existing legal and political structures but also hides the acting subjects under its fantasy. In this chapter, through an analysis of *Leviathan*, I disclosed the state's modern (bodily) construction. Again, the point that is worth noting in this construction is the issue of responsibility, as Hobbes's social contract theory attributes responsibility to the victims of state violence. Indeed, the mythical imaginary of the state may show nuances in its construction and operation due to different socio-political contexts; in the following chapter I explore this operation within the context of contemporary Turkey.

References

Amnesty International. 2013. 'Gezi Protests: The Brutal Denial of Right to Peaceful Assembly'. 2 October. Accessed 16 July 2024. https://www.amnesty.org/en/documents/EUR44/022/2013/en/.

Amnesty International UK. 2014. 'Turkey: Gezi Park Protests On Year On – Police Remain Unpunished, Demonstrators Go on Trial'. *Press Release*. 9 June. Accessed 16 July 2024. https://www.amnesty.org.uk/press-releases/turkey-gezi-park-protests-year-police-remain-unpunished-demonstrators-go-trial.

Althusser, Louis. 2014. 'Ideology and Ideological State Apparatuses'. In *On the Reproduction of Capitalism*. London: Verso. 232–272.

Aretxaga, Begoña. 2005. *States of Terror: Begoña Aretxaga's Essays*. Edited by Joseba Zulaika. Nevada: Center for Basque Studies.

Benjamin, Andrew. 2012. 'Fate and Character'. In *Working with Walter Benjamin: Recovering a Political Philosophy*.. Edinburgh: Edinburgh University Press. 69–93.

Benjamin, Walter. 2007. 'Critique of Violence'. In *Reflections: Essays, Aphorisms, Autobiographical Writings*. New York: Harcourt Inc. 277–300.

Benjamin, Walter. 2009. 'The Task of the Translator'. *One-Way Street and Other Writings*. London: Penguin Books. 29–45.

Benjamin, Walter. 2021. *Toward the Critique of Violence: A Critical Edition*. Edited by Peter Fenves and Julia Ng. Stanford, CA: Stanford University Press.
Butler, Judith. 1997. *The Psychic Life of Power: Theories in Subjection*. Stanford, CA: Stanford University Press.
Butler, Judith. 2011. *Bodies that Matter: On the Discursive Limits of 'Sex'*. Oxford: Routledge.
Butler, Judith. 2014. 'Walter Benjamin and the Critique of Violence'. In *Parting Ways: Jewishness and the Critique of Zionism*. West Sussex: Colombia University Press. 69–98.
Berkin Elvan Indictment: Republic of Turkey, Istanbul Office of the Chief Public Prosecutor, Investigation no: 2013/155787, Case no: 2016/42124, Indictment no: 2016/4484.
Derrida, Jacques. 1992. 'Force of Law: The "Mystical Foundation of Authority"'. In *Deconstruction and the Possibility of Justice*, edited by David Gray Carlson, Drucilla Cornell and Michel Rosenfeld. New York and London: Routledge. 3–67.
De Pizan, Christine. 1994. *The Book of the Body Politic*. Edited by Kate Longdon Forhan. Cambridge: Cambridge University Press.
Dworkin, Ronald. 1986. *Law's Empire*. Cambridge: Harvard University Press.
Ertür, Başak. 2019. 'Conscription and Critique'. *Critical Times* 2(2): 270–284.
Fenves, Peter. 2019. 'Intervention, Encroachment'. *Critical Times* 2(2): 209–220.
Forhan, Langdon Kate, and Cary Joseph Nederman, eds. 1993. *Medival Political Theory: A Reader: The Quest for the Body Politic 1100–1400*. London: Routledge.
Genet, Jean. 2019. *The Thief's Journal*. London: Faber & Faber Limited.
Gilloch, Graeme. 1997. *Myths and Petropolis: Walter Benjamin and the City*. Cambridge: Polity Press.
Gönen, Zeynep, and Deniz Yonucu. 2012. 'Legitimizing Violence and Segregation: Neoliberal Discourses on Crime and the Criminalization of Urban Poor Populations in Turkey'. In *Lumpencity: Discourses of Marginality/ Marginalizing Discources*, edited by Alan Bourke, Tia Dafnos and Markus Kip. Ottawa: Red Quill Books. 75–103.
Hart, H. L. A. 2012. *The Concept of Law*. Oxford: Oxford University Press.
Hobbes, Thomas. 1991. *Leviathan*. Edited by Richard Tuck. Cambridge: Cambridge University Press.
Kantorowicz, Ernst H. 1997. The King's *Two Bodies: A Study in Mediaeval Political Theology*. Princeton and Princeton, NJ: Princeton University Press.
Lamb, Melayna Kay. 2024. *A Philosophical History of Police Power*. London: Bloomsbury Academic.
Martel, James R. 2012. *Divine Violence: Walter Benjamin and the Eschatology of Sovereignty*. Oxon: Routledge.
Martel, James R. 2018. *Bodies Unburied: Subversive Corpses and the Authority of the Dead*. Amherst, MA: The Amherst College Press.
Navaro-Yashin, Yael. 2002. *Faces of the State: Secularism and Public Life in Turkey*. Princeton and Oxford: Princeton University Press.
Rose, Jacqueline. 1996. *States of Fantasy*. New York: Oxford University Press.
Ross, Alf. 1961. 'On the Concepts "State" and "State Organs" in Constitutional Law'. *Scandinavian Studies in Law* 5: 111–130.
Schmitt, Carl. 1996. *The Leviathan in the State Theory of Thomas Hobbes: Meaning and Failure of a Political Symbol*. London: Greenwood Press.

Sharma, Aradhana, and Akhil Gupta. 2006. *The Anthropology of the State: A Reader*. Oxford: Blackwell Publishing.

Sherman, Claire Richter. 1995. *Imaging Aristotle: Verbal and Visual Representation in Fourteenth Century France*. California and London: University of California Press.

Skinner, Quentin. 2007. 'Hobbes on Persons, Authors and Representatives'. *The Cambridge Companion to Hobbes's Leviathan*, edited by Patricia Springborg. Cambridge: Cambridge University Press. 157–180.

Skinner, Quentin. 2018. *From Humanism to Hobbes: Studies in Rhetoric and Politics*. Cambridge: Cambridge University Press.

Taussig, Michael. 1992. *The Nervous System*. New York and London: Routledge.

Yonucu, Deniz. 2014. 'Okmeydanı Üzerine Notlar (1)'. *Evrensel*. 1 June. Accessed 28 September 2021. https://www.evrensel.net/haber/85437/okmeydani-uzerine-notlar-1.

Yonucu, Deniz. 2022. *Police, Provocation, Politics: Counterinsurgency in Istanbul*. Ithaca and London: Cornell University Press.

Žižek, Slavoj. 2008. *The Sublime Object of Ideology*. London and New York: Verso.

Chapter 2

Stately Performatives

Two days after Berkin Elvan's funeral, on 14 March 2014, the then-Prime Minister, and now-President, R.T. Erdoğan responded to his killing during a rally speech. In the trajectory of Berkin Elvan's case, this five-minute mention has a significant place as it was the first time Erdoğan commented on Elvan's case.[1] In his hour-long address, Erdoğan commented on Elvan's killing in these words:

> There was a funeral in Istanbul a couple of days ago. Unfortunately, a child who was among the terror groups, whose face was masked, with a slingshot put into his hand and iron marbles in his pocket, was exposed to teargas. How could the police identify the age of a masked person throwing iron marbles with a slingshot?[2]
>
> (Parti Mitingleri 2014).

In his speech, Erdoğan presents the killing of Elvan as a tragic but expected consequence of Elvan's own actions. In order to do so, Erdoğan evokes a common visual description of a so called violent protester who throws iron marbles and firecrackers at police while in disguise. Although there is no evidence supporting this description of Elvan at the time of the incident, Erdoğan refers to an earlier image of Elvan that has been circulated by the People's Front, which I discuss in the following chapter. Erdoğan later insinuates that Elvan's actions are an outcome of his bad upbringing by his terrorist-sympathiser family. Then he diverges his attention from the Elvan family

1 A year later, the Turkish newspaper *BirGün* published Erdoğan's remarks on Elvan's killing. The text demonstrates that Erdoğan's response had not changed throughout the time and that he argued against his responsibility, although, as the newspaper article demonstrates, he once said that he had given the orders to clear the park and to put an end to the demonstrations. 'Unutulmasın Diye...Berkin İçin Nerede Ne Demişti?' *BirGün*, 16 June 2015. Accessed 16 July 2024. www.birgun.net/haber/unutulmasin-diye-berkin-icin-nerede-ne-demisti-82892.

2 Translation from its Turkish original belongs to me. Erdoğan's full address can be reached at Parti Mitingleri (2014).

DOI: 10.4324/9781032690070-3

to his opponent, the then-Opposition leader Kemal Kılıçdaroğlu, and accuses him of being a terrorist sympathiser due to his support of the Elvan family. This time, almost in a shouting voice, Erdoğan addresses the following words to the rally crowd:

> Despite the facts, Kılıçdaroğlu refers to Elvan as a child who was on the way to buy bread. Be honest, he was not on the way to buy bread! And what is remarkable is that Elvan's mother says it is the Prime Minister who killed my child. I can relate to the love of a child, but I did not understand why you [Elvan's mother] throw carnations and iron marbles on your child's grave. What message are you trying to give by throwing those iron marbles on his grave?
>
> (Parti Mitingleri 2014)

Iron marbles are considered a common weapon used against the police by protesters; combined with slingshots and firecrackers, they are the everyday weapons of resistance. However, marbles bear an interesting double symbolism as glass marbles are also a common symbol of childhood. Remarkably Erdoğan sees terrorism in a symbol of childhood. In return to Erdoğan's words, the crowd expresses their disapproval of the mother with boos. There is something scandalous in this call and answer. It is something beyond the scandal of accusing Elvan and his family, which has resonated with discontent in the Turkish media[3] as well as in the international media under the titles such as: 'Berkin Elvan: Turkish PM accuses dead boy of terror links'[4] and 'Erdoğan makes crowd boo Berkin Elvan's family'.[5] In his response, Erdoğan does not comment on any legal or political processes regarding Elvan's killing, yet claims the righteousness of facts. Although he adopts a casual tone, his address is a pre-written and practised speech, a performance that transmits

3 The scene of the booing of Elvan's mother had preoccupied public discussion for a while. Even so, a Turkish singer, Yavuz Bingöl, who appeared to be close to Erdoğan at the time, excused the booing in an interview on 3 December 2014. Bingöl suggested that Erdoğan made the crowd boo the mother because people had cursed Erdoğan's mother; see Ahmet Hakan, 'Bütün Yönleriyle Yavuz Bingöl Olayı'. Hürriyet, 5 December 2014. Accessed 16 July 2024. www.hurriyet.com.tr/yazarlar/ahmet-hakan/butun-yonleriyle-yavuz-bingol-olayi-27711761. The statement caused yet another wave of uproar in public; even so, Elvan's mother responded to Bingöl, asking whether he would have joined the booing crowd. See 'Berkin'in Annesinden Bingöl'e: Sen de Yuhalayacak Mıydın?' Ege'den Son Söz, 3 December 2014. Accessed 16 July 2024. www.egedesonsoz.com/haber/berkin-in-annesinden-bingol-e-sen-de-yuhalayacak-miydin/884951

4 'Berkin Elvan: Turkish PM Accuses Dead Boy of Terror Links'. *BBC*, 15 March 2014. Accessed 16 July 2024. www.bbc.co.uk/news/world-europe-26594922.

5 'Erdoğan Makes Crowd Boo Berkin Elvan's family'. *Al-Monitor*, 16 March 2014. Accessed 16 July 2024. www.al-monitor.com/pulse/originals/2014/03/Erdoğan-terrorist-elvan-crowd-incitement-elections.html.

the Hobbesian message, as discussed in the previous chapter, that those who rebel against the sovereign are the ones responsible for their deadly fate. In that regard, Erdoğan's rally speech performance responds to the political and legal demands of accountability by their rejection. Furthermore, what is worth our attention is the way in which he communicates this rejection. He does not reject the demands for accountability and his responsibility through directly addressing such arguments, but rather, he does so by shifting the discussion from political and legal processes of accountability to a family matter. This shift peaks at the moment of the call and answer of booing Elvan's mother, the failed mother who raised a disobedient son.

Indeed, Erdoğan's rally speech is built on a family analogy. While referring to a time before the AKP rule, he presents personal anecdotes from his own family. He discloses the hard decisions he had to make as the father as if he is having a heart-to-heart with the rally crowd. This father figure, which he performs, serves as a passage from personal to national, as he tacitly invokes a common political imaginary of modern Turkey: *devlet baba*. In the reading I provide in this chapter, *devlet baba*, which translates as *father-state*, is the myth of the Turkish state that Erdoğan consults in his response to Elvan's killing as well as to the dissolution of the unified state imaginary. The two aspects, which are uniting the state and the subjection of Elvan and his family, are intertwined under the mythical stately image of the *father-state*. Thus, in this chapter, I refer to Erdoğan's *father-state* performance as a *stately performative*. My suggestion of the term *stately performative* is not only to highlight its magnitude, as the word 'stately' would suggest in its common usage; rather, I use *stately performative* in reference to performatives which are performed by the ones who claim, and acclaim, the mythical imaginary of the state and its powers. My objective in suggesting the term *stately performative* is associated to the task of understanding how the state acts, and how it is constructed through such acts. As I explain further in this chapter through Erdoğan's rally speech, what I read as a *stately performative* is Erdoğan's enactment of a political myth, namely the *father-state,* which is deeply rooted in Turkey's political culture, and which constructs a certain knowledge of the (Turkish) state. In that regard, as I discuss further in this chapter, Erdoğan's rally speech, as a *stately performative*, performs and reconstructs the state by evoking majestic, mythical, and *stately* constellations within which Elvan has a role as a misbehaving, disobedient son.

As the chapter inquires into the doings of Erdoğan's rally speech, it contributes to the existing literature on performative utterances while focusing on the reciprocal operation of Erdoğan's *stately performative*, which plays out in the form of a call and an answer. The call – that is Erdoğan's accusation of Elvan, his mother and the opposition leader – is complemented by and completed with the audience's boos. As I unpack further below, I read the call-and-answer format of Erdoğan's *stately performative* as something challenging the absolute (sovereign) authority that is commonly attributed to the utterer and which exposes the mythical performance of this assumption. In relation to the discussion in Chapter 1 on the mythical existence of the state and its manifestation through the everyday performance of statecraft, this chapter suggests that Erdoğan is not the only (sovereign) utterer of the *stately performative*. Although his call intends to receive a certain answer, it still bears a potential for its refusal, a refusal of the mythical imaginary of the state and its powers, which is situated between the gap of the call and the answer. The chapter first carries out a conceptual discussion on Erdoğan's rally speech to locate this potential within the operation of his *stately performative*. Then, through a close reading of the rally speech, the chapter discloses the making of political myths and introduces the Turkey-specific mythical framework of the *father-state*. Finally, the chapter elaborates on Elvan's disposition within the mythical state imaginary of the *father-state*.

Between Performance and Performativity

I read Erdoğan's rally speech, in which he addressed the death of Berkin Elvan, in two parts. The first part is when Erdoğan accused Elvan of imitating terrorists, if not actually being one, and the second part is when Erdoğan extends this accusation to his opponent and, more significantly, to Elvan's mother who, in turn, received boos from the rally crowd. The first part, in which Erdoğan likens Elvan to a terrorist, 'whose face was masked, with a slingshot put into his hand and iron marbles in his pocket', utters an accusation without pronouncing the exact words: *I accuse*. This accusation is a performance of the Hobbesian maxim, as discussed in the previous chapter, which accuses the victims of state violence of violating the covenant, hence finding the victims responsible for the violence inflicted upon them. In that regard, with the accusation, Erdoğan responds to the demands of accountability by subjectifying Elvan as a disobedient son, which I discuss further in the following sections. In the second part of his rally speech, however, as he extends the accusation towards his opponent and Elvan's mother, Erdoğan performs a *stately* imaginary. His *stately performative* then receives a confirmation, a validation from the rally crowd in the form of boos. I present the meanings behind his *stately performative* in detail in the following sections; in this section, however, I present a discussion regarding the conceptual framework of performative utterances which allows us to register the many doings of Erdoğan's rally speech.

At this point, it is necessary to present a brief account of performative utterances. Linguistic philosopher J.L. Austin's work on performative utterances, introduced in a series of lectures in 1955 and later published under the title of *How to Do Things with Words* (1975), constitutes the foundation of studies on performativity. Austin's notion of performative utterances is a rather strict linguistic category with many conditions to fulfil, which even Austin himself fails to obey. Scholars (such as Derrida 1988; Felman 2003) who follow Austin and reconsider his notion understand his failings in terms of unexplored potentials of performative utterances. In Austin's words, performative utterances are the ones 'in which to *say* something is to *do* something; or in which *by* saying or *in* saying something we are doing something' (12). Although, according to Austin, performative utterances grammatically appear like statements, which Austin calls constative utterances, performative utterances diverge from constatives as they are neither true nor false, and they do not describe, report or constate anything (5). It is necessary to note that, throughout his lectures, Austin struggles with this constative/performative distinction, which he addresses in the final lecture. Shoshana Felman (2003), in her cross-reading of Austin with Moliere's play *Don Juan*, presents an analysis of Austin's notion of performative utterances while considering Austin's own performance in delivering lectures. Felman notes that 'Austinian analysis, if it is an act, is only the act of *failing to grasp the constative of the performative*' (43). Felman reads this as a scandal in which Austin scandalously realises that the constative/performative distinction does not hold. The scandal, however, is not in the failure of performativity as a pure linguistic form but rather, as Felman suggests, its own subversion while performing the performatives. Thus, Felman argues that Austin's theory of the performative includes all its exclusions and failures: 'the capacity for failure is situated not outside but inside the performative, both as speech-act and as theoretical instrument' (45).

Furthermore, Austin's performative utterances follow a specific sentence syntax; they are all 'verbs in the first person singular present indicative active' (1975, 5). Austin provides examples such as: 'I promise', 'I apologize', 'I dare you', 'I bet', 'I sentence you' and 'I do' (as in a marriage ceremony). Although, according to Austin, the performative utterances do not have a true/false judgement, they nonetheless must fulfil certain conditions to be successful, all of which are related to having the right context, procedure and actor (14–15). Austin lists those conditions under three categories; while the first category has to do with having 'accepted conventional procedures' (A.1) in which the performative utterance is uttered by the appropriate person (A.2), the second category has to do with the execution of the procedure (B.1 and B.2), that it must be completely executed by all appropriate actors (ibid.). In other words, for Austin, conventions are essential in defining and performing performative utterances; and, hence, failure in both categories results in void performative utterances, which he refers to as *misfires*.[6] The third category, on the other hand, has to do with thoughts, feelings and emotions.

6 Austin names the failure of the first category as *misinvocations* and the failure of the second category as *misexecutuions* (18). It is necessary to note that the names Austin gives to infelicities are not definite; as the publisher notes, in his lectures, from time to time Austin refers to them by different names, such as non-plays for A.1, misplays for A.2 ... etc. (1975, 5).

For example, the person who says 'I do' in a wedding ceremony could be unwilling to do so. However, regardless of their insincerity, the convention validates the performative utterance and they are married. Austin refers to failures of all the categories as *infelicities* and considers the third case as *abuses*; the 'act [is] professed but hollow' (18). In that regard, for Austin, neither feelings nor emotions are factors determining the validity of a performative utterance; nor do they have the potential to trigger a convention-like process, which I observe in Erdoğan's exchange with the rally crowd, as I explain further below.

Austin's treatment of emotions and feelings within his coinage of performative utterances interests me, as Erdoğan's accusation, *I accuse*, provoked certain feelings and moved the rally crowd. Not only did his accusation of Elvan and his mother initiate the rally crowd to express their feelings in boos, but his initiation, which was captured by the media as Erdoğan's doing, as mentioned above, also generated certain feelings in the public. Thus, it is possible to argue that in both cases Erdoğan's accusation produced certain effects. Indeed, later on in his lectures, while aiming to clarify the borders of performative utterances, Austin suspends the performative/constative distinction and introduces another set of categories, namely *locutionary, illocutionary* and *perlocutionary* acts in which he addresses the issue of speech-acts that produce certain effects. To introduce these briefly, Austin describes *locutionary* acts as acts 'in which to say something *is* to do something', *illocutionary* as '*in* saying something we do something' and *perlocutionary* as '*by* saying something we do something' (94). Austin then focuses on *illocutionary* acts to reintroduce performative utterances; however, what is significant here in relation to Erdoğan's rally speech is his distinction between *illocutionary* and *perlocutionary* acts, as he writes:

> to perform a locutionary act, and therein an illocutionary act, may be to perform an act of another kind. Saying something will often, or even normally, produce certain consequential effects upon the feelings, thoughts, or actions of the audience, or of the speaker, or of other persons: and it may be done with the design, intention, or purpose of producing them [....] We shall call the performance of an act of this kind the performance of a 'perlocutionary' act'.
>
> (101)

Austin suggests that we have 'to draw the line between an action we do (here an illocutionary) and its consequences' (111) while admitting that this is not an easy task. Indeed, following the distinction, he points out certain cases in which *illocutionary acts* must produce certain effects in order to be successful:

> Unless a certain effect is achieved, the illocutionary act will not have been happily, successfully performed. This is not to say that the illocutionary

> act is the achieving of a certain effect. I cannot be said to have warned an audience unless it hears what I say and takes what I say in a certain sense. An effect must be achieved on the audience of the illocutionary act is to be carried out.
>
> (116)

Despite such occasions in which the distinction between *illocutionary* and *perlocutionary* acts appears blurry, for Austin, the main point of separation is the force of *illocutionary* acts, as Austin classifies them as 'utterances which have a certain (conventional) force' (109). In that regard, when an *illocutionary* act produces a certain effect, it is due to its conventional force. In other words, in *illocutionary* utterances, what produces an aftereffect is not feelings, or emotions, but the force of the convention. Furthermore, in Austin's coinage the context of conventional force limits the effects to the moment of utterance, whereas Erdoğan's utterance, *I accuse*, produces effects exceeding the moment of its utterance. Indeed, in *Excitable Speech* (1997), Judith Butler, while elaborating on how hate speech injures its addressee, identifies the issue of temporality within Austin's coinage of performative utterances. Butler indicates that for a performative utterance to be 'not only conventional, but in Austin's words, "ritual or ceremonial"', it must be 'repeated in time, and hence, maintain a sphere of operation that is not restricted to the moment of the utterance itself' (3). Hence, Butler points out that even *illocutionary* acts are not limited to the moment of their utterance, and points to the blurring of *illocutionary* acts and *perlocutionary* effects of utterances:

> The illocutionary speech act performs its deed at the moment of the utterance, and yet to the extent that the moment is ritualized, it is never merely a single moment. The "moment" in ritual is a condensed historicity: it exceeds itself in past and future directions, an effect of prior and future invocations that constitute and escape the instance of utterance.
>
> (ibid.)

Following Austin's explanation and Butler's expansion on the effects of *illocutionary* acts, it is possible to argue that the rally crowd's booing is the *perlocutionary* aftereffect of Erdoğan's accusation. This effect, I suggest, complements, in other words validates, Erdoğan's accusation with an affirmative response. If this is the case, Erdoğan's accusation must have a force that moves the rally crowd; this force, I argue, is driven by the mythical imaginary of the state that Erdoğan performs. In other words, in addition to Erdoğan's accusation against Elvan, his utterance does something to the rally crowd; or, to put it in another way, the reciprocal operation of Erdoğan's call in conjunction with the crowd's answer does something. In the absence of a conventional procedure as Austin understands it, how do we address the reciprocal doings of Erdoğan's accusation, *I accuse*, and the rally crowd's affirmation in boos? I suggest the rally speech has both *illocutionary* force and *perlocutionary* effects that become difficult to distinguish and that complement one another.

It is necessary to address the distinct form of a rally speech in which, resembling a mobile theatre, the utterer travels from city to city to deliver a pre-written and rehearsed speech. Although the speech is often pre-written and read before an audience, it is not limited to a conventional procedure. Within its ritualistic repetitiveness, there are temporal alterations and breaks. The speech goes through alternations that are specific to the time and space of the address, such as listing all the investments made in that specific city, as Erdoğan does at the end of his rally speech. However, more significantly, it bears the potential to break off from its ritualistic repetitiveness as it invites the audience to respond, just as in the case of Erdoğan's accusation, which I read as his call to the rally crowd. In that regard, it is possible to argue that Erdoğan's rally speech resembles the form of a performance in which the measure of its success or failure depends on whether it moves the audience, a movement which often materialises in the form of clapping, chanting slogans or exclamations such as booing. However, this resemblance interferes with its recognition as a performative utterance in Austinian terms. Although for Austin (1975), it is significant that the term 'performative' derives from the verb 'to perform' to indicate 'that the issuing of the utterance is the performing of an action' (6), it is important to note that, by suggesting a term derived from 'to perform', Austin does not aim to highlight a theatrical aspect. On the contrary, Austin considers what is theatrical as parasitic, rendering a performative utterance void:

> a performative utterance will, for example, be in a peculiar way hollow or void if said by an actor on the stage, or if introduced in a poem, or spoken in soliloquy [....] Language in such circumstances is in special ways – intelligibly – used not seriously, but in ways parasitic upon its normal use – ways which fall under the doctrine of the etiolations of language. All this we are excluding from consideration.
>
> (22)

Regardless of Austin's exclusion, Andrew Parker and Eve Kosofsky Sedgwick (1995) address the intersection between performative and performance. Later Sedgwick (2003) proposes a conceptual framework of *periperformatives* as a formula to attach performance and theatrical performativity to Austin's peculiar notion: 'though not themselves performatives, they are *about* performatives and, more properly, thatthey cluster *around* performatives' (68). In doing so, surprisingly, Sedgwick accepts the Austinian separation of performance and performative utterances.

However, in the quote above, it appears that the reason for Austin's exclusion of the theatrical is its unserious nature, perhaps something related to having certain effects. At this point, if we return to the rally speech, despite its theatricality in terms of performance, would it be possible to say that Erdoğan's speech was not serious or that it did not have any serious implications? I would suggest that seriousness cannot be a criterion for excluding performance from the performative. For instance, in 1999, when Erdoğan was the governor of Istanbul, he was sentenced to ten months in prison, which also barred him from running for public office and prevented him from participating in parliamentary elections. He was charged with 'inciting hatred based on religious differences' according to article 312/2 of the previous Penal Code (no: 765),[7] after reading a verse of the well-known nationalist poet Ziya Gökalp at a rally speech in 1997.[8] It is possible to suggest that Erdoğan's poem invited the legal performative, *I sentence you*, which had serious consequences for Turkey's political trajectory. In that regard, I locate the rally speech between performance and performativity. Furthermore, a rally speech invites a response – either a momentary one from the audience or a future response in the form of votes – but it may also have further effects and implications that may or may not be predicted at the time. In other words, as Butler indicates, the utterance of a rally speech exceeds the moment of its utterance, and, in addition, its force comes from the feelings and emotions that it produces.

Stanley Cavell's notion of *passionate utterances*, which he develops following Austin's illocutionary/perlocutionary distinction, could be illuminating to address how feelings and emotions in Erdoğan's call produce an effect. As Cavell explains in 'Performative and Passionate Utterance' (2005), in Austin's project, he observes a 'continued neglect of the passions', which leads him to extend Austin's theory with a focus on perlocutionary utterances to register the doings of *passionate utterances* (159).[9] Cavell observes that Austin's definition of performative utterance 'relies on the idea of appropriateness', or,

7 This article existed in the 1926 Turkish Penal Code (law no: 765). The article was repealed when a new Penal Code came into force on 1 June 2005.

8 The poem included the lines, "The mosques are our barracks, the domes are our helmets, the minarets our bayonets and the faithful our soldiers"; see: 'Profile: Recep Tayyip Erdoğan". *Aljazeera*, 25 June 2018. Accessed 16 July 2024. www.aljazeera.com/indepth/spotlight/turkeyelection/2011/05/2011526121054590355.html.

9 In an earlier text in which Cavell inquires into Austin's illocutionary/perlocutionary distinction through responding to Derrida's reading of Austin, Cavell comments on the privileged place of *illocutionary* utterances in Austin's notion of performative utterances. While noting that 'illocutionary utterances take over and further articulate the cases Austin began by simply calling performatives' (1994, 81), Cavell raises his objection that Austin would fail to acknowledge the performative operation of *perlocutionary* utterances: 'Now since there is no reason to believe that Austin for some reason fails to regard annoying or wounding someone, or persuading them of something, as something language is as fully capable of conveying as it is of conveying bets and gifts' (82). I understand Cavell's objection as an intervention to readings that exclude *perlocutionary* utterances from the category of performative utterances.

in other words, relies on having conventional procedures, which *passionate utterances* exceed (164). Cavell notes, '[a] performative utterance is an offer of participation in the order of law. And perhaps we can say: A passionate utterance is an invitation to improvisation in the disorders of desire' (185). In that regard, *passionate utterances* do not operate through a conventional procedure but rather '[t]he speaker is on his or her own to create the desired effect' (180). Considering Erdoğan's call as a *passionate utterance* allows us to register the doings of the rally speech and how Erdoğan creates the desired effect of declaring Elvan and his mother guilty of disobeying the *father-state*. I observe a convention-like process in Erdoğan's rally speech in which *perlocutionary* effects and *passionate utterances* complement where the force of convention falls short. Although Erdoğan does not have the authority and the context to pronounce Elvan and his mother guilty in a rally speech, by calling on the passions of the rally crowd, he nonetheless delivers a guilty verdict and institutes a law where there has not been a legal process. However, this does not mean that Erdoğan is the only utterer, as Erdoğan's call for a boo is an invitation to exchange as his accusation invokes a procedure that demands an answer: 'Demand from you a response *in kind*, one you are in turn *moved* to offer, and moreover [...] Now' (182).

Following Austin and Cavell, in *Our Word Is Our Bond*, Marianne Constable (2014) challenges the authority of 'I' as the utterer. She notes in a dialogue 'I' and 'you' keep changing places (91). I understand the reciprocal call and answer in a similar manner; however, I do acknowledge that there is a force in Erdoğan's call which directs the crowd's response. In her elaboration of legal speech-acts, Constable exposes that by responding affirmatively to imperatives, both 'I' and 'you' become actors of the speech-act:

> Insofar as this "I" unites with other subjects, a collective of "I"s becomes possible. A collective of "I"s is a "we" of sorts. On its own, this collective "I" is not the "we" whose "word is bond" [....] For the *we* of "our word" or "our bond" to emerge, *I* must become *you*, and *you*, *I* to one another'. (93)

As mentioned before, I understand the rally crowd's boos as an affirmation of Erdoğan's passionate accusation against Elvan and his mother. I suggest that by making the crowd co-authors of his accusation, Erdoğan constructs a 'we', which corresponds with his construction of a nation, which I discuss in the following sections. That is what I refer to as Erdoğan's *stately performative,* since his accusation reconstructs a mythical imaginary of the state by singling out Elvan and his mother from this imaginary. This constructs an imaginary "we" through the reciprocal operation of the call and the affirmative answer in boos. As Cavell (2005) writes regarding *passionate utterances*, 'if I generalize my standing in singling you out, and attempt to recognize or create a group to whom I speak, in its difference from another group, then I undertake political oratory' (182).

Furthermore, I suggest Erdoğan's call carries a force which resembles the force in Althusser's police-hailing analogy, which I discussed in the previous chapter. In his *stately performative*, Erdoğan claims – and acclaims – the state; in other words, he performs the state as he embodies the mythical (bodily) imaginary of the state, which I unpack further through his *father-state* performance in the following sections. His accusation of Elvan and his mother, *I accuse,* subjectifies Elvan as a disobedient son and, similar to the myth of Niobe, aims to subjectify his mother through guilt as a failed mother. What is more striking in a similar manner to Althusser's hailing analogy, in which the hailed gets subjectified as they turn to the hailer, Erdoğan's call subjectifies the rally crowd as they respond affirmatively in boos. However, to remember Cavell's point on *passionate utterances* being invitations to disorder, '[i]n the mode of passionate exchange there is no final word, no uptake or turndown until a line is drawn, a withdrawal is effected, perhaps in turn to be revoked' (183). In that regard, complementary to Butler's objection to the absolute authority of subjection that was discussed in Chapter 1, Erdoğan's call is also an invitation for its refusal and disobedience. As Cavell notes, 'in the realm of the perlocutionary, refusal may become part of the performance' (ibid.). Indeed, Erdoğan's call also demands an answer from those who Erdoğan deems as terrorists, and whom, he claims, Elvan was imitating, which I discuss in Chapter 3.

Situated between a performance and a performative utterance, where *illocutionary* acts and *perlocutionary* effects blur, Erdoğan's rally speech swings from official to unofficial. In that regard, it is remarkable that Erdoğan chooses to comment on Elvan's killing and respond to demands of accountability within this peculiar context. In relation to the discussion on the seriousness of an utterance, on the one hand, this may serve as an official response, but, on the other hand, it cannot be held into account. The force of Erdoğan's call derives from his repetitive performance of the mythical imaginary of the state, as Butler (1997) reminds us:

> Social action requires a performance which is repeated. This repetition is at once a re-enactment and reexperiencing of a set of meanings already socially established; it is the mundane and ritualized form of their legitimation [....] Understood in pedagogical terms, the performance renders social laws explicit.
>
> (277)

As Erdoğan accuses Elvan of his own death, he embodies Turkey's bodily state myth, the *father-state*, and hence performs his accusation from a force that derives from its repetition. His embodiment of the *father-state* indicates the significance of the body in his *stately performative*. In order to unpack this aspect, I refer to Butler's revision of performativity. As Elena Loizidou points out in *Judith Butler: Ethics, Law, Politics* (2007), 'Butler situates bodies (both literally and figuratively) at the centre of her analysis' (23). Considering Butler's criticism of the title of the first English edition of Felman's work on performative utterances (*The Literary Speech Act*), that it 'lost the body', for Butler (2003), the body is the main component of performative speech: 'they draw upon the body to articulate their claims, to institute the realities of which they speak' (113). However, Butler's emphasis on the body is not to highlight the authority of the speaking body but rather to expose the transformation the body goes through while speaking or rather, speak-acting. In that regard, Butler (1990) reads performative utterances as constituting acts, 'constituting acts not only as constituting the identity of the actor, but as constituting that identity as a compelling illusion, an object of belief' (271). In a similar vein, I read Erdoğan's rally speech as a *stately performative* which constructs two bodies simultaneously as he performs the *father-state*; his own and the *body politic* of the Turkish state. In Erdoğan's speech, the paternal right to punish the disobedient son merges with the stately right to kill as Erdoğan accuses Elvan of his own death. As a final point, as Loizidou (2007) also points out, Butler reads performativity as a way of writing history, 'in reconstructing the past and refiguring the future' (20). Performative speech as a form of history writing, which consists of erasing and rewriting, exposes 'the active role played by both language and bodies' (ibid.). Erdoğan, in his accusation against Elvan for his own death, aims to erase and rewrite history by portraying Elvan with a face mask and a slingshot. His account of events contests the Elvan family's and witnesses' accounts. Erdoğan claims to speak the truth by performing the all-knowing and undisputed *father-state*, which demands an affirmative response from its addressee. Through his bodily performance of the *father-state*, Erdoğan intends to constitute his own identity in terms of authority and to reconstruct a unified political body that materialises in his body. As I discuss further in the following sections, he does so by excluding the Elvan family and his opponents from the Turkish *body politic* as he directs the rally crowd to affirm his accusation in boos.

The Father-State

In *Mythologies*, Roland Barthes (2009) writes, '[w]hat the world supplies to myth is an historical reality, defined, even if this goes back quite a while, by the way in which men have produced or used it; and what myth gives in return is a natural image of this reality' (169). Barthes's *Mythologies* mainly focuses on myths as anonymous tales which are significant to a culture and which have a semi-historical, or rather pseudo-historical, quality, such as the myth of Niobe. In his work, Barthes also presents a linguistic analysis of myths in which he refers to myths as metalanguage, that locates myth within a separate terrain, second-language order in comparison to statements (183). Although it is possible to carry out a linguistic cross-reading of Barthes' definition of myths with the Austinian notion of performative utterances, this research is rather interested in the performative function of political myths in terms of their performance and repetition. Thus, although what I refer to as myth, or to be precise political myths, does not precisely fit to this classical form, I argue that they, nonetheless, function in a similar manner. Moreover, although Barthes does not use this term, I read his quote above, in which he summarises the meaning and function of myths, as something disclosing its performativity. I propose a cross-reading of Barthes's quote above with another quote from Butler on performativity:

> Performativity is thus not a singular 'act', for it is always reiteration of a norm or set of norms, and to the extent that it acquires an act-like status in the present, it conceals or dissimulates the conventions of which it is repetition. Moreover, this act is not primarily theatrical; indeed, its apparent theatricality is produced to the extent that its historicity remains dissimulated [....] Within the speech-act theory, a performative is that discursive practice that enacts or produces that which it names.
>
> (Butler 2011, xxi)

Myths live through their repetition; they reflect societal, cultural and political norms. In other words, as Barthes (2009) puts it in the quote at the beginning of this section, 'what the world supplies to myth is an historical reality' (169). However, as Butler points out, this set of norms does not exist prior to the myths; but rather, they are constructed, deconstructed and reconstructed through repetition. In return, myths give a natural, or objective, image of this constructed reality. They produce that which they name. In terms of political myths, towards the end of his study of myths, Barthes discusses bourgeois ideology as a form of myth. He notes the work of myth in today's context: 'For the very end of myths is to immobilize the world: they must suggest and mimic a universal order which has fixated once and for all the hierarchy of possessions' (183). And he continues, '[m]yths are nothing but this ceaseless, untiring solicitation, this insidious and inflexible demand that all men recognize themselves in this image, eternal yet bearing a date, which was built of them one day as if for all time' (184).

The state has a specific mythical bodily image in Turkey. *Devlet baba*, literally translating as *father-state*, is the dominating imaginary of the state in Turkey, establishing the relationship between the state officials and the people. It is a bodily image of the state; a *body politic* of the Turkish state. Prominent law professor Ergun Özbudun (1993) locates the origin of this imaginary in the Ottoman Empire, in the Sultan's duty to maintain order through his absolute power, which 'was to be exercised with justice and with the aim of promoting public welfare' (190).[10] Özbudun concludes that '[t]his last notion gave the Ottoman-Turkish state its paternalistic character [....] Interestingly, not only the ruling class but also the subject masses seemed to share this belief in the paternalistic nature of the state, as evidenced by the popular expression of "father-state" (*devlet baba*)' (ibid.). This book does not trace the Ottoman experience of the state, as it focuses on the contemporary political and legal constructs. However, Özbudun's observations can guide us to comprehend how the *father-state* myth has constructed the meaning of the state and, to put it in Barthes's words, demanded everyone – citizens and state officials alike – to recognise themselves in this image and, to add in Butlerian terms, to perform this image.

The nuclear family was a significant unit and metaphor of the nation-state building process in the early years of the Turkish Republic, and it continued to be a significant metaphor in the education of the upcoming generations to maintain the unity of the nation.[11] Carol Delaney's (1995) 'Father State, Motherland, and the Birth of Modern Turkey' provides an overview of the peculiar overlap of state and fatherhood within the Turkish context. As is explicit in the title, in the essay Delaney suggests that the modern Turkish nation was conceived by the *father-state*, Atatürk, and motherland. Delaney, through highlighting the commonly used phrases of *devlet baba* (father-state) and *anavatan* (motherland) suggests that this gendered parental image is carefully constructed during the transition from the Ottoman Empire to Modern Turkey, which is then referred to and accepted as the rebirth of a nation. Although Delaney's observations could apply to any nation-state building project, especially in the eighteenth century, nonetheless, Delaney exposes the kinship relations enacting within the national consciousness of Turkey through the newly coined political term for citizen, which is significant in defining the state and society relations:

> All those born upon and nurtured by her [motherland] soil were henceforth to be related like siblings. *Vatandaş*, the word coined to mean 'citizen', is literally 'fellow of the motherland'; it is like the word *kardeş*, which means both brother and sibling, literally 'fellow of the womb'.
>
> (186)

10 Regarding the Turkish Republic's adaptation of the welfare state, it is possible to trace secularised versions of Ottoman practices. In this regard, the transformation of the Ottoman's state-supported religious philanthropic system called vakıfs to a secular civil society in modern Turkey provides an interesting trajectory in tracing adaptations and discontinuities of values in state and society relations. For more on this see Zencirci (2014).

11 The notion of *father-state* or *fatherly state* is commonly used in Turkish literature, especially in children's books. One of the best-known contemporary examples is by the prominent children's book writer Muzaffer İzgü's *Devlet Babanın Tonton Çocuğu* (1981), which translates as 'perky child of father state'; see Muzaffer İzgü, *Devlet Babanın Tonton Çocuğu*. Istanbul, 1981. Bilgi Yayinevi.

Yiğit Akın, in a similar vein to Özbudun's remark on the promotion of public welfare, elaborates further on the reproduction of the Ottoman paternal image during the early years of the Turkish Republic and suggests that '"benevolent father" (*devlet baba*) was one of the regime's legitimacy-providing myths' (444–445). Akın reads this as an attempt to fill the mythical gap left by the fall of the Ottoman Empire and to replace it with a modern state imaginary of a caring father (ibid.). The national-family reference that is constructed around a paternal figure is performed by Mustafa Kemal Atatürk, who was granted the surname of Atatürk which translates as 'Father Turk', or 'father of the Turks', by the national assembly in 1934.[12] Atatürk's image as the 'father of the Turks' is accompanied by this personal but publicly known 'benevolent father' image to his adopted children. The fact that he did not have a child of his own to suggest a patrilineal system of power made this father-of-the-nation image stronger. Indeed, Özyürek (2006), in her analysis of Atatürk as a parent, mentions how followers of Atatürk (commonly referred to as Kemalists) feel indebted to him, and she associates this feeling with cultural parenthood practices in Turkey: 'When parents are the only providers, children are always considered indebted to them [....] According to the nationalist discourse, Atatürk is another parent, particularly a father, to whom citizens should feel indefinitely indebted' (109).

I suggest, that in his rally speech, Erdoğan resurrects, and reappropriates, this *father-state* myth to reunify the dissolving *body politic* of the state. Regarding the importance of political myths, in *Reflections on Violence*, Georges Sorel (1999) suggests that myths are 'expressions of a will to act' (28). He writes in his letter to Daniel Halévy, which is included in place of an introduction to the 1908 publication, '[a]s long as there are no myths accepted by the masses, one may go on talking of revolts indefinitely without ever provoking any revolutionary movement' (ibid.). What is noteworthy in Sorel's account is the crucial role myths, or political myths to be more precise, play in persuading the masses to be willing to kill or be killed for a cause. In a similar fashion, the mythical imaginary of the *father-state,* embodied in the material body of Atatürk, had been the uniting glue of the newly founded

12 In that regard, Vamik D. Volkan and Normal Itzkowitz's work titled *The Immortal Atatürk: A Psychobiography*, presents a psychological study of Atatürk's life. This work, in a nutshell, suggests that the loss at an early age of his father, who sent him to a secular school, which symbolised modernisation, and his Oedipal desire to save his religious mother impacted on Atatürk's vision on modern and secular reconstruction of the Turkish state as well as 'his own fullfillment of the role of "father" at the birth of Turkey'. (Volkan 2007: 239). The prominent Turkish historian Kemal Karpat disagrees – 'the development of Mustafa Kemal's personality and his ideas of reform appear to have resulted more from the existing socio-political and historical conditions than from oedipal complexes' – but does not provide an explanation for his adaptation of the father image except in the form of a general statement of its representation of authority (Karpat 1985, 896).

Turkish Republic. This time, Erdoğan is embodying the *father-state* through its repetition. The rally speech sounds rather informal and personal precisely because of the paternal style of his address. Erdoğan's *father-state* performance blends stately affairs with family affairs as if the rally crowd is his confidant. Although at first it seems otherwise, this blend of state and family through his imaginary role of *father-state* does not depoliticise the killing of Elvan. Instead, it carries a Hobbesian political claim that attributes all the responsibility to those who protest and revolt against the sovereign, even in the case of their death. In *Leviathan*, Hobbes (1991) writes that there are two forms of sovereign power, one paternal and the other by the voluntary engagement through the covenant: 'The attaining to this Sovereigne Power, is by two ways, One, by Naturall force; as when a man maketh his children, to submit themselves, and their children to his government, as being able to destroy them if they refuse' (121). Although Hobbes categorises the paternal form of sovereign power as despotic and instead proposes *Leviathan* as its replacement, nonetheless both give the same reflex to opposition, whether it is children rebelling against their father or people rebelling against the sovereign.[13] In that regard, the Turkish state myth, *father-state,* is situated at the intersection of *Leviathan*, the modern Western state myth, and paternal power. Erdoğan's performance of the *father-state* is a performative response to the disobedient child and to the opposition at once, which he combines in his enemy assemblages.[14]

Constructing the Enemy

In order to comprehend Erdoğan's assemblages of enemies, it is necessary to present the turbulent political climate of the time briefly. The local elections of 30 March 2014 had borne the added significance of being the first election to be held after the Gezi protests of June 2013. The nationwide protests, which lasted throughout the summer of 2013, were followed by a high-profile corruption scandal which shook the AKP government until the

13 Elsewhere, I provide a cross-reading of this family metaphor with the possibility of civil war (*stasis*) in the context of what is commonly referred as Turkey's 'Kurdish Question' in Ceylan Begüm Yıldız, 'A State in Anomie: An Analysis of Modern Turkey's States of Exception' in *States of Exception: Law, History, Theory*. Eds. Cosmin Sebastian Cercel, Gian-Giacomo Fusco and Simon Lavis. Oxon: Routledge, 2021.

14 Here I use assemblages in reference to Jasbir K. Puar's (2017) *Terrorist Assemblages* in which Puar borrows the term assemblage from Deleuze and Guattari: 'A multiplicity has neither subject or object, only determinations, magnitudes and dimensions that cannot increase in number without the multiplicity changing in nature (the laws of combination therefore increase as the multiplicity grows) .... An assemblage is precisely this increase in the dimension of a multiplicity that necessarily changes in nature as it expands its connections' (212).

local elections.[15] This is a period of what I refer to as the state being undone. It is when the state's imaginary *body politic* dissolves and when the omnipotent and omnipresent power attributed to this imaginary is scrutinised and challenged by the masses. Hence, the local elections of 2014 were burdened with the AKP government's desire to unite the imaginary once again. In order to do so, Erdoğan, with a paternal tone, consulted the Schmittian rulebook for creating ghostly enemies. At this point, the question is not whether such enemies do really exist but rather the 'conspiratorial imagination' that flourishes in the state in crises (Ertür 2016) and which, in turn, defines, unifies and materialises the margins of the state. Erdoğan's rally speech frames a certain picture of the Turkish state by constructing an enemy with a capital 'E'. This giant enemy is as mythical as the *body politic* of the state with a capital 'S'. As its assemblage frames the borders of the state, it simultaneously contains the dissolving unity.[16]

Erdoğan claims that the ones who were involved in the nationwide Gezi protests and corruption-scandal operation are elites whom previous governments had favoured. He underlines over and over that it was him and his party who fought for the rights of veiled women. At this point, he recalls his paternal role once again and provides personal examples from the hardships of his daughters while mentioning the 28 February 1997 military memorandum, which is commonly referred to as the post-modern coup.[17] As he

15 Between the 17th and 25th December some tape recordings began to circulate on social media: these were of a series of phone conversations between cabinet members and their sons, and between Erdoğan and his family. It was claimed that those phone conversations took place on 17 December, when police conducted raids on some high-profile businessmen and relatives of cabinet members with corruption and money-laundering charges. The high-profile corruption investigation was later considered as the first action by the Gülen sect to influence politics in Turkey before the coup attempt of July 2016, which was claimed to be orchestrated by the Gülen sect. The prosecutor and police officers involved in the corruption investigation were either dismissed and arrested or fled the country. Although Erdoğan and AKP members argued against the authenticity of the leaked tapes, there is little clarity on the falsehood of the corruption operation and the content of the leaked tapes. For more on this issue, see 'Leaked Tapes Prompt Calls for Tukish PM to Resign' (*The Guardian*, 25 February 2014. Accessed 16 July 2024. www.theguardian.com/world/2014/feb/25/leaked-tapes-calls-Erdoğan-resign-turkish-pm) and 'Turkish PM Says Tapes of Talk with Son a Fabrication'. (*Reuters*, 25 February 2014. Accessed 16 July 2024. www.reuters.com/article/us-turkey-Erdoğan/turkish-pm-says-tapes-of-talk-with-son-a-fabrication-idUSBREA1N1ZX20140225).

16 Here I am referring to Judith Butler's use of 'frame' in *Frames of War*, which at the same time recalls the meaning of 'to be framed', but more significantly the frame or the necessity to frame exposes the fact that there is something uncontainable, something that is already outside, which (is supposed to) make 'the very sense of inside possible, recognizable' (Butler 2010, 8–9).

17 After the National Security Council meeting on 28 February 1997 which was attended by the top generals of the armed forces and the prime minister. The PM at the time, Necmettin Erbakan from the Welfare Party, resigned after being forced to sign a list of decisions during

addresses the women in the crowd, he says the post-modern coup was carried out against their freedom to wear veils. While the first enemy is the ghost of pre-AKP times, the second enemy is a familiar one. Erdoğan accuses Fethullah Gülen, the head of the Gülen sect, of treason and gives guidelines to the crowd to follow against the Gülen sect's operations.[18] Erdoğan continues by suggesting that people who were involved in the Gezi protests and corruption-scandal operation are neither concerned with environmental issues nor issues of corruption but rather those people are reacting against losing their advantageous position in society and that, since the beginning of the AKP regime, the political power of the state no longer favours them. Erdoğan says, 'it is you they are concerned about, your sovereignty brought discomfort to them', and then he begins counting all the investments made in Gaziantep and in other south-eastern and eastern cities during the more-than-a decade-long AKP government.

Tanıl Bora (2018) analyses the political terminology commonly used by Erdoğan. In reference to Erdoğan's rhetoric during the Gezi protests, Bora suggests that Erdoğan is choosing a nation, people or a folk for himself (41–43). What Bora means by that is that, while Erdoğan excludes those who participated in the protests by relating them to some phantasmatic enemy powers, he is constructing in turn 'the true nation' ('asıl millet'), referring to those who supported his government during the protests (41). In Erdoğan's political terminology, Bora observes the Schmittian friend/enemy distinction, which aims to unite a group of people, a nation, through declaring a common enemy. To briefly present this, according to Schmitt an enemy can simply mean one who is in opposition: '[a]n enemy exists only when, at least potentially, one fighting collectivity of people confronts a similar collectivity' (2007, 28). He takes a leap in his train of thought and argues that such an enemy 'is solely the public enemy, because everything that has a relationship to such a collectivity of men, particularly to a whole nation, becomes public by virtue of such a relationship' (ibid.). In a similar fashion, Erdoğan declares

the meeting. The decisions were announced by the National Security Council's website, hence giving rise to the name 'post-modern coup'. Erbakan and his party were known for their conservative stance and were often referred to as the founders of the National Vision movement from which the AKP originates. For more on this see 'Turkish Military Leaders Held for Role in '97 Coup'. *The New York Times*, 12 April 2012. Accessed 16 July 2024. www.nytimes.com/2012/04/13/world/middleeast/turkey-detains-military-leaders-for-role-in-1997-coup.html.

18 Before the 2016 coup attempt, AKP and the Gülen movement were allies. It is commonly understood that the December 2013 corruption investigations, which involved Erdoğan's cabinet ministers and his family members and which were believed to be orchestrated by Gülenist prosecutors, shattered this allyship. For more on the AKP and Gülen sect, see Kareem Shaheen, 'Erdoğan v the Gülenists: From Political Allies to Turkey's Bitter Rivals'. *The Guardian*, 19 July 2016. Accessed 28 September 2021. www.theguardian.com/world/2016/jul/19/thousands-detained-as-turkey-vows-to-smoke-out-gulen-supporters.

anyone critical of him and his party's government as enemies. He continuously repeats the list of enemies and, according to the context, stacks up new ones to the existing assemblage, as he does in this rally speech regarding Elvan and his family.

However, I would argue that Schmitt's friend/enemy distinction actually signposts the existential crisis of the state, a state of being undone. It is a state of undoing the unified imaginary of the state when the fantasy of its omnipotent and omnipresent power, the mythical body politic, comes into question. Therefore, what Schmitt suggests through his friend/enemy distinction, which he presents as an unescapable necessity, is rather a quick fix to overcome this existential crisis of the state. It is not a coincidence that, for Carl Schmitt, political myths are driving forces to mobilise the masses for political ends. In the final chapter of *The Crisis of Parliamentary Democracy* (1988), originally published in 1923, Schmitt refers to George Sorel's work on myth, and he writes, '[i]n direct intuition the enthusiastic mass creates a mythical image that pushes its energy forward and gives it the strength for martyrdom as well as the courage to use force. Only in this way can a people or a class become the engine of world history' (68).[19] In that regard, Erdoğan's revitalisation of the *father-state* is a performance of a fantasy which aims to mobilise the masses and unite them under its mythical bodily image.

In *the Sublime Object of Ideology*, Slavoj Žižek (2008) compares the political performative of a king and a totalitarian leader. For the former, Žižek writes, 'a king is a king because we treat him like one' and to keep this illusion the king relays his power to an 'external authority' – Žižek gives 'God, nature and some mythical past event' as examples – and that 'as soon as the performative mechanism which gives him his charismatic authority is demasked, the Master loses his power' (163). However, Žižek argues that this is not the case for the totalitarian leader, as their claim is rather, '[i]n myself, I'm nothing, I am what I am only as an expression, an embodiment, an executor of your will' (164). In other words, the totalitarian leader's reference to the People, the Class and the Nation 'exists only through and in its fetishistic representative, the Party and its Leader'; and he adds, 'the People are the 'real People' only in so far as they are embodied in their representative, the Party and its Leader' (ibid.). It is possible to cross-read Žižek's remarks in reference to Bora's note to conclude that Erdoğan chooses a nation for himself, and I

19 Schmitt refers to George Sorel's work on myth to conclude that parliamentary democracy is not the great political myth which mobilises the masses. However, Schmitt argues that it is not the project of parliamentary democracy but, on the contrary, the political ideas against parliamentary democracy which had been able to create such myths which successfully mobilised the masses; he quotes Mussolini: '"[w]e have created a myth, this myth is a belief, a noble enthusiasm; it does not need to be reality, it is a striving and a hope, belief and courage. Our myth is the nation, the great nation which we want to make into a concrete reality for ourselves"' (1988, 76).

propose an amendment that Erdoğan does not choose a nation to himself, but he constructs, or rather reconstructs, a nation that is embodied in the *father-state* image that he performs through his own material body.

Two Sons

In the last part of his speech, Erdoğan compares the killing of Berkin Elvan with the killing of Burakcan Karamanoğlu, who died during the clashes that took place right after Elvan's funeral ceremony in Kasımpaşa, a working-class neighbourhood situated next to Okmeydanı. As Toyar Sinan Baykan (2018) explains 'Kasımpaşa is located in the immediate periphery of the cosmopolitan Beyoglu sub-province of Istanbul, alongside other conservative and low-income neighbourhoods, and has always been home to new provincial and poor immigrants of the city' (126). Despite their shared working-class fabric, while Okmeydanı has an established reputation of being a leftist and revolutionary neighbourhood, Kasımpaşa is a conservative neighbourhood with a strong AKP support. With the rise of Erdoğan, Kasımpaşa has also become a political signifier since Erdoğan is from this neighbourhood. 'Being from Kasımpaşa' is not only a signifier for a poor, conservative, domestic-immigrant population which greatly contributed to Erdoğan's 'people's leader' image as 'their savior against Turkish elites and Western imperialism' (Önder 2018), but also has given him a 'no-nonsense character' (Krajeski 2014), because the neighbourhood 'is also known for its strict conservative, moralist and macho subculture' (Baykan 2018, 126). As a result, Erdoğan often attributes his leadership qualities to the neighbourhood: 'my manliness, bluntness, and principled conduct derive from my roots [in Kasımpaşa]' (ibid.). Kasımpaşa and Okmeydanı are two neighbourhoods next to one another, representing two polar opposites of Turkey's politics. From time to time, groups within those rival neighbourhoods organise provocative attacks on one another. Shortly after Elvan's burial at the cemetery, police attacked the funeral crowd without warning. The police's intervention was exceptionally violent. In 2019, in regard to a case file on the police's conduct on the day, the Constitutional Court noted that 'the police attacked without any warnings beforehand' and concluded the prohibition of ill treatment (Art 17/3) had been violated.[20] Clashes resulted in the death of a Kasımpaşa veteran, Burakcan Karamanoğlu. Erdoğan, in the final part of his speech, compares Karamanoğlu and Elvan. While labelling the latter as a terrorist, Erdoğan publicly mourns for the former:

20 'Non-Pecuniary Damages for Police Attack at Funeral of Berkin Elvan'. *Bianet*, 10 December 2019. Accessed 16 July 2024. https://bianet.org/english/law/216901-non-pecuniary-damages-for-police-attack-at-funeral-of-berkin-elvan.

> That evening of the funeral, the Revolutionary People's Liberation Party-Front terrorist organisation comes to my hometown and martyrs our son Burakcan, who came back from his military service just three months ago. Burakcan did not have a slingshot in his hand, he did not have any weapon on him. He was just in front of his house, and they martyred him. The number of bullets collected from the street is 42! 42! The opposition party is acting together with such terrorists. The ones who killed our son are the illegal executioners of Kılıçdaroğlu [former opposition party leader]. Yes, his illegal executioners!
>
> (Parti Mitingleri 2014)

In this dramatic ending, Erdoğan's slip of the tongue reveals that, for Erdoğan, there can be legal executioners in a jurisdiction that has abolished the death penalty. Perhaps by legal executioners, Erdoğan refers to those who kill on behalf of the state, such as the police officer Dalgalı, who is the main officer suspected of killing Elvan. I discuss the legal handling of the officer Dalgalı in Chapter 4. In this section, however, what interests me is Erdoğan's comparison of Elvan and Karamanoğlu, which also serves as a signpost for Erdoğan's criteria of sanctioned and unsanctioned violence, and hence for accountability. As mentioned before in this chapter, Erdoğan responds to the killing of Elvan and responds to the accountability demands as a family matter. However, as I demonstrated above through the Turkish state myth of the *father-state*, Erdoğan's reference to the family is political; and, furthermore, as I propose in this section, it appears as a criterion for accepting or rejecting accountability demands. At this point, it is important to stress that Erdoğan does not deny that Elvan was hit by a tear gas canister, but rather, he intends to free the police from their responsibility as he asks the crowd, 'How could the police identify the age of a masked person throwing iron marbles with a slingshot?' Erdoğan presents the killing of Berkin Elvan as an unfortunate incident caused by Elvan's own poor decision in joining the protests and as an expected outcome of Elvan's own actions in mimicking terrorists. His description of Elvan, with a face covering and throwing iron marbles with a slingshot, although disproved during the trial process, serves as a reply to accountability demands. For Erdoğan, this description demonstrates the legitimacy of his killing. In the manner of the *father-state*, he exempts the police officers from being held accountable – *I forgive you* – and accuses Elvan of his death – *I accuse you*.

Erdoğan's comparison of two deaths is reminiscent of Sophocles' famous tragedy *Antigone* (1994). To briefly recount the story, two brothers, Eteocles and Polyneices, lead opposite sides in Thebes's civil war, and they both die fighting against each other. Creon, ruler of Thebes, orders Eteocles to be honoured, while he publicly shames Polyneices by ordering him to be left unburied. In his speech, Erdoğan is performing the role of Creon in glorifying the death of Karamanoğlu and shaming Elvan. Furthermore, in the foreword of Žižek's *Antigone* (2016), Hanif Kureishi, while unpacking the complex family relations within the tragedy that bind Antigone to Creon, defines Creon in these words; 'Creon is a leader, a clever politician with a Mafia don side, a primal father to whom all the women must belong' (viii). In that regard, Creon shares similar traits with Erdoğan who is proudly bringing his Mafia don upbringing to politics, who performs *father-state* – or, in Kureishi's words, 'primal father' – and who considers women as his responsibility, either solving their abiding difficulties (lifting the veil ban) or publicly shaming the ungrateful ones (Elvan's mother).

Timothy Gould, in 'The Unhappy Performative' (1995), remarks that Creon's announcement regarding Polyneices is an order and a performative speech: 'I here proclaim to the city that this man shall no one honor with a grave and none shall mourn' (35).[21] In a similar vein, by depicting the killing of Elvan as the tragic, but expected, death of a boy who was masked and armed with a slingshot and marbles, like a terrorist, Erdoğan accuses Elvan of his own death: *I accuse you*. In other words, he orders the public not to hold anyone else accountable. Similar to what Gould observes in Creon's lines, Erdoğan's performative speech is intended 'to have the force of a stigmatizing, descriptive fiat' (35) as he describes Elvan as a terrorist, a disobedient son.

Karamanoğlu stands as a model of a good son who served in the military, and hence Erdoğan refers to him as a martyr, although his death is unrelated to his military service. Erdoğan defines both Karamanoğlu and

21 Those lines do not appear in H.D.F. Kitto's translation of the play that is used in this book. We rather hear of the Creon's orders indirectly from Antigone when she reports to her sister Ismene:

> 'Our brother's burial. – Creon has ordained
> Honour for one, dishonour for the other.
> Eteocles, they day, has been entombed
> With every solemn rite and ceremony
> To do him honour in the world below;
> But as for Polyneices, Creon has ordered
> That none shall bury him or mourn for him;
> He must be left lie unwept, unburied,
> For hungry of prey to swoop and feast
> On his poor body, So he has decreed,
> Our noble Creon, to all the citizens:
> To you, to me. To me! And he is coming
> To make It public here. That no one may
> Be left in ignorance: nor does he hold it
> Of little moment: he who disobeys
> In any detail shall be put to death
> By public stoning in the streets of Thebes
> So it is now for you to show if you
> Are worthy, or unworthy, of your birth (Sophocles 1994, 3–4).

Elvan's deaths, and their meaning in reference to the role he performs as the *father-state*. By juxtaposing Karamanoğlu's death with Elvan's, Erdoğan constructs yet another friend/enemy narrative. This time, the mythical body of the friend, which constitutes the *body politic,* and its enemy, which frames the *body politic* to unify and contain it, materialises through the dead bodies of Karamanoğlu and Elvan. The former, 'our son', whose obedience to *father-state* grants him martyrdom, and the latter, the disobedient other who should not be honoured with accountability. In this process of subjection in Erdoğan's speech, which 'is not only a subordination but a securing and maintaining, a putting into place of a subject, a subjectivation' (Butler 2011, 9), it is possible to hear resonances of Creon's orders: *I here proclaim to the city that this boy shall no one honour and none shall be punished but him.* In return, the rally setting provides Erdoğan the audience, or rather the witness, for his performativity to be effective; the 'performative utterance is to be characterized as a kind of verbal performance or artefact, and hence it is to be assessed by its effectiveness with an audience (whether real or implicit or constructed)' (Gould 1995, 24). The audience for the rally speech, however, is not in the position of a passive witness, but becomes a co-author to Erdoğan's punishing act by booing the mother. Furthermore, it is possible to suggest that the violence inflicted on the mother, Gülsüm Elvan, is due to her non-acceptance of her son's death as his fate. Recalling Benjamin's reading of Niobe, it is possible to say that Elvan's mother challenges the fate that comes from state violence, as she does not obediently seek help from the *father-state* but rather accuses the *father-state* of killing her son.

Nonetheless, Erdoğan's subjection of Elvan as a terrorist and a disobedient son whose death does not deserve an accountability process is the intentional doing of his *father-state* performativity which contains the possibilities of its failures. Erdoğan exposes that the paternal care of the *father-state* kills his children for their own sake to save them from being disobedient. In that regard, while Erdoğan performs the *father-state* as a state myth to unite the Turkish state's dissolving fantasy, he simultaneously, performs the horrors of this fantasy.

However, in *States of Terror*, Aretxaga (2005) reminds us, in reference to Derrida (1994), that state violence and its countering violence are reciprocal. She writes:

> [They] are produced, not arbitrarily, but within what Derrida (1994:97) has called a 'phantomatic mode of production': a structure and modus operandi which produce both the state and terrorism as fetishes of each other, constructing reality as an endless play of mirror images. This play of terrorism is what makes the State (with a capital *S*) and Terrorism (with a capital *T*) so real, organizing political life as a phantasmatic universe where the "really real" is always somewhere else, always eluding us'.
> (229)

It is possible to cross-read Aretxaga's remarks above with Cavell's notion on *passionate utterances*, in which he read these as invitations to disorder. Indeed, Erdoğan's call, which accuses Elvan and his mother, and which demands an affirmative response from the rally crowd, receives yet another response, this time from those he refers to as 'terrorists'. By owning Berkin Elvan's legacy, the Revolutionary People's Liberation Front (Party-Front), responds to the unaccountability of Elvan's killing by taking hostage the then prosecutor in charge of the Elvan investigation, which I discuss in the following chapter.

References

Aretxaga, Begoña. 2005. *States of Terror: Begoña Aretxaga's Essays.* Edited by Joseba Zulaika. Nevada: Center for Basque Studies.

Austin, J. L. 1975. *How to Do Things with Words.* Oxford: Oxford University Press.

Barthes, Ronald. 2009. *Mythologies.* London: Vintage.

Baykan, Toyar Sinan. 2018. *The Justice and Development Party in Turkey: Populism, Personalism, Organization.* Cambridge: Cambridge University Press.

Bora, Tanıl. 2018. *Zamanın Kelimeleri: Yeni Türkiye'nin Siyasi Dili.* İstanbul: İletişim Yayınları.

Butler, Judith. 1990. 'Performative Acts and Gender Construction: An Essay in Phenomenology and Feminist Theory'. *Performing Feminisms: Feminist Critical Theory and Theatre.* Ed. Sue-Ellen Case. Baltimore: The John Hopkins University Press. 270–282.

Butler, Judith. 1997. *The Psychic Life of Power: Theories in Subjection.* Stanford, CA: Stanford University Press.

Butler, Judith. 2000. *Antigone's Claim: Kindship Between Life and Death.* New York: Colombia University Press.

Butler, Judith. 2003. 'Afterword'. In Shoshana Felman. *The Scandal of the Speaking Body: Don Juan with J.L Austin, or Seduction in Two Languages*, Stanford, CA: Stanford University Press. 113–123.

Butler, Judith. 2010. *Frames of War: When Is Life Grievable?* London: Verso.

Butler, Judith. 2011. *Bodies that Matter: On the Discursive Limits of 'Sex'.* Oxford: Routledge.

Cavell, Stanley. 1994. 'Derrida's Austin and the Stake of Positivism'. In *A Pitch of Philosophy: Autobiographical Exercises.* Cambridge, MA: Harvard University Press. 77–96.

Cavell, Stanley. 2005. 'Performative and Passionate Utterance'. In *Philosophy the Day After Tomorrow.* Cambridge, MA: Harvard University Press. 155–191.

Constable, Marianne. 2014. *Our Word Is Our Bond: How Legal Speech Acts.* Stanford, CA: Stanford University Press.

Delaney, Carol. 1995. 'Father State, Motherland and The Birth of Modern Turkey'. In *Naturalizing Power: Essays in Feminist Cultural Analysis,* edited by Sylvia Yanagisako and Carol Delaney. New York and London: Routledge. 177–200.

Derrida, Jacques. 1988. *Limited Inc.* Evanston, IL: Northwestern University Press.

Derrida, Jacques. 1994. *Specters of Marx: The State of the Debt, the Work of Mourning and the New International*. New York: Routledge.
Ertür, Başak. 2016. 'The Conspiracy Archive: Turkey's "Deep State" on Trial'. In *Law, Memory, Violence*, edited by Stewart Motha and Honni van Rijswijk Oxford: Routledge. 177–194.
Felman, Shoshana. 2003. *The Scandal of the Speaking Body: Don Juan with J.L Austin, or Seduction in Two Languages*. Stanford, CA: Stanford University Press.
Gould, Timothy. 1995. 'The Unhappy Performative'. In *Performativity and Performance*, edited by Andrew Parker and Eve Kosofsky Sedgwick. New York: Routledge. 19–44.
Hobbes, Thomas. 1991. *Leviathan*. Edited by Richard Tuck. Cambridge: Cambridge University Press.
İzgü, Muzaffer. 1981. *Devlet Babanın Tonton Çocuğu*. Istanbul, Bilgi Yayinevi
Karpat, Kemal. 1985. 'The Personality of Atatürk'. *The American Historical Review* 90(4): 893–899.
Krajeski, Jenna. 2014. 'Turkey's Erdoğan Retains Working-Class Roots'. *Al Jazeera*, 28 March. Accessed 16 July 2024. https://www.aljazeera.com/indepth/features/2014/03/turkey-pm-retains-working-class-roots-2014327113735373532.html.
Kureishi, Hanif. 2016. 'Foreword'. In Slavoj Žižek. *Antigone*. London: Bloomsbury. vii–x.
Loizidou, Elena. 2007. *Judith Butler: Ethics, Law, Politics*. Oxford: Routledge-Cavendish.
Önder, Engin. 2018. 'Global Justice: The Man from Kasımpaşa'. *Boston Review*, 11 January. Accessed 16 July 2024. http://bostonreview.net/politics-global-justice/engin-onder-man-Kasımpaşa.
Özbudun, Ergun. 1993. 'State Elites and Democratic Political Culture in Turkey'. In *Political Culture and Democracy in Developing Countries*, edited by Larry Diamond. Colorado: Lynne Rienner Publishers. 189–210.
Özyürek, Esra. 2006. *Nostalgia for the Modern: State Secularism and Everyday Politics in Turkey*. Durham and London: Duke University Press.
Parker, Andrew, and Eve Kosofsky Sedgwick. 1995. 'Introduction'. In *Performativity and Performance*. New York: Routledge. 1–18.
Parti Mitingleri. 2014. 'Başbakan Recep Tayyip Erdoğan Ak Partı Gaziantep Mitingi'. *YouTube video*, 1:04:30, 14 March. Accessed 16 July 2024 https://www.youtube.com/watch?v=qAKzFThXo-w.
Puar, Jasbir K. 2017. *Terrorist Assemblages: Homonationalism in Queer Times*. Durham and London: Duke University Press.
Schmitt, Carl. 1988. *The Crisis of Parliamentary Democracy*. Cambridge: MIT Press.
Schmitt, Carl. 2007. *The Concept of the Political*. London: University of Chicago Press.
Sedwick, Eve Kosofsky. 2003. *Touching Feeling: Affect, Pedagogy, Performativity*. Durham: Duke University Press.
Sorel, George. 1999. *Reflections on Violence*. Cambridge: Cambridge University Press.
Sophocles. 1994. *Antigone, Oedipus the King, and Electra*. Edited by Edith Hall, Translated by H. D. F. Kitto. Oxford: Oxford University Press.

Volkan, Vamık D. 2007. 'On Kemal Atatürk's Psychoanalytic Biography'. *International Journal of Turkish Studies* 13(1&2): 229–241.
Volkan, Vamık D., and Normal Itzkowitz. 2007. *The Immortal Ataturk: A Pscyhobiolography*. Chicago: University of Chicago Press.
Zencirci, G. (2014). 'Civil Society's History: New Constructions of Ottoman Heritage by the Justice and Development Party in Turkey'. *European Journal of Turkish Studies* 19: 1–20.
Žižek, Slavoj. 2008. *The Sublime Object of Ideology*. London and New York: Verso.

Chapter 3

Countering Violence

It is 31 March 2015. It has been two years since Elvan was shot by a police tear-gas canister and a year since he died. The Elvan family has already filed a criminal complaint on the grounds of direct intention to kill. On 25 June 2013 the Istanbul prosecution office accepted the complaint on the grounds of excessive use of force, and the investigation has been ongoing ever since, while the prosecutor in charge of the investigation has kept changing. The footage, which becomes breaking news in Turkey on 31 March, is a video statement which shows a man wearing a red face covering holding a gun to the head of the prosecutor Mehmet Selim Kiraz, who is by then the fifth prosecutor in charge of Berkin Elvan's investigation at the time, in his office at the Istanbul courthouse.[1] As Kiraz sits under the pointed gun with his hands tied and mouth gagged, the man with the red face cover begins to speak: 'We are Revolutionary People's Liberation Front fighters. Here, today we are holding this prosecutor in hostage, as he is the chief prosecutor of Berkin Elvan's murder investigation. And yet, the police officers, who are responsible for Elvan's death, still have not been punished. Hence, we are holding the prosecutor hostage' (Boran Yayınları 2017, 59).[2] As the hostage-taking

1 The video statement is no longer accessible through online media channels and social media after a court order issued on 6 April 2015 ('Turkey Threatens Google with Ban Over Hostage Image'. BBC News, 7 April 2015. Accessed 16 July 2024. www.bbc.co.uk/news/technology-32194913.) Although, it is possible to find national and international media coverage on the issue, at times I refer to my personal archive unless noted otherwise.

2 Translation from its Turkish original belongs to me. For this translation, I compared the video statement from my personal archive with the one published by the Revolutionary People's Liberation Front's publishing house, Boran Yayınları, in a booklet they released on 19 June 2017 (see Boran Yayınları 2017). The booklet is dedicated to Şafak Yayla, Bahtiyar Doğruyol and Elif Sultan Kalsen. The first two are the militants who conducted the hostage-taking action, and the latter is the militant who carried out an armed attack at a police headquarters in Istanbul to commemorate the martyrdom of the former two militants. The booklet is an important source as it contains information which had been removed from the internet, such as the transcript of the statement, the transcript of some phone interviews conducted by the militants during the action, as well as biographies of the militants and a brief report on the negotiations written by the mediating lawyers. Since the booklet does not have a publishing date, I take its release date as the publishing date. Although the book is accessible online at

DOI: 10.4324/9781032690070-4

event suspends the everyday legal operation through a violent intervention in the prosecutor's office at the courthouse, the video statement reaches beyond these spatial limits and takes every spectator hostage. The hostage-taking video statement punctures the overstretching of time with urgency; it marks a date on the prolonged investigation over Elvan's killing – justice *here-now*.

The Revolutionary People's Liberation Party-Front (Devrimci Halk Kurtuluş Partisi-Cehpesi, DHKP-C), commonly referred to as People's Front or Party-Front, is an armed leftist organisation which is known for sensational violent actions. The People's Front has been listed as a terrorist organisation in Turkey, as well as in the European Union and US.[3] As I explain further in the first section of this chapter, the People's Front is organised within the predominantly Alevi working-class, urban neighbourhoods of Istanbul, especially in Okmeydanı, where the Elvan family resides. It is necessary to note here that they are the terrorists who, according to Erdoğan, Elvan had imitated. In that regard, Erdoğan's *father-state* performance can be considered as a call, a provocation, directed towards the People's Front. In this chapter, I approach the hostage-taking action as countering violence, which, I argue, exhibits that Elvan's death was not the tragic fate of a disobedient son, but rather it was an active killing by the ones who performed violence on behalf of the state. The first section of this chapter unpacks the People's Front's countering violence in relation to the state violence, while suggesting that the People's Front's countering violence is more than a simple reaction but rather imitates, and aims to replace, the state violence and its legal system. Thus, I suggest the term counter-violence to emphasise the double movement within the People's Front's violent action which, on the one hand, refuses the existing political and legal order and, on the other hand, reperforms an idealised version of it. I explore this through the conceptual framework of *counter*. In addition to countering state violence with counter-violence, I understand their act as a form of disobedience against the state's subjection of naming the terrorist. In a performative manner, the People's Front militants' act is a performance that reconstructs their subjectivity against the state. I consider the People's Front's counter-violence as an act of counter-subjection, while exploring the agency of the figure of the revolutionary martyr in relation to its appropriation of deadly fate, 'a grim yet political act of resistance or refusal of the injustice of an order that has become some kind of fate [...] a way of grappling with this fate by taking it into his [one's] own hands' (Bargu 2016, 29).[4]

Halkın Sesi, a website which is the People's Front's media and communications channel, the exact link of the website changes occasionally due to censorship.

3 For a brief profile of the People's Front see: 'Profile: Turkey's Marxist DHKP-C'. BBC News, 2 February 2013. Accessed 16 July 2024. www.bbc.co.uk/news/world-europe-21296893.

4 Banu Bargu (2016) makes this comment in relation to Mohammed Bouazizi, the 26-year-old street vendor who set himself ablaze in 2010 in Tunisia, whose action sparked the nationwide protests which soon spread regionally, commonly referred to as the Arab Spring.

In that regard, it is possible to suggest that the hostage-taking action enacts a tragedy. In a similar fashion to tragedy, as in the literary genre, the hostage-taking operation ended with a catastrophe. At around eight-thirty in the evening, Special Forces carried out an operation which ended with the death of the People's Front militants and the prosecutor.[5] In *The Origin of German Tragic Drama* (1998), while analysing the differences and connections between Greek tragedy and German tragic drama (*Trauerspiel*), Walter Benjamin notes the juxtaposition of what he calls as the *martyr-drama* and the *drama of the tyrant*, a peculiar form which, according to Benjamin, originally belongs to tragedy but is later adapted by the baroque drama (69). To put it briefly, while the former is a tale of the personal sufferings of 'a radical stoic', the latter refers to the difficult decision-making process of a sovereign,[6] which is followed by 'the downfall of the tyrant' (72–73). According to Benjamin, these two figures appear to be intertwined: 'the tyrant and the martyr are but the two faces of the monarch' (69). Following Benjamin's remarks, I read the hostage-taking action as a real-life tragedy which shines a light onto the state and onto its violent manifestation from the other side of the monarch, which uncovers the *stately performative*'s disguise of state violence as the protagonists, in other words, the martyrs, progress towards their deadly fate – a heroic act that is conditioned to the death of the martyr. As the mythical construction of the state and the state's claim on the monopoly of violence dissolve before our eyes, the hostage-taking action reveals the *drama of the tyrant*.

In order to address the self-sacrificial act of defiance in the People's Front's hostage-taking action, I present a cross-reading of Sophocles' *Antigone* (1994). To briefly recall the plot of Sophocles's famous tragedy, the heroine Antigone goes against the unjust, tyrannical and sovereign law of Creon, who orders Polyneices to be left unburied. Her defiance brings her death, but it also reveals the *drama of the tyrant* as the defiance reveals Creon's tyrannical violence and brings his ruin. In the previous chapter, I mentioned Creon's order and his comparison of the two dead brothers while unpacking Erdoğan's comparison of Berkin Elvan and Burakcan Karamanoğlu. In this chapter, I draw parallels between the People's Front militants and Antigone's claim to bring justice to the dead as Antigone's self-sacrificial action sheds

5 The footage of the operation was circulated via the national news agency, Anadolu Ajansı (Anadolu Agency), to respond to criticism over the handling of the hostage-taking event. The CCTV footage claims to demonstrate that the operation took place right after hearing gunshots from the room. However, from the released footage, it is not possible to locate the origin of the gunshots. See Anadolu Agency, 'Savcı Kiraz'ın Şehit Edildiği Ana İlişkin Operasyonun Görüntüleri', YouTube video, 0:31, 28 March 2016. Accessed 16 July 2024. www.youtube.com/watch?v=ODnfoCUCTUg.

6 It is possible to trace a Schmittian vein in Benjamin's reading of the drama of the tyrant, as he writes: 'The function of the tyrant is the restoration of order in the state of emergency a dictatorship whose utopian goal will always be to replace the unpredictability of historical accident with the iron constitution of the laws of nature' (1998, 74).

light on the People's Front militants' self-sacrificial action. Although I present a detailed discussion on the matter later in this chapter, it is necessary to note there that I do not disregard the gendered aspect of Antigone, the celebrated woman heroine who rebels against the male sovereign and his tyrant (male) laws. However, my cross-gendered reading of Antigone with the two male People's Front militants offers an alternative reading beyond gender norms, emphasising her disposition as a defiant subject beyond the limits of a grieving sister or a mad woman. From that perspective, Antigone presents to us a unique lens to consider the militants' positions, as well as the meanings and claims of their self-sacrificial action against the state. In addition, as I argue in this chapter, when Antigone is stripped of her gender norms, in other words, when her action is considered as something more than a heroic enactment of her womanly fate, it reveals a question – *Why must Antigone die?* – which I ask in relation to the deadly fate of the People's Front militants. I inquire into the self-sacrificial character of the action to reveal the interplay between the *martyr-drama* and the *drama of the tyrant*; when the latter gets exposed as the former approach to its end.

Militant-Martyrs

In Sophocles's tragedy, the heroine Antigone buries her unburied brother despite knowing this act is punishable by death.[7] Antigone's act of defiance defies reason, through which the law operates. The act is irrational and unintelligible to Creon as he asks whether Antigone knew her act was forbidden: 'Did you not know that this had been forbidden?' When Antigone affirms that she knew, Creon asks, 'And so you dared to disobey the law?' (Sophocles 1994, 16).

Judith Butler (2000), in their reading of Antigone in *Antigone's Claim*, registers this as a sovereign expectation: 'He [Creon] expects that his word will govern her deeds, and she speaks back to him, countering his sovereign speech act by asserting her own sovereignty' (11). As I draw parallels between Creon's order and Erdoğan's *stately performative* in the previous chapter, it is possible to observe a similar expectation in Erdoğan's *father-state* performative of accusing Elvan of his own death, that Erdoğan expects everyone to accept his word and not hold anyone else accountable for Elvan's death. As for Erdoğan, Elvan's death serves as evidence for his disobedience of the *father-state;* there is no one else to be held accountable. This dynamic

7 Antigone tells her sister: 'he who disobeys
In any detail shall be put to death
By public stoning in the streets of Thebes.
So it is now for you to show if you
Are worthy, or unworthy, of your birth' (Sophocles 1994, 4)

between the sovereign expectation of obedience and its defiance recalls the discussion on subjection, or *interpellation*, in Chapter 1. I read this along the lines of the expectation of *interpellation*, which I explain in relation to the hailer police officer's expectation to dominate and subjugate the hailed subject. Both Antigone and the militants of the hostage-taking action defy their subjection as they disobey the legal order, even though this brings their own deaths. In that regard, both acts are self-sacrificial actions which are unintelligible to the ones who claim the powers of the state and perform the state and its laws: *Why would someone abandon their life in the name of someone else who is already dead?* To unpack this, below I present a reading of the People's Front militants' act of defiance in response to the state's subjection. To do so, first, I introduce the figure of the martyr, or revolutionary martyr to be precise, within the repertoire of Turkey's radical left, and then I discuss this disposition in relation to the state and its subjection through the cross-reading of Antigone.

Shela Sheikh (2013), in her doctoral thesis on Lebanese martyrdom testimonies – which consist of a series of martyrdom video recordings that originated in Lebanon after the Israeli invasion of June 1982, provides a detailed account of the etymology and history of the word 'martyr'. She writes:

> The English word 'martyr' originates from Old English *matir*, via the ecclesiastical Latin *martyr*, from the Greek *martur*, meaning 'witness'; an expression used in Greek courts. It was not until the second century AD that the word acquired the technical signification within Christian discourse of dying for a cause; choosing to suffer death rather than renouncing one's beliefs; of one whose suffering and death bore witness to the truth of Jesus' passion and resurrection. With this new meaning, the old sense of bearing witness (testifying) in a court gradually became blurred. This same conjunction is evident in Arabic, in which the word *shahīd* (pl. *suhadā*), meaning 'martyr'.
>
> (31)

Furthermore, it is possible to observe a common trait between the Lebanese martyrdom videos and the hostage-taking video statement, as both mediums reach the spectators who serve as witnesses to the martyrdom of the militants, which is a condition for their martyrdom to be recognised. However, martyrs, too, claim to be witnesses, i.e., witnesses of the truth or violence. Sheikh explains the intertwined relationship between the martyr and witness:

> Upon a brief survey of historical and religious studies, as well as etymological analyses, it quickly becomes apparent that the concept of martyrdom entails or implies some form of witnessing and/or testifying (i.e. bearing witness); that [...] the martyr is a witness and that his/her martyrdom testifies and is subsequently witnessed by an audience, with the witnessing

> and bearing witness of the audience being necessary for the martyrdom to be recognised and authenticated as such; in other words, for the "martyrdom" to take place.
>
> (18)

To follow Sheikh's explanation on the etymology of 'martyr', the Turkish word for martyr, *şehit*, which derives from its Arabic origin, also bears the same meaning. Although in Turkish *şahit* is more commonly used for witness, both *şehit* and *şahit* derives from the same Arabic root *sh-h-d* which, as Sheikh explains through citing from Nader el-Bizri by providing an Islamic reading of its etymology, 'refer to the experience of being present in a spectacle and assembly, or to having evidential attestation of the happening of an event, while also being a literal manner of affirming the beholding of an incident with ones' own eyes' (32). Here I do not aim to present a reading of the meaning of martyrdom solely based on its etymological roots;[8] nonetheless, it provides us with an orientation to grasp its usage in Turkey's radical left. What is striking in Sheikh's definition, however, is that despite the common belief, the martyr is not foundationally a religious figure but rather a figure related to legal procedure as it is used in Greek courts. This finding can be associated with the People's Front militants' claim of bringing justice to Berkin Elvan through the hostage-taking event. Not only do they claim to bear witness to Elvan's killing at an imaginary court, but they also aim to carry out a public tribunal and prosecution to bring justice, which I discuss further in the next section while analysing their demands.

Regarding the figure of the martyr in Turkey's radical left, however, it is possible to trace a combination of religious and non-religious connotations of martyrdom. On the one hand, Turkey's radical left is known to be a non-religious, secular movement, while, at the same time, its discourses and especially martyrdom practices are heavily influenced by Alevi culture, which is an Islam-orientated belief system that is referred to as a heterodox Islamic belief due to diverging from common practices of Sunni and Shia. As Martin van Bruinessen (1996) notes, 'Prayer (*namaz*), the fast in Ramadan, zakat and hajj are alien practices to most Alevi communities. Instead, they have their own religious ceremonies (*cem*), officiated by holy men (*dede*) belonging to a hereditary priestly caste' (7). Alevi ceremonies and rituals have strong references to martyrdom. Michael Reinhard Hess (2007), in his detailed study on the issue titled 'Alevi Martyr Figures', highlights that there are four martyr figures, al-Hallag, al-Husayn, Fazlollah Astarabadi and Nesimi, all of whom 'are regarded as martyrs in the true sense of the world.

8 Likewise, despite providing a detailed analysis on its etymology, Sheikh (2013) also approaches such readings with caution: 'whilst we draw from etymological sources as catalyst for readings to follow, the authority of etymology is always regarded with some degree of suspicion' (33).

For they are believed to have been killed for the public profession of their faith' (275). Furthermore, Reinhard Hess notes that martyrdom is not only a religious symbol in Alevi practices but 'is also an integral element of the ceremony itself' as 'the ceremony includes a declaration of one's willingness to go so far as to die for the Way if necessary' (276). In her chapter on the construction of martyrdom in radical-left organisations in Turkey, Eylem Özkaya Laselle (2016) points out the overlapping of the radical left and Alevi culture during the politicisation of Alevism. Özkaya Laselle notes that this process resulted in members of the Alevi community being active members of Turkey's radical left, which, on the one hand enabled the radical left to reach out to the rural areas and, on the other hand, transformed and modernised Alevi culture (325). This overlap of the Alevi community and radical left can be observed in a number of working-class neighbourhoods in Istanbul where the People's Front is active and strong, such as Okmeydanı, where the Elvan family resides.

Deniz Yonucu (2022), in her book *Police, Provocation, Politics: Counterinsurgency in Istanbul*, offers an ethnographic study of Alevi working-class neighbourhoods in Istanbul. While disclosing the mimetic co-existence of policing practices and revolutionary activities in these neighbourhoods, Yonucu emphasises the significance of the figure of the revolutionary martyr within the collective memory of the neighbourhoods' residents. Yonucu mentions that the names of the revolutionary martyr figures decorate the streets of the neighbourhoods in the form of graffiti and stencils. Landmarks within the neighbourhoods carry the name of the revolutionary martyrs, such as 'Berkin Elvan Park in Güzeltepe', as Yonucu exemplifies (17). The martyr figures not only haunt the public space but continue to live through the next generations as newborns are named after them. These practices could be understood as a counter-subjection, a form of resisting the subjection, or *interpellation*, of the state. In reference to Foucault (1988), Yonucu highlights these practices are also practices of 'ethical self-formation' that inspire the youth, as she writes, 'martyrs are the spirits of resistance and solidarity who help enable dissident political activity to continue' (ibid.). Yonucu considers the revolutionary martyr figures as ghosts and suggests their memory haunts the residents and inspires 'them to take defiant action', which she refers to as '*inspirational hauntings*' (121). Yonucu also mentions 'the burden of being a witness' experienced by the residents and especially the youth of these neighbourhoods (129). Following Yonucu's observations, I suggest that *inspirational hauntings* of the past revolutionary martyrs, on the one hand, allow the youth to reconstruct their agency against the subjection of the state; on the other hand, however, the figure of the revolutionary martyr becomes an idealised subject, a desired subject. In other words, a revolutionary martyr becomes a desired future.

Banu Bargu (2014), in her detailed work titled *Starve and Immolate* on the People's-Front-led prison hunger strikes of the early 2000s in Turkey, elaborates on the significance of martyrdom in Turkey's radical left tradition. In October 2000, a mass hunger strike was launched by prisoners in a protest against high-security prisons, commonly referred to as F-type cellular imprisonment in Turkey. The People's Front-led death fasts called on other radical leftist organisations to join, to which the Turkish radical left responded with temporary solidarity hunger strikes while the Kurdish movement withheld participation. Nonetheless, what initially began as a hunger strike of some eight hundred prisoners escalated into a nationwide movement against F-type prisons as it gained momentum outside of prisons through the initiatives of various civil-society organisations, bar associations, trade unions, human-rights organisations and artist initiatives within Turkey. It also triggered solidarity hunger strikes to take place in European prisons. The government carried out a violent security operation, 'Operation Return to Life', in the prisons involved in the hunger strike which caused even more casualties. Hunger strikes to the death continued until May 2006, and one hundred and twenty-two people died in the death-fast struggle. Bargu lists the causes of death as self-starvation due to a death fast, self-immolation (self-immolation while on a death fast or suicide attack) and killed (killed while on a hunger strike or died of medical neglect) (196–213). Bargu argues that it would be wrong to relate the martyrdom practices of Turkey's radical left only to Alevi martyrdom culture; instead, she refers to such practices as *sacrificial Marxism* which, she suggests, corresponds to 'a secularised political theology', as a form of 'political mysticism' (237). Regarding the discourse and practice of martyrdom in Marxist leftist organisations in Turkey, Bargu writes, '[i]n the theologization of leftist politics, martyrdom combines the secular and the sacred, the past and the present, the living and the dead' (260). Bargu gives the name *militant-martyr* to define this subject who operates 'as a dialectic between the militant and the martyr, the human and the weapon, the living and the dead, steered by the "consciousness of sacrifice", which now replaces "class consciousness" in more conventional Marxism' (241). Furthermore, Bargu describes the People's Front ideological strategy as 'vanguardist warfare' which carries out sensational actions against agents of imperialism, finance capitalism, state officials, torturers and drug dealers 'to display the vulnerability of existing order and [to] expose the political "truths" that are concealed from the masses by the "artificial balance"' (234).

Following Bargu's observations, I consider the People's Front militants Şafak Yayla and Bahtiyar Doğruyol, who carried out the hostage-taking action, as *militant-martyrs*. Not only were they *militant* subjects who were devoted to a cause, that is, devoted enough to sacrifice themselves on behalf of the cause, but also *martyrs* in the sense that they believed their self-sacrifice would reveal the truth of Elvan's death and of state violence. This devotion has a transforming effect on the subject, as Bargu notes: 'In the transformation of human life into a weapon, there is both the desire to pursue particular political goals and an assertion of subjectivity' (17). In that regard, the transformation of the subject 'from human life into a weapon' indicates a process of counter-subjection that rejects its subordination. As Butler (1997) puts it, 'subjection is a subordination that the subject brings on itself; yet if subjection produces a subject and a subject is the precondition of agency, then subjection is the account by which a subject becomes the guarantor of its resistance and opposition' (14). In other words, the People's Front militants' state subjection as terrorists serves as a ground, a guarantor, for their resistance and hence for their transformation into *militant-martyrs*. However, this process of counter-subjection is rather entangled with its subjection, as is evident in its reappropriation of the deadly fate that is attributed to the subject by the state. At this point, I recall Antigone to disclose this entanglement.

To begin with, I would like to address the gender aspect of Antigone, as her entanglement with the state, or rather with the sovereign, occurs in a gendered form. Judith Butler (2000) reminds their readers in *Antigone's Claim* that 'women were not citizens in classical Athens, even though the civic culture was imbued with valences of femininity' (86 n.15). This fact highlights the significance of gender and gender roles in Sophocles' *Antigone*. The interest in reading *Antigone* begins in political philosophy with G.W.F. Hegel, who establishes the relationship between Antigone and Creon as the clash between natural law and state law; Hegel attributes the former to womanhood and the latter to manhood. As Butler (2000) summarises, in *the Phenomenology of the Spirit*, 'Hegel claims that Antigone represents the law of the household gods [...] and that Creon represents the law of the state. He insists that the conflict between them is one in which kinship must give way to state authority as the final arbiter of justice' (4–5). Hegel also writes about Antigone in *Aesthetics: Lectures on Fine Art Volume II* (1975), in which he elaborates in a similar vein: 'in Antigone, the "spiritual power" of family piety is independently personified in her, while Creon is the independent personification of law and the state' (1163 n.1). What is interesting is that Hegel presents the clash in terms of the state's expectation of obedience and paternal responsibility to care that arises from Creon representing the *father-state*:

> Antigone lives under the political authority of Creon [the present King]; she is herself the daughter of a King [Oedipus] and the fiancée of Haemon [Creon's son], so that she ought to pay obedience to the royal command. But Creon too, as father and husband, should have respected the sacred tie of blood and not ordered anything against its pious observance.
>
> (Hegel 1975, 1217)

Although there are differences in the readings of Antigone and her legacy in the literature, there seems to be a consensus over the significance of her gender. In feminist scholarship and critical literature, Antigone is celebrated as a heroine, a rebel, a martyr and an unruly woman who exposes the limits of (manly) sovereignty.[9] In *Antigone Interrupted*, Bonnie Honig (2013) summarises the canonised readings of Antigone as 'heroic conscience objector who on political grounds violates an unjust law, challenges a powerful sovereign, and all by herself dares speak truth to power', 'humanist lamenter of the dead, grieving sister/mother/daughter' and 'monstrous creature of desire [...] even passionately eager, to die for her cause' (7). Although there are apparent similarities between the People's Front militants and Antigone in carrying out self-sacrificial actions with the claim of bringing justice to the dead, how is it possible to read Antigone beyond her most significant trait? Or, to put it in other words, what does Antigone as a man tell us?

Nüket Sirman's (2016) 'When Antigone Is a Man' provides an opening to cross-read Antigone with the two male militants. Sirman analyses 'the case of a man who demands that the state return the remains of his dead guerrilla brother and then goes on a hunger strike [...] a woman journalist links his act to Antigone and finally the man ends up accepting the Antigone name' (192). Sirman reads this act as an act of transgression towards 'both gender and kinship norms', as she notes, '[i]f Antigone occupied the place of the man in deciding to bury her brother, Hüsnü Yıldız seems to occupy the place of the woman in claiming the right to bury his brother's remains' (198). Indeed, in *Antigone's Claim*, Butler points to the passage in which Creon responds to Antigone's act in these words: 'Now I am no man, but she the man [*aner*]' (9). Elena Loizidou (2007) suggests that Butler uses this passage 'to demonstrate that there is no stabilisation of gender in the play or, more generally, there is rather a flowing temporality of genders' (83). In Sirman's reading, what results in the naming of the man as Antigone is his self-sacrificial act for the burial right of his dead brother, who, in a similar vein to Antigone's unburied brother, was considered an enemy of the state. Sirman reads the man's self-sacrificial act, in relation to Antigone's, as 'an act that places the actor in a position of vulnerability' and elaborates further:

> What these actions undertake in response to necropolitics is to remove the repressive policies from the domain of the political and place them with the domain of the moral. This amounts to an attempt to delegitimize the state itself, as it is presently constituted. The immorality of denying a proper burial becomes equivalent to letting a man die a little every single day in full view of the public.
>
> (Sirman 2016, 197)[10]

9 The edited collection by Fanny Söderbäck presents a good selection of feminist readings of *Antigone*. See Söderbäck (2010).

10 Sirman refers to *necropolitics*, a term coined by Achille Mbembe (2003), which suggests 'to exercise sovereignty is to exercise control over mortality and to define life as the deployment and manifestation of power' (12).

Sirman's analysis of Antigone as a man coincides with the previous remarks by Bargu's, as discussed above, which suggest that the self-sacrificial actions aim to reveal the truth of the state. Surely, the People's Front's hostage-taking action is not only a self-sacrificial action, but rather, it is a violent action that targets the prosecutor. I unpack this further in this chapter. However, my inquiry here is regarding the agency of *militant-martyr*. Although the People's Front's action is not simply a self-sacrificial action, similar to Antigone, as mentioned at the beginning of this section, the militants know very well that their act would bring them death. In that regard, to put it in Sirman's perspective, I suggest Antigone's and the militants' defiance indicate vulnerability as a position; 'I would like to be able to talk about the becoming vulnerable not of a subject, but a position, a relation to power, that brings with it unintelligibility and thereby vulnerability' (Sirman 2016, 192). What is striking in Sirman's analysis is her reading of vulnerability beyond the subject, which, on the one hand, sheds light on the agency of Antigone beyond gender norms, i.e., as a vulnerable woman who mourns eternally, and, on the other hand, reveals that vulnerability is something related to 'the existing scheme of power and intelligibility' (ibid.). Following Sirman's observations, I argue that the two male militants of the hostage-taking action not only act vulnerably as they carry out a self-sacrificial action but also act from a position of vulnerability which, similar to Antigone, transgresses kinship roles. Although they are not related by blood to Berkin Elvan, they share a kinship through their position of being the vulnerable ones in relation to the state who are subjectified as the disobedient sons of the *father-state*, a kinship through a shared deadly fate which they reconstruct through the codes of camaraderie, militancy and martyrdom. Indeed, in her ethnographic work in the working-class neighbourhoods of Istanbul, Yonucu (2022) observes two types of martyr figures: 'those revolutionaries and rebels who lost their lives while fighting against oppression and those who lost their lives at the hands of the state and state-backed violence' (16). In the hostage-taking action, the two martyr figures, Elvan, the one who lost his life at the hands of the state, and Yayla and Doğruyol, the militants who fight in his name, intertwine with one another, establishing a kinship through the figure of the martyr.

Following Sirman's observations, I read her analysis on vulnerability in relation to fate, or rather the state violence that disguises itself as fate, which I introduced in Chapter 1. What Sirman registers as vulnerability is the deathly fate that is attributed to some subjects by the *father-state*, that is, when their death is disguised as fate. Regarding this, Banu Bargu's (2016) reading of the death of Mohamed Bouazizi, the street vendor who set himself ablaze in Tunisia in 2010, presents an analysis of self-immolation and self-sacrificial actions through the lens of fate. Her analysis on the deadly fate of Bouazizi shares similarities with Sirman's reading of vulnerability, as Bargu emphasises Bouazizi's position within, as Sirman puts it, 'the existing scheme of power'. In a similar vein to Sirman, Bargu (2016) notes: 'Bouazizi's self-killing is a testament to the absence of a collective movement and the helpless solitude experience by the individual before an existing order, whose oppression and injustice now appear to be some kind of fate' (28). Furthermore, after briefly elaborating on fate, Bargu concludes that the Hobbesian figure of the sovereign is the bearer of fate in the modern state and explains how the various meanings 'of fate are brought together in the figure of the sovereign, a figure that now gains an impersonal, public, even collective meaning (31), as Bargu explains further;

> On the one hand, the sovereign speaks (*fari*) and his speech becomes the law; this fits both with his role as the "mortal god" and, because sovereignty is produced through the authorization of individuals constituting the commonwealth, with the idea that it is the people speaking though the sovereign. On the other hand, the speech of the sovereign, the "thing spoken" (*fata*) is the allocation to each man what will fall to his lot by law, that is, the dispensation of punishments, including death (*fatalis*), in return for the defiance of the law or the disruption of security. In each sense, the sovereign and, indirectly, the individuals in their collective capacity of authorizing the sovereign, are substituted for the divine as the ultimate arbiter of fate'.
>
> (ibid.)

According to Bargu, the Hobbesian imaginary of sovereignty does not only signify a control over fate through reason, but more importantly indicates an economy of fate, 'to control fate by deciding and distributing fatality' (ibid.). Finally, Bargu notes that the distribution of fatality is unequal, which 'does not merely produce some populations always closer to death than the rest. It also leads to new forms of resistance that emerge out of these increasingly invisibilized, alterized, "surplus" populations that are ever more criminalized, demobilized, punished, or left to die' (32).

Berkin Elvan and the militants Şafak Yayla and Bahtiyar Doğruyol share a vulnerable position in relation to the state. They are the ones whom the police hail as suspects, who are already subjectified as disobedient sons, even before enacting their disobedience. They are those who are closer to death, whose fate is death and whose deaths are fate in the economy of the modern state. Following the discussion on fate in Chapter 1 and Chapter 2, in which I suggest Berkin Elvan's deadly encounter with the police is rendered as his own fate due to his subjection as a disobedient son, it is possible to argue that People's Front militants re-enact this scenario by putting themselves in a vulnerable position which exposes the distribution of deadly fate.[11]

11 Indeed, Julia Ng, in her keynote address at the 'Working with Benjamin on Law' workshop organised by the International Walter Benjamin Society, the Walter Benjamin Archive and the Leibniz-Zentrum für Literatur- und Kulturforschung, held between 15 and 17 July 2021,

As a final point, I would like to turn my focus to the significance of the imaginary used in the video statement to expand on the militants' association with Berkin Elvan. The video statement captures a usual office setting disturbed by an extraordinary event. As the militants list their demands, three posters stand out which clearly do not belong to the prosecutor's office. The posters set the scene not only because they served as décor for the video statement, but also because they convey the message of the action. What is significant in this constellation is Berkin Elvan's image, which is placed next to two organisational flags, one red with a yellow star, the other red with a hammer and sickle placed inside a red star circled in yellow. The third image displays Berkin Elvan with a slingshot in one hand and making a victory sign with the other. His face is disguised with a red face cover similar to that worn by the People's Front militant, and below his picture is written: 'We want Berkin's killers' (Berkin'in katillerini istiyoruz). Berkin Elvan is usually referred to by his forename rather than his surname as a sign of familiarity, kinship and camaraderie. While the two organisational flags and symbols locate the action's place within the complex map of Turkey's leftist organisations, relating the action to specific revolutionary historiography, the image of Berkin Elvan sets out the objective of the action while associating Elvan with the revolutionary legacy.[12] In that regard, this constellation consisting of party flags, revolutionary symbols, and Elvan's image transgresses traditional kinship norms and binds Elvan and the militants in a kinship of martyrdom, and, in doing so, reconstructs both their own and Elvan's subjection.

presented a reading on Benjamin's elaborations on law. Ng points out that, in a Benjaminian sense, what transforms Niobe into stone is guilt and that by turning into a stone her life transforms into materiality. At this point, Ng recalls *Antigone* and notes that Benjamin would have known Hölderlin's translation of *Antigone*. By drawing parallels between Niobe and Antigone, Ng suggests that for Benjamin law is established at the moment when life transforms into matter. Law, which operates through guilt and governs debt, invests in life as matter. Furthermore, Ng relates the law's operation to the position of vulnerability by noting that the law imputes violence onto beings that are relationally vulnerable. I relate Ng's observations to Bargu's analysis of the economy of deadly fate, which could be read as the transformation of life into a matter. Thus, the law renders life vulnerable and creates vulnerable positions against the state and its violence. Finally, Ng concludes with an observation on how the police and their violence operate more crudely in vulnerable areas, which recalls the police's violent presence in the poor urban neighbourhood of Okmeydanı, where Elvan was shot and where the People's Front is organised. (See ZfL Berlin 2021.)

12 Banu Bargu (2014) skilfully summarises the complex family tree of the extra-parliamentary left in Turkey while tracing their common grounds which enabled all factions to work together during the period of the death fasts. (227–236). Bargu describes the People's Front ideological strategy as 'vanguardist warfare' which carries out sensational actions against agents of imperialism, finance capitalism, state officials, torturers and drug dealers 'to display the vulnerability of existing order and [to] expose the political "truths" that are concealed from the masses by the "artificial balance"' (234).

Significantly, the image of Elvan corresponds with Erdoğan's description of him at the rally speech: 'a child who was among the terror groups whose face was masked, with a slingshot put into his hand and iron marbles in his pocket' (Parti Mitingleri 2014). In the aftermath of his death, this image of Elvan was circulated in the media, casting doubts on his innocence. Even though the Elvan family objected to these manipulations, stating that the picture did not belong to the day he was shot, Erdoğan and other state officials kept referring to this image of Elvan as if it belonged to that day. At first, the People's Front's usage of this image might appear contradictory; however, I suggest its usage can be understood in relation to the previous discussion on the shared position of vulnerability and deadly fate. The People's Front's usage of this particular image serves as a reply to Erdoğan's subjectification of Elvan as the disobedient son of the state, which is replaced with revolutionary martyrdom. Indeed, the book dedicated to Berkin Elvan (Köse 2015), published by a publishing house associated with the People's Front, mentions the significance of this portrayal while criticising the 'petite bourgeoise' for owning the legacy of Berkin Elvan based on the innocence of a child and rejecting his political agency. 'They refused to show his photograph with the red face cover and throwing stones with slingshot. Instead, they publicised childhood photographs of him swinging or flying a kite' (Köse 2015, 9).[13]

It is necessary to note here that, although the People's Front militants are *militant-martyrs*, who consciously decide to carry out a deadly and sacrificial action, this is not the case for Berkin Elvan. As if Elvan's death was a self-fulfilling prophecy of his militancy, Elvan becomes a martyr after his death, without any pronounced decision to be a *militant-martyr*. This, however, can be understood as a re-subjectification of Elvan against his subjectification by the *father-state*. The People's Front's re-adaptation of the image can be read as a refusal of the state's expectation of obedience that suggests Elvan was already a *militant-martyr*; already a disobedient subject, before the state's subjection of him as such. In that regard, I propose to read it as a counter-subjection that aims to take the power of subjection from the state to reject being a part of the stately economy of obedience and disobedience. However, this gesture of counter-subjection also contains the assimilation of the subjection it opposes. To put it in other words, the *militant-martyr* is both a refusal and a reappropriation of the deadly fate that is attributed to disobedient subjects by the state, as it replaces the state's subjection of the terrorist with the *militant-martyr*.

Indeed, this double movement of refusal and replacement through reappropriation extends throughout the hostage-taking. The People's Front's

13 'Berkin'in sapanla taş atan kızıl fularlı resimlerini görmeyip uçurtma uçuran salıncakta sallanan çocukluk resimlerini öne çıkarttılar' (Köse 2015, 9). Translation from its Turkish original belongs to me.

action is significantly different from that of Antigone and her male counterparts. Although the People's Front's action is self-sacrificial, it carries the objective of issuing violence to the other, not only to the self. The action of the People's Front aims to prosecute the ones who claim the powers of the state, who embody and perform the state and its violence. In that regard, it aims to replace state violence and its legal system, which I analyse further below through the list of demands.

Counter

The People's Front militant lists their demands while holding the prosecutor at gunpoint:

> Our first demand is a live, public confession by the police officers who shot Berkin, who witnessed it and who gave orders. Our second demand is the public prosecution of those police officers in a people's court at a public square by a committee of our choice. Our third demand is the acquittal of all people who are on trial for seeking justice for Berkin. Our fourth demand is to exit safely with the prosecutor. Once our three demands are met, we will leave the prosecutor in a safe place. The prosecutor lives.
>
> (Boran Yayınları 2017, 59)

At first, the demands appear exaggerated and unattainable as they push the boundaries of the existing legal and political order. The hostage-taking action *counters* the juridical system by enacting a violent act, which counters Elvan's violent encounter. It is a spectacle of punishment that targets the representative of the legal system. Regarding Elvan's case, this representative is the prosecutor, Selim Kiraz, who, according to the militants, failed to bring the perpetrators before justice and hold them accountable. In other words, the hostage-taking action serves as a response to the killing of Berkin Elvan and the failures of its legal aftermath. What is significant, however, is that the hostage-taking action simultaneously challenges and replaces the existing political and legal order by enacting its alternative. Below, I unpack this double movement through a discussion on the conceptual framework of *counter*.

Banu Bargu (2014) reads the self-destructive and self-sacrificial death fast campaign of the 2000s through the conceptual lens of *counter-conduct*: 'a *counterconduct* against dominant forms of conduct prescribed by the state, a selfless, ethical performance for the revolution, potent with symbolic and political significance' (243). Bargu emphasises the sacrificial character of the hunger strikes while registering those acts as 'heroic deeds based on the performance of acts of sacrifice on behalf of the working and oppressed classes' which target official, economic or political institutions of strategic value 'to expose political "truths" [and] to expose the "truth" of the state' (238). The case of the hostage-taking action, too, can be considered an act of sacrifice on behalf of Berkin Elvan and on behalf of the public, which demands justice for Elvan. I discuss the sacrificial character of the action in the following section. It is important to note that the action targeted the state juridical system, which failed to bring justice to Berkin Elvan, by directly targeting the prosecutor in charge of the investigation. The hostage-taking action is not only self-sacrificial, as was the case of the death-fast campaign, but more so a violent act that was directed towards the prosecutor, as the representative of the state juridical system. In that regard, the action aimed to punish the state for its crime, echoing the chant 'the murderer state will be held to account'.

Bargu borrows the term *counter-conduct* from Michel Foucault, who presented the term in his 1977–78 lectures, later published under the title *Security, Territory, Population* (Foucault 2009). Foucault initially presents the terms *conduct* and *counter-conduct* in relation to pastorate (191–226). As the lectures progress, Foucault carries these terms to the modern state (333–361).[14] Foucault uses the term 'counter-conduct in the sense of struggle against the processes implemented for conducting others' (201) while introducing the term in relation to the pastorate's power 'of conducting men' (194). Rather than the term 'misconduct', which for him 'refers to the passive sense of the word, of behavior: not conducting oneself properly', Foucault suggests *counter-conduct* to capture the active form of resistance which he favours in 'reference to the active sense of the word "conduct"' (201). To note, Foucault uses *conduct* and *counter-conduct* to emphasise the power of the pastorate's operation through the governance of people's *conduct*, 'that takes as its instrument the methods that allow one to direct them (*les conduire*), and its target the way in which they conduct themselves, the way in which they behave' (194). Foucault elaborates on the various aspects of the word conduct:

> Conduct is the activity of conducting (*conduire*), of conduction (la conduction) if you like, but it is equally the way in which one conducts oneself (*se conduit*), lets oneself be conducted (*se laisse conduire*), is conducted (*est conduit*), and finally, in which one behaves (*se comporter*) as an effect of a form of conduct (*une conduite*) as the action of conducting or of conduction (*conduction*).
>
> (193)

14 Foucault (2009) initially uses the term 'conduct' only in relation to the pastorate power. In his 1 March 1978 lecture, he notes that 'what I would like to show you is that they [revolts of conduct] are distinct from political revolts against power exercised by a form of sovereignty, and they are also distinct [from economic revolts against power] inasmuch as it maintains or guarantees exploitation' (196). In his 5 April 1978 lecture, however, he carries his analysis on 'the pastoral art of conducting men and the counter-conducts' to modern forms of governmentality (355–356).

In that regard, it is possible to argue that Foucault's reading of the pastorate conduct echoes his notion of biopower. By *counter-conduct* then, Foucault refers to 'movements of resistance' against pastoral conduct, which he reads as 'movements whose objective is a different form of conduct, that is to say: wanting to be conducted differently, by other leaders (*conducteurs*) and other shepherds, towards other objectives and forms of salvation, and through other procedures and methods' (194–5). In other words, Foucault's notion of *counter-conduct* targets existing institutional structures which design and order *conduct*; the movement of countering does not only object to such structures but also presents or enacts its alternative with an aim of replacing the *conduct*. This replacement aspect is missing in Bargu's adaptation of the term *counter-conduct*, although it is something Foucault (2009) wrestles with throughout his lectures: 'Are we not merely dealing with the same phenomena in reverse, from the negative or reactive side?' (196). Moreover, it is possible to detect an undertone of concern regarding *counter-conduct* replacing *conduct* via adapting its operation of conducting life. Foucault ends his lectures with an insinuation on this matter, this time in relation to the modern state: 'the history of *raison d'État*, the history of the governmental *ratio*, and the history of the counter-conducts opposed to it, are inseparable from each other' (357). Although the editors try to conclude this open-ended final remark by noting that Foucault initially had two more pages in which he explains how revolutionary movements adapt the 'government of men', it is unclear how Foucault understands their inseparability.[15]

On the other hand, the reciprocal relationship between what Foucault refers to as *conduct* and *counter-conduct* takes a more direct form in Frantz Fanon's dialectical reading of violence and counter-violence in the 'Concerning Violence' chapter of *The Wretched of the Earth* (2001). Fanon discusses violence and counter-violence in the context of colonial violence, as he suggests it is the coloniser, through its agents such as the police and army, who initially brings 'violence into the home and into the mind of the native' (29). In a similar vein to Foucault, Fanon also points to state institutions as the origin of this dialectic, but this time explicitly referring to those enacting the state's monopoly on violence. In that regard, while Foucault indicates the indirect, or rather structural, violence of conducting life, Fanon refers to a direct use of physical violence. Fanon concludes that '[t]he violence of the colonial regime and the counter-violence of the native balance each other

15 The editors follow the final sentence with a note: 'Foucault leaves out here the two final pages of the manuscripts in which, defining revolutionary movements as "counter-conducts, or rather types of counter-conducts that correspond to these forms of society in which the 'government of men' has become one of the attributes of the society, if not even its essential function," he briefly examines the question of their "religious inheritance"' (Foucault 2009, 357).

and respond to each other in an extraordinary reciprocal homogeneity' (69). This reciprocity also has a subjective aspect; Fanon presents a dialectical relationship between the subjectivities of the coloniser and the colonised; as he famously writes, 'the settler and the native are old acquaintances. In fact, the settler is right when he speaks of knowing "them" well. For it is the settler who has brought the native into existence' (28). However, Fanon does not suggest that violence and counter-violence have the same impact, as he reminds us of the dissymmetry within this reciprocal relationship: 'for machine-gunning from aeroplanes and bombardments from the fleet go far beyond in horror and magnitude any answer the natives can make' (70).

Following the discussion on the conceptual framework of countering, I register the hostage-taking event as a counter-violence which reciprocates state violence; however, while doing so, as Foucault highlights, it also aims to replace the existing structures, that is, the existing legal structures of accountability. At this point, I would like to return to the demands. The first demand calls for the police officers to admit the violence in the form of a confession. The performative utterance of the confession, *I confess*, indicates an acceptance and taking ownership of the violent act. Through the act of confessing, the police officers would render their actions as something to confess, a wrongdoing. In that regard, this demand counters the state's legitimate claim to violence and its execution through the police officers by exposing its criminality. Furthermore, it transforms the subjectivity of the police officer from someone bearing the state and its powers, to a wrongdoer, a perpetrator and a criminal. In other words, the demand, even when it is not fulfilled, bears a process of counter-subjection. Similar to the process of the counter-subjection of Berkin Elvan from a disobedient son to a revolutionary martyr, which I discussed in the section above, this demand reveals the fallacies of the state's power of subjection by enacting its refusal, in other words, by demonstrating the possibility of its refusal. In that regard, it is an act of disobedience and a display of power. It is worth noting that the People's Front militants lift the disguise of subjection through its appropriation, in other words, through utilising the power of subjection to counter the state's performance of subjection. To put it in terms of Althusser's hailing analogy, which I discussed in Chapter 1, the demand reverses the direction of *interpellation*, this time from the hailed suspect to the police officers, who then become the suspect. To put it in terms of Butler's remarks on the Althusserian *interpellation* then, this time the demand calls for the police officers to align themselves with the law (Butler 1997, 107).

This brings us to the second demand, which challenges the existing legal structures of accountability by proposing an alternative, which is to publicly prosecute the police officers by a committee of their own choice. This demand exposes the failings of the existing legal structures of accountability by presenting its replacement. Their demand recalls a discussion between Foucault and a Maoist on public prosecutions – or, rather, on people's courts

– that is published in the edited collection *Power/Knowledge* (1980). In that discussion, the Maoist discussant advocates the necessity to establish people's courts rather than immediately prosecuting the counterrevolutionaries by death to ensure that the 'particular act of vengeance is not simply a matter of an individual settling of accounts' (3). Foucault disagrees that setting up a people's court 'is the natural expression of popular justice, but rather that its historical function is to ensnare it, control it and to strangle it, by re-inscribing it within institutions which are typical of a state apparatus' (1). In other words, Foucault argues, in a similar vein to his remarks on *conduct* and *counter-conduct*, that people's courts imitate the state juridical system, and hence, it is the 'first deformation' of popular justice' (2).

Indeed, an alternative proposal to set up people's courts would necessitate its own procedural system and criminal codes and perhaps even require establishing its own accountability process. In fact, the People's Front militants' demand for a people's court has its roots in the people's committee and people's court practices in the working-class neighbourhoods of Istanbul. Yonucu's (2022) ethnographic work on working-class neighbourhoods displays the origins and operation of people's committees and people's courts in the predominantly Alevi working-class neighbourhoods (36–44). As Yonucu explains, these neighbourhoods were established as shantytowns by internal migration from rural to the city of the Alevi Turks and Kurds in the 1960s and 1970s, and, soon after, neighbourhood people's committees and people's courts were established to govern the neighbourhoods and to resolve conflicts (36). Yonucu's interlocutors express that these were formed out of necessity, as the state did not recognise these neighbourhoods as residential areas and thus did not provide any services, including security (36–37). The state did not have any presence in these neighbourhoods, rather only had a violent presence by demolishing or threatening to demolish these neighbourhoods, which led to practices of self-governance and dispute resolution. Yonucu concludes that 'both the urgent infrastructural needs and the historical Alevi experience of informal justice played a part in their creation' (36). Yonucu mentions that these practices were revived in the late 1990s, and, this time, they were associated with the People's Front by the national media (48).

The historical practice of people's committee and people's court in the working-class neighbourhoods reveals that these practices aimed to fill the gap of the state and its failings, rather than aiming to topple over the bourgeois state and its institutions as aspired in the discussion between Foucault and the Maoist. I suggest the demand of public prosecution of the police offers responsible for killing Elvan does something similar here. The demand aims to fill the gap of the state legal system, which had failed to bring the police offers before the law for two years. Despite his general opposition to people's courts, at the very end of the discussion Foucault (1980) accepts their use only on one condition: 'where one can, in parallel with a bourgeois trial, conduct an alternative trial which can expose as lies what is taken as truth in the former' (36). However, what has to be done when there is not a state trial? When the state withdraws, and its legal apparatus withholds its legal power, or rather utilises its powers to stall the legal process and suspend accountability? The People's Front militants' demand, with knowing that the demand would not be accepted, exposes the fallacy of the state legal apparatus. The demand exposes the state law's inability to hold the police officers accountable and offers its alternative by demanding to set up an accountability process that is not carried out by the state representatives. By this, the demand reveals the fantasy of accountability regarding the cases of state violence. Recalling the almost tragic situation that Navaro-Yashin notes about complaining about the state to the state (167), which I mentioned in Chapter 1, the People's Front's demand exposes the fallacy of the processes of accountability. The state cannot sit simultaneously in the seat of the perpetrator and the prosecution. A moral argument follows from this point that if the state is the perpetrator of violence issued by state officials to the people, then the state should not be the one conducting the processes of accountability.

While the listed demands expose the fallacies of the state juridical system in holding the state to account, their action already enacts the public spectacle of punishment by holding the prosecutor hostage. Indeed, the hostage-taking event is a re-enactment of the state violence that killed Berkin Elvan. Yonucu (2022) also observes a similar mimetic relationship between the policing practices and extralegal security practices conducted by revolutionary groups in working-class neighbourhoods (109). However, this mimetic relationship is not a crude imitation of state violence; it is counter-violence which challenges the state's monopoly on violence and also exposes the links between law and violence. It reminds the public that Elvan's death was not the tragic fate of a disobedient child, but, rather, it was an active killing by those who performed violence in the name of the state and that the legal processes had been reluctant to identify the perpetrators and to bring them before the law. As a result, the hostage-taking action responds to the killing of Elvan and its unaccountability by claiming to perform something that the state juridical system failed to perform, and it does so by claiming state's sanctioned violence. In other words, the People's Front militants appropriate the two monopolies of the state: violence and law.

To expand further on this countering movement of refusal and adaptation, I consult Judith Butler's reading of Sophocles's tragedy Antigone. In *Antigone's Claim* (2000), Butler reads Antigone's act of defiance as a double movement which operates simultaneously through her appropriation of stately power; Butler writes, 'her autonomy is gained through the appropriation of the authoritative voice of the one she resists, an appropriation that has within it traces of a simultaneous refusal and assimilation of that very authority' (11). In their reading of Antigone's act of disobedience, Butler suggests that Antigone appropriates the authoritative voice of Creon:

> Her agency emerges precisely through her refusal to honor his command, and yet the language of this refusal assimilates the very terms of sovereignty that she refuses. He expects that his word will govern her deeds, and as she speaks back to him, countering his sovereign speech act by asserting her own sovereignty.
>
> (11)

Indeed, as discussed above, the People's Front's appropriation of the state monopolies of violence and law assimilates the stately sovereign power. Although the People's Front militants use the word 'to punish' rather than 'to prosecute' or 'to sentence', it is possible to recognise a similar authoritative and assertive tone to those of *stately performatives*. Moreover, differently from Antigone, it is possible to read the militants' appropriations as an exaggerated imitation, to the point of ridicule, of state violence and its unaccountability. There is an element of mockery of the state's actual powerlessness, which can be detected at the end of the statement. The People's Front militant concludes the video statement by noting that if their demands are not met, they will kill, or in his own words 'punish', the prosecutor and die fighting. He presents the options in a cheerful manner, as if he is a game-show host presenting the game's rules. As he concludes:

> We are addressing the President and the Prime Minister; who is more valuable? Your murderer police, and the ones who gave the orders, or your precious prosecutor? It is yours to decide. We are giving you three hours. This is not a joke. It's 12:37 now; you have until 15:37 and if those demands are not met by that time, as the DHKC [People's Front] fighters, we will punish the prosecutor with death.
>
> (Boran Yayınları 2017, 59)

This mocking undertone runs throughout the statement. To note, this mocking undertone differs from Navaro-Yashin's (2002) reading of cynicism, which I mentioned in Chapter 1. Rather than cynicism, which, according to Navaro-Yashin's analysis, keeps people performing everyday statecraft although they are aware of its non-existence, here mockery appears as an expression of breaking off from this power relation. In that regard, the People's Front's mockery is an active counter-performance. The hostage-taking event, through the medium of live video coverage and interviews, exposes the scandals of the *father-state*, its violence, its powerlessness, its incompetence and its unaccountability to the public. The mockery contains an undertone of contempt for state power, a cheerfulness in exposing its limits and its 'truth', as Bargu puts it. However, the People's Front militants counter-act at the expense of their own life. To put it in Benjaminian terms, the *drama of the tyrant* comes to light as the martyrs approach their deadly fate.

Martyr's Promise

In a phone interview, one of the militants, Bahtıyar Doğruyol, utters the words below:[16]

> We salute Berkin Elvan, all other Gezi martyrs [...] and their families from here. We love them; we love our martyrs. We repeatedly stated that we would seek revenge. Today is the day to retaliate; it is a part of it. May they be at peace [....] We stated that we will bring justice, we are bringing justice. The Revolutionary People's Liberation Front will bring justice. We salute our organisation, our movement and all our comrades from here. We love them. We are here for them. We are here to bring justice.
>
> (Boran Yayınları 2017, 250–251)

It is possible to hear the echoes of the chant, 'The murderer state will be held to account' in the militant's words. If the chant verbalised a wish that has taken the form of an oath through the cross-generational rituals of Turkey's leftist dissent, the hostage-taking action is a manifestation of the chant, an act that is holding the state accountable. The act of holding the state to account, however, is conditioned to the militants' deadly fate. To begin unpacking this interdependence, Jacques Derrida's (2000) remarks on witnessing can be illuminating:

> The witness marks or declares that something is or has been present to him, which is not so to the addressees to whom the witness is joined by a contract, an oath, a promise, by a pledge of sworn faith whose performativity is constitutive of the witnessing and makes it a pledge [*gage*], an engagement'.
>
> (190)

Although the quote above gives the impression of witnessing in a court setting, Derrida elaborates on witnessing, or bearing witness, in more general terms through Paul Celan's poems. What the quote above reveals, when it is cross-read with the words of the militant, is that the militants claim the position of a witness. Through their act, they address the public, declaring what is present to them: that Berkin Elvan was killed by the police, and the juridical process is hiding their identities, and hence the state is responsible for this killing and its disguise. In that regard, the militants are enacting according to the responsibility of witnessing, as ones who have taken an oath. Of course,

16 The phone interview was circulated on the day from the People's Front's online media channel, Halkınsesi TV. Shortly after the hostage-taking event, all video footage, voice recordings and Twitter feeds were erased, and all People's Front-related internet websites were shut down. However, the full transcript of this interview can be found in the booklet that is dedicated to the People's Front fighters. See Boran Yayınları (2017).

there are issues with this metaphor, as the witness is the person who witnesses the event, who was present as it unfolds; hence, the truth is present to them through their presence. This is not the case for the People's Front militants. However, it is possible to argue that their witnessing comes from the repetition of the event, as they bear witness to history and thus become martyrs. Other than the etymological bonds between witness and martyr, what entwines the act of bringing justice for their dead?

In 'Force of Law', Derrida (1992) elaborates on the possibility of justice, and he interprets justice as something yet to come – 'Justice remains, is yet, to come, *à avenir*' (27) – but also as an urgency, as justice does not wait (26). The issue of bringing justice, however, is rather complicated for Derrida due to its entanglement with the law, which I elaborate in further detail in the following chapter. Here, I suggest, the People's Front militants were responding to this urgency, something the state juridical system failed to acknowledge as the investigation on Elvan's killing had been ongoing for two years. As the militant Bahtıyar Doğruyol continues, it becomes apparent that the action is an attempt to make justice possible not only for Berkin Elvan but for the peoples of Turkey:

> We are patriot Marxist-Leninist revolutionaries. If necessary, we are ready to die for our people's liberation. And surely, we will bring good days to our people. Together with our people, we will bring revolution. We will bring justice and establish a just country. We salute and send our love to all comrades.
>
> (Boran Yayınları 2017, 251)

Their promise of justice not only indicates the failings of the state juridical system but also, as I discussed above, uncovers the fallacy of the law's legitimising claim that it is bringing or enforcing justice. While doing so, however, the militant simultaneously expresses acceptance of their death. The promise communicates the demand for justice, and a just future, and exposes the state's inability to provide it while verbally registering their deadly determination. This linkage between the possibility of the future and deadly fate is what I inquire into in this section. Following the discussion on counter-subjection, I suggest this is a troubled relationship. On the one hand, it is an act of agency; however, on the other hand, it is a reappropriation, and hence a replay, of the deadly fate attributed by the state to disobedient subjects.

Dying for the future is something Fanon mentions within the context of counter-colonial violence. In *A Dying Colonialism* (1965), while differentiating between the terrorist and the *fidaï*, Fanon writes:

> The "terrorist," from the moment he undertakes an assignment, allows death to enter into his soul. He has a rendezvous with death. The *fidaï*, on the other hand, has a rendezvous with the life of the Revolution, and with his own life. The *fidaï* is not of the sacrificed.
>
> (57)

The booklet dedicated to the militants of the hostage-taking action (Boran Yayınları 2017) refers to the term *fedai* and describes the subjectivity of *fedai* as someone who sacrifices themselves for the future (158). Although both Fanon's and the People's Front's usage of the term refers to acting for the future, there is a significant difference regarding whether to register such actions as sacrifice. Bargu (2014) also differentiates acts of terror from self-sacrificial acts, which she refers to as weaponization of life, and reads this responsibility to act for the future as 'consciousness of sacrifice' (241). In that regard, sacrificing worldly joys, including life, becomes a condition for the future, or rather for the possibility for the future. Although Fanon does not read this in terms of sacrifice, he suggests a transformation in which the death of the *fedai* breathes life into the possibility of the future. All these comments above indicate the transformation of the subject, counter-subjection, through which the future becomes possible. Although this transformation breaks off from the state's subjection, it brings a loss, that is, the loss of life. In that regard, even if, as Fanon suggests, the *fedai* lives on through the life of the revolution, this transcendental transformation of the subject is only possible through sacrificing one's own life, which then, in a cyclical manner, gives life to the possibility of the future. To complement this, Butler (2000) also reads Antigone's self-sacrificial act as something exceeding the mortal life: 'She acts, she speaks, she becomes one for whom the speech act is a fatal crime, but this fatality exceeds her life and enters the discourse of intelligibility as its own promising fatality, the social form of its 'aberrant, unprecedented future' (82). Both Butler and Fanon point out, in their potential to construct a future, the aspect of sacrificial acts beyond the limit of death. This future, as is also the case in the hostage-taking action, is enacted in the form of a threat as it aims to rupture and reconstruct the existing order. In other words, the promise of justice is, at the same time, a promise of death.

Indeed, in Sophocles's tragedy, nothing can intervene between Antigone and her deadly fate, although she is interrupted several times on her path towards death. Bonnie Honig, in *Antigone, Interrupted* (2013), offers a reading of the tragedy through these interruptions to highlight Antigone's determination and her political agency; something, according to Honig, is disregarded in the canonical readings of Antigone: 'She [Antigone] is pointedly political not transcendently universal but she can still speak to us, centuries later, nonetheless. She laments, but she does so in a way that is also partisan, vengeful, not just mournful or humanist' (7–8). Indeed, first, her sister Ismene tries to convince Antigone not to disobey Creon's orders, then her fiancé, Haemon, attempts to reason with his father Creon and comes to save her right after her burial. Finally, at the very end, Creon repents and comes back to release her from the cave where she is buried alive with some amount of food to see that Antigone has killed herself. Despite all the interruptions which could have saved Antigone, she reaches her glorious death by taking her own life inside the stone vault where she is imprisoned. This deadly trajectory resonates with the hostage-taking action as the militants too refuse any interruption.

At this point, one may wonder: *Why must Antigone die?* I suggest the tragedy insinuates that there is no other option for the disobedient ones but death, not to mention its gendered implications that disobedient women must kill themselves for their words to have any authority, to be taken seriously or for men to finally comprehend their wrongdoings. In relation to the hostage-taking action, it exposes how the People's Front militants failed to break off the deadly fate that is attributed to them by the state's subjection. Sophocles's tragedy teaches its audience that an act of disobedience always requires its actors to sacrifice their life, sacrifice their material existence for their transcendence as a martyr or they should be ready to sacrifice their future for the prospect of an idealised future for others. This, I argue, is a version of the Hobbesian motto that those who disobey and rebel are responsible for their own deaths, this time from a subjective realm. Perhaps it is possible to argue there is an expectancy of subjection, that the disobedient subject would accept its deadly fate at the expense of exposing the truth. In that regard, the glorified and transcendental figure of a martyr consolidates the association between speaking the truth and death and even transforms the deadly fate into something desirable. In relation to the discussion above on vulnerability and the distribution of deadly fate, it is possible to argue that the state delivers its deadly fate in direct and indirect forms. In direct form, the state directly targets the disobedient ones; in indirect form, the state expects the disobedient ones to deliver their own death at the expense of their act of disobedience. In reference to the discussion on subjection and guilt, there is an expectation of acceptance, that is, accepting the guilt of disobeying the *father-state*. Although in both forms, it is the state that causes such a distribution of deadly fate, in the latter, it appears as if the death is an outcome of the subject's own agency – whereas I argue that it is a reappropriation of the state's subjection of the disobedient ones.

Returning to the events of 31 March 2015: despite the publication ban on the hostage-taking event, a Europe-based Kurdish broadcast-media channel, Med Nûçe TV, conducts a live phone interview as a part of their evening news coverage. In the middle of the interview, Berkin Elvan's father Sami Elvan calls the fighters from the other line. As the news presenter requests for the fighters to stay on air, anyone who watches the news report suddenly becomes a part of the negotiations.[17] Similar to Antigone, just before their death, the militants refuse to allow Elvan's father, Sami Elvan, to enter the room, their stone vault, their death chamber. The interruption takes place at the final stages of negotiations. In what appears to be the last communica-

17 See Korhan Çaycı, 'Berkin'in Babası Eylemcilerle Canlı Yayında – Çağlayan Adliyesi – Savcı Mehmet Selim Kiraz – DHKP-C'. YouTube video, 19:20, 31 March 2015. Accessed 16 July 2024. www.youtube.com/watch?v=2LsW-MERJFs.

tion between the negotiators and the militants, Sami Elvan suggests entering the room; 'Now you are asking me to return to 16 June, you want me to go through the same grief. Look my dearest, I do not want you to get hurt. If you allow me, let me come next to you, let me come there'. The militants refuse. This is the last time we hear from the militants, as the operation begins soon after the phone conversation. The conversation between the father, Sami Elvan, and the militant transgresses traditional kinship norms, as the militant calls him Uncle Sami, and the father addresses the militants as if they are his own sons. The father Elvan already mourns their death – 'I cannot explain the feelings I am going through right now, I am trembling' – and he begs the militants, 'do not make me leave empty-handed, please. Do not return me to 16 June, to 11 March. Do not make me live those feelings again'. Sami Elvan refers to the day Elvan was shot on 16 June 2013 and to the day he died, 11 March 2014. This conversation reveals the repetitive nature of state killings that the militants reveal in the injustice of Elvan's killing through appropriating the deadly fate that had found and killed him. Furthermore, according to the negotiating lawyers' notes, the militants wanted to be addressed as Berkin. By doing so, they re-enacted his death (Boran Yayınları 2017, 115–119). Berkin Elvan's father responds to this repetition and trembles for their lives just as Ismene, the sister of Antigone who had refused to join her in the act of burying their brother, trembles for Antigone's life: 'You reckless girl! I tremble for your life' (Sophocles 1994, 5). Similar to Ismene, Berkin Elvan's father's attempt to interrupt their deadly fate fails.[18]

In his book titled *Greek Tragedy* (2011), Classical scholar H.D.F. Kitto, who translated Sophocles's tragedies into English, mentions that, *Antigone*, as a play, is accused in the literature of being off balance, as 'the heroine drops out half-way through and leaves us to do our best with Creon, Haemon, and their fortunes' (106). Kitto argues that, although this may appear as a fault, it is a deliberate choice which reveals at the halfway point of the tragedy that there is not one but two main characters: 'the last part of the *Antigone* makes no sense until we realize that there is not one central character but two'; the second is Creon (107). In a similar vein, as the militants progress towards their deadly fate – or to put it in Benjaminian terms, as the *martyr-drama* comes to its end – at that point we come to realise the other main character who had been there all along: the prosecutor. In that regard, although the exchange between the militants and the father of Berkin Elvan declares the end of the militants, it calls our attention to the as yet unknown fate of the prosecutor Mehmet Selim Kiraz.

18 Sami Elvan's position is reminiscent of Ismene's in Antigone. In *Mourning Sex*, Peggy Phelan (1997) elaborates on the role of Ismene as she writes: 'Ismene attempts to cut her losses and to choose life over death. But instead, she becomes absorbed in the terrible economy of death, an accelerating multiplication' (13).

In *The Scandal of the Speaking Body*, Shoshana Felman (2003) considers commitment as something between a promise and a threat: 'if promising consists in committing oneself to do something for someone, then similarly, threatening consists in committing oneself to do something against someone' (13). In a similar vein, when the oath of 'the murderer state will be held to account' transforms into a promise through the self-sacrificial commitment of its utterers, it simultaneously serves as a threat to the state. Felman adds right after pointing out their similarity, '[a]lthough the meaning of promise (love and marriage) is of course different from that of the threat (revenge and punishment), the force behind both is the same' (ibid.). In the case of the hostage-taking action, the meaning of promise and threat is entangled through the deed. At this point, it becomes evident that the militants' commitment to the promise of bringing justice to Berkin Elvan is materialised and enacted through a physical, bodily, sacrificial and violent threat. As the militant utters his love for the Gezi martyrs and his comrades, his commitment of love manifests as a threat to the prosecutor's life.

Martyr of Law

Shortly after the phone conversation with Sami Elvan, at around eight-twenty-two in the evening, Special Forces mount an operation. While the militants die at the scene, the prosecutor Mehmet Selim Kiraz is rushed to hospital, where he loses his life. The next day, the prosecutor is buried following a visually spectacular ceremony at the courthouse. The prosecutor's funeral ceremony is televised live. We hear the Minister of Justice calling the event a terrorist attack that not only targeted the prosecutor but the justice system as a whole and the people of Turkey. He adds that the methods for demanding justice are known, with all other methods being illegal and immoral.[19] During the ceremony, Kiraz is called a martyr – in fact, often referred to as the *martyr of law* (hukuk şehidi) – and his name is given to the justice palace complex, where the hearings of Berkin Elvan's case are later to take place.

The prosecutor's death is thus transformed into a spectacle of the state and its legal system, into a stately performance of power and authority over law. However, despite the heroic speeches by the state official against terrorism, I argue that the ceremony actually serves the purpose of restoring the damaged almighty *father-state* imaginary and its force of law. The renaming of the justice palace complex symbolises this reparation, as the prosecutor's name attaches to the massive building compound as if it is a good-luck charm. In relation to the discussion on martyr and witness, his being referred to as the

19 See BBC News Türkçe's 'Öldürülen Savcı Mehmet Selim Kiraz için Tören', YouTube video, 1:30, 1 April 2015. Accessed 16 July 2024. www.youtube.com/watch?v=11iP9tCHuUM.

martyr of law serves the purpose of indicating his devotion to justice and truth. Indeed, media coverage that ensued about him after his death mentioned that he was close to solving the case of Elvan before he died, suggesting that the truth also died with him. This could be read as a cover to disguise the truth. More significantly, however, it is the state's attempt to bind the truth to law, in response to the People's Front claim of exposing the truths of the state and its legal system. It is an act of reclaiming authority over truth and justice: suggesting that justice only comes through the state and its legal representatives and that only they have the power to reveal or conceal the truth.

It is possible to observe the reconstruction of the mythical *father-state* imaginary through the discourses of martyrdom. Such discourses of martyrdom, in a performative manner, (re)construct the omnipotent and omnipresent stately power, as they gain official recognition. Indeed, the two martyr figures, the *martyr of law* and the revolutionary martyrs, are positioned against one another. The contestation between the state and its *counter* continues through the ideal subjects in a transcendental, mythical realm. At this point, the remarks of the prosecutor's family on their son's death allow us to analyse the performative remaking of the *father-state* further. After the prosecutor's death, the family, especially the father, Hakkı Kiraz, have become the centre of attention. This is partly due to the fact that Kiraz's family portrays a perfect representation of a conservative, potentially AKP-supporting, family. However, beyond this, it is possible to observe a *father-state* constellation that is constructed around the state's discourse of martyrdom. Hakkı Kiraz has given several interviews and made several public appearances with and without Erdoğan since his son's death. On every occasion, the father of Mehmet Selim Kiraz expressed his acceptance of his son's martyrdom, registering it as a glorious gift from God. Even so, in a 45-minute interview conducted two years later with the father on his son and his son's death, the older Kiraz shared an anecdote about his son, which implied that his son desired martyrdom. He considers this memory of his son as if it were a prophecy of his glorious deadly fate.[20] Surely the father's words can be read as a form of endurance. However, in their public speeches, both Hakkı Kiraz and Erdoğan stress the prosecutor's disposability for the state's sake, almost with the same exact words. In 2019, Erdoğan, in his address to prospective judges and prosecutors, mentions Selim Kiraz as an ideal to follow: 'one brother Selim gets martyred, thousands of Selim follow' and adds that he was martyred because he was just.[21] In a similar vein, in 2021 commemorations of Mehmet Selim Kiraz's death, his father echoes Erdoğan's

20 See Doğru Tarih's 'Sonra Ne Oldu - Şehit Savcı Selim Kiraz - 11 Şubat 2017', YouTube video, 45:09, 11 February 2017. Accessed 16 July 2024. www.youtube.com/watch?v=vTY5-nJJFu8&t=189s.

21 See 'Erdoğan, Hakim ve Savcılara Seslendi', *Sözcü*, 22 May 2019. Accessed 16 July 2024. www.sozcu.com.tr/2019/gundem/erdogan-hakim-ve-savci-kura-toreninde-4892646/.

words: 'one Mehmet Selim dies, thousands are born. Had we had thousands of lives, let all be sacrificed for the state, for this nation, for this nation-state'.[22] This reveals that the *father-state* performance attributes deadly fate not only to its disobedient sons but also to his obedient sons, the only difference being the glorification of their deaths as martyrs.

I read this as *the drama of the tyrant*, or to put it in Turkey's context, the drama of the *father-state*. Turkey's *father-state* drama reperforms the drama of Creon, whose decision causes the death of his own son as well. The drama of the *father-state* exposes that the state does not only distribute its deadly fate to the disobedient ones. The myth of the state relies on the death of everyone, its supporters and opposers alike, in order to sustain its existence and authority. The only difference is that the ones who act on behalf of the state are valued and glorified by the *father-state* after their death. The drama of the *father-state* is then something related to its mythical grip which distributes death to its opposers and supporters alike once it is challenged. The drama of the *father-state* is indeed its deadliness, its worldliness, that brings its own end as it distributes death also to the subjects who act on its behalf.

References

Bargu, Banu. 2014. *Starve and Immolate: The Politics of Human Weapon.* New York: Columbia University Press.

Bargu, Banu. 2016. 'Why Did Bouazizi Burn Himself? The Politics of Fate and Fatal Politics'. *Constellations* 23(1): 27–36.

Benjamin, Walter. 1998. *The Origin of German Tragic Drama.* Translated by John Osborne. London: Verso.

Boran Yayınları. 2017. Biz de Sizi Seviyoruz!. Accessed 16 June 2024. http://www.halkinsesitv.info/2017/06/boran-yaynlarndan-yeni-kitap-biz-de.html.

Butler, Judith. 1997. *The Psychic Life of Power: Theories in Subjection.* Stanford, CA: Stanford University Press.

Butler, Judith. 2000. *Antigone's Claim: Kinship Between Life and Death.* New York: Colombia University Press.

Derrida, Jacques. 1992. 'Force of Law: The "Mystical Foundation of Authority"'. In *Deconstruction and the Possibility of Justice,* edited by David Gray Carlson, Drucilla Cornell and Michel Rosenfeld. New York and London: Routledge. 3–67.

Derrida, Jacques. 2000. '"A Self-Unsealing Poetic Text": Poetics and Politics of Witnessing'. In *Revenge of the Aesthetic: The Place of Literature in Theory Today,* edited by Michael P. Clark, translated by Rachel Bowlby. Berkeley, CA: University of California Press.

Fanon, Frantz. 1965. *A Dying Colonialism.* New York: Grove Press.

22 See 'Savcı Mehmet Selim Kiraz'ın şehadetinin 6.yılı! Baba Hakkı Kiraz: Bir Tane Mehmet Selim Gider Bin Tane Mehmet Selim Doğar!', *A Haber*, 31 March 2021. Accessed 16 July 2024. www.ahaber.com.tr/ozel-haberler/2021/03/31/savci-mehmet-selim-kirazin-sehadetinin-6yili-baba-hakki-kiraz-bir-tane-mehmet-selim-gider-bin-tane-mehmet-selim-dogar-savci-mehmet-selim-kiraz-kimdir.

Fanon, Frantz. 2001. 'Concerning Violence'. In *The Wretched of the Earth*. London: Penguin Books. 27–84.
Felman, Shoshana. 2003. *The Scandal of the Speaking Body: Don Juan with J.L Austin, or Seduction in Two Languages*. Stanford, CA: Stanford University Press.
Foucault, Michel. 1980. *Power/Knowledge: Selected Interviews and Other Writings 1972–1977*. New York: Vintage Books.
Foucault, Michel. 1988. *Technologies of the Self: A Seminar with Michel Foucault*. Amherst, MA: University of Massachusetts Press.
Foucault, Michel. 2009. *Security, Territory, Population: Lectures at the Collége de France, 1977–78*. Hampshire and New York: Palgrave Macmillan.
Hegel. 1975. *Aesthetics: Lectures on Fine Art*. Translated by T. M. Knox. Oxford: Clarendon Press.
Honig, Bonnie. 2013. *Antigone, Interrupted*. Cambridge: Cambridge University Press.
Kitto, H. D. F. 2011. *Greek Tragedy: A Literary Study*. London and New York: Routledge.
Köse, Ali Osman. 2015. *Onbeşinde bir Fidan Umudun Çocuğu Berkin Elvan*. İstanbul: Boran Yayınları.
Loizidou, Elena. 2007. *Judith Butler: Ethics, Law, Politics*. Oxford: Routledge-Cavendish.
Mbembe, Achille, and Libby Meintjes. 2003. 'Necropolitics'. *Public Culture* 15(1): 11–40.
Navaro-Yashin, Yael. 2002. *Faces of the State: Secularism and Public Life in Turkey*. Princeton and Oxford: Princeton University Press.
Özkaya Lasalle, Eylem K. 2016. 'Radikal Sol Örgütlerde Şehitliğin İnşası'. In *Öl Dediler Öldüm: Türkiye'de Şehitlik Mitleri*, edited by Serdar M. Değirmencioğlu. İstanbul: İletişim Yayınevi. 291–329.
Parti Mitingleri. 2014. 'Başbakan Recep Tayyip Erdoğan Ak Parti Gaziantep Mitingi'. *YouTube video*, 1:04:30, 14 March. Accessed 16 July 2024. https://www.youtube.com/watch?v=qAKzFThXo-w.
Phelan, Peggy. 1997. *Mourning Sex: Performing Public Memories*. Oxon: Routledge.
Reinhard Hess, Michael. 2007. 'Alevi Martyr Figures'. *Turcica* 39: 253–290.
Sheikh, Shela. 2013. *"I Am the Martyr (x)" Philosophical Reflections of Testimony and Martyrdom*. PhD Thesis. Goldsmiths: University of London.
Sirman, Nükhet. 2016. 'When Antigone Is a Man'. In *Vulnerability in Resistance*, edited by Judith Butler, Zeynep Gambetti and Leticia Sabsay. Durham and London: Duke University Press. 191–210.
Sophocles. 1994. *Antigone, Oedipus the King, and Electra*. Edited by Edith Hall, Translated by H. D. F. Kitto. Oxford: Oxford University Press.
Söderbäck, Fanny. 2010. *Feminist Readings of Antigone*. New York: SUNY Press.
Van Bruinessen, Martin. 1996. 'Kurds, Turks and the Alevi Revival in Turkey'. *Middle East Report* 200: 7–10.
Yonucu, Deniz. 2022. *Police, Provocation, Politics: Counterinsurgency in Istanbul*. Ithaca and London: Cornell University Press.
ZfL Berlin. 2021. 'Julia Ng: Benjamin on Law'. *YouTube video*, 33:43, 9 July. Accessed 16 July 2024. https://www.youtube.com/watch?v=DnGaTvvJU-Q&list=PLRwXH9t33XB4-69pnvx8i_Ykmv2ZY9Nu1.

Chapter 4

State Violence on Trial

In June 2013, the Elvan family filed a criminal complaint against the police with the accusation of a direct intention to kill right after Berkin Elvan was hit by a tear-gas canister. At the time, the prosecutor opened an investigation into charges of excessive use of force, which is described in the Turkish Penal Code article 256(1) as, 'any public officer, having the authority to use force, who uses an amount of force in the course of his duty which exceeds that required by such duty, shall be subject to the provisions relating to intentional injury'.[1] In March 2014 Elvan died after being in a coma for almost a year. One year later, in 2015, the People's Front took as their hostage the fifth prosecutor in charge of Berkin Elvan's case. After a criminal investigation lasting for three years under six different prosecutors, in December 2016, the indictment was finalised, which brought probable intent to kill charges against one police officer, Fatih Dalgalı.[2] Probable intent to kill is a reduced homicide charge in comparison to direct intention to kill.[3] Following the indictment, the first court hearing took place in April 2017, and the final hearing was held in June 2021.[4] Throughout the trial process, Officer Dalgalı

1 The English version of the Turkish Penal Code can be accessed from the Council of Europe. Penal Code of Turkey. 2016. Trans. European Commission for Democracy Through Law (Venice Commission). 15 February. Strasbourg. Accessed 16 July 2024. https://www.google.com/url?sa=t&source=web&rct=j&opi=89978449&url=https://www.venice.coe.int/webforms/documents/default.aspx%3Fpdffile%3DCDL-REF(2016)011-e&ved=2ahUKEwjqicWb5seJAxW3W0EAHQwbJo4QFnoECBUQAw&usg=AOvVaw1_mP6WZwdzR4314SK5Gx0

2 See Berkin Elvan Indictment: Republic of Turkey, Istanbul Office of the Chief Public Prosecutor, Investigation no: 2013/155787, Case no: 2016/42124, Indictment no: 2016/4484.

3 According to the Turkish Penal Code, criminal charges including homicide are classified according to two categories of intent (article 21) and recklessness (article 22). Intent is also considered in terms of direct intent and probable intent. For homicide charges, the sentence for the former is an aggravated life sentence (article 82) and, for the latter, it is a life sentence, which may be subject to further deductions in the penalty (article 22(2)).

4 The Berkin Elvan trial has been observed by many national and international human-rights organisations. The most detailed account of the hearings can be found at Faili Belli (Perpetrator Unknown), a project which provides detailed reports on the hearings of Turkey's

DOI: 10.4324/9781032690070-5

held the right to bear arms while carrying out his duty as a police officer in the eastern province of Van. In the final hearing, Fatih Dalgalı was found guilty on the charge of probable intent to kill and was sentenced to sixteen years and eight months in prison.[5] Despite the verdict, however, the court did not order Officer Dalgalı's arrest; instead, he was put under juridical control until the appeal process was concluded.[6] Although, according to juridical control provisions, Officer Dalgalı was prevented from leaving the country, he still continues to carry out his duties as a police officer. The decision was carried to the Regional Court of Appeal by the Istanbul Bar Association to challenge the reduced sentence. In March 2023, the Regional Court of Appeal rejected the application by majority, stating that there are no violations on the grounds of law and its application.[7] Nonetheless, one judge raised opposition to the verdict by stating that the sentence was incomplete as it did not take into consideration that Elvan was a minor and concluded that the sentence should have been higher. In other words, the Regional Court of Appeal's decision validates the sixteen years and eight months sentence given to the police officer Fatih Dalgalı; however, the conviction could still be overturned by the Supreme Court. The Elvan family has been seeking justice and accountability for more than a decade, and the legal process is still ongoing. The family is entangled with the law and held in suspense between the law's promise of justice and its reluctance to deliver it. As Özgür Sevgi Göral (2019, 2021) also observes in relation to the cases of enforced disappearances in Turkey, waiting, or rather keeping justice-seeking subjects waiting, appears to be a common practice of law in state-violence cases. By following the Elvan case, this chapter expands on the literature on waiting and exposes the operation of law as a *waiting apparatus* and registers it as a form of legal violence. While the Elvan family's wait for justice and accountability dominates their life, the legal process has had little impact on the perpetrator. Despite the verdict, and the Regional Court of Appeal's verification, the perpetrator police officer has not been arrested and still continues to carry out his duties as a police officer. The court's conflicting verdict of sentencing him to prison but not ordering his arrest interests me. This could be noted

state-violence trials, including the Elvan trial. In this chapter, I take their reports on Elvan trial hearings as the main resource. See: 'Berkin Elvan Davası' n.d. Faili Belli. Accessed 16 July 2024. www.failibelli.org/dava/berkin-elvan-davasi/.

5 Berkin Elvan Verdict: Republic of Turkey, Istanbul, 17. High Criminal Court, Case no: 2016/325, Verdict no: 2021/189.

6 According to the Turkish Criminal Procedure Code (article 109), the court may put the suspect under juridical control in cases that would have resulted in an arrest. The obligations under juridical control may include travel restrictions, informing authorities regularly and obeying the conditions and restrictions set by the authorities.

7 Regional Court of Appeal Verdict: Republic of Turkey, Istanbul, 1. Criminal Chamber, Case no: 2021/1375, Verdict no: 2023/398.

as the court's reluctance to prosecute, and sentence, the ones responsible for Elvan's killing. However, following the Elvan trial, I argue that the trial process and the verdict expose a form of legal decision: that law as a *waiting apparatus* operates through delivering inconclusive verdicts and performing legal failure.

In addition to the criminal complaint against the police officers, the Elvan family also filed a criminal complaint against the then-prime minister, the minister of the Interior, Istanbul's governor and Istanbul's chief of police on the grounds of their criminal liability arising from giving orders for the violent suppression of the Gezi protests and their lack of cooperation in identifying the suspect after the incident. Their complaint resulted in a criminal investigation against Istanbul's governor and chief of police, an investigation dropped in 2014. As a result, in 2015, the family appealed to the Constitutional Court. In 2019, the Constitutional Court rejected their application by concluding that criminal liability for the high public officers was not established.[8] The Constitutional Court decision stated that the applicant – the Elvan family – had failed to provide evidence that proved a direct relationship between the police officer's actions and orders given by high public officers, although Erdoğan repeatedly stated that he gave the orders to the police to disperse the Gezi protests. In reference to the Act on Prosecution of Public Servants and Other Public Officers (Memur ve Diğer Kamu Görevlilerinin Yargılanması Hakkında Kanun, Law no: 4483), the Court noted that complaints against public officers cannot be on general grounds.[9] In other words, the Constitutional Court's refusal singled out the incident and dismissed the organised and systematic nature of the police violence during the Gezi protests. However, it did so by pointing to the possibility of accountability, i.e., that it would have been possible had there been enough evidence. The rejection does not say *no*, but *not now*. Following this, the Constitutional Court rejected yet another application in 2020 by the Elvan family, this time regarding the criminal liability of the other police officers who were present at the scene, by stating that 'one police officer is already on trial'.[10] This time, the Constitutional Court told the family to wait. The Constitutional Court's decisions remove Elvan's killing from its historical context and reduce it to the possible wrongdoing of one bad cop. The legal conventions on accountability fail to *see*, or turn a blind eye to, the

8 The Constitutional Court Application 2019: Gamze Elvan and others, Application no: 2015/5718, Decision date: 9/05/2019.

9 Article 4 of the Act states that complaints against public servants and other officers cannot be on general grounds, that the complaints must specify a person and event, claims must rely on serious evidence and the complaint document must include the complainant's full name, contact details and signature.

10 The Constitutional Court Application 2020: Sami Elvan, Application no: 2017/15640, Decision date: 13/02/2020.

systematic and organised nature of police violence, and hence fail to *see* the state and its violence.

Shoshana Felman (2002), in *The Juridical Unconscious*, notes that '[l]aw itself is [...] both redemptive and oppressive; and so is in potential every trial. Every trial can be both at the same time, or it can be rather the one or the other' (17). Regarding the Elvan case, as is often the case in state-violence trials, the possibility of redemption manifests in the form of accountability, which translates into justice, a sense of closure. However, as I disclose in this chapter, what we witness rather in the Elvan trial is an interplay between those two potentials, redemption and oppression, which also illustrate the family's association with the law through the court case. Furthermore, the interplay between the two possibilities, namely redemption and oppression, keeps the Elvan family in suspense, waiting for accountability, which I examine in this chapter as a form of legal violence in itself.

Legal violence is often considered in terms of its force; a force with *mystical* foundations, as Derrida (1992a) refers to it in 'Force of Law'. In the context of a trial, as Robert Cover (1986) exposes in his famous essay 'Violence and the Word', this force operates through the medium of legal interpretation. As Cover explains:

> Legal interpretive acts signal and occasion the imposition of violence upon others: A judge articulates her understanding of a text, and as a result, somebody loses his freedom, his property, his children, even his life. Interpretations in law also constitute justifications for violence which has already occurred or which is about to occur.
>
> (1601)

Cover's analysis not only exposes how the violence of legal interpretation is at the heart of juridical operation but also, more importantly, points to a continuity of violence. This continuity can be understood within the context of the repetitiveness of legal conventions, something specific to the legal field; as Cover brings to light in the quote above, it announces future violence by repeating the former. Cover's emphasis on the violence of legal interpretation also allows us to consider the force of law as a performative thing, which is established through a repetition of legal interpretation. This repetitive, almost ritualistic, utterance and performance of legal interpretation solidifies law and legal convention.

Furthermore, I suggest that the continuity of violence that Cover exposes, can also be considered in terms of its connections to other forms of violence, such as police violence. As I present in my reading in this chapter, the Elvan trial displays the continuity of violence while making the transformation between police violence and legal violence intelligible. To clarify my position here, by suggesting an association between the police violence that is inflicted upon Berkin Elvan and the legal violence that manifests during the legal processes of accountability, I do not imply the existence of a conspiring, evil, omnipotent omnipresent state with a capital 'S'. On the contrary, I argue that the legal aftermath of Elvan's death exposes the ordinariness of violence that is infused within the everyday operation of state institutions.

Following Cover, Austin Sarat (2001) notes that '[l]aw without violence is unthinkable [....] Law depends on violence and uses it as a counterpunch to the allegedly more lethal and destructive violence situated just beyond law's boundaries' (3). Sarat concludes that 'law sits poised between the present reality of violence and the promise of a justice not yet realised' (8). Regarding the case of Berkin Elvan, what Sarat refers to as the more lethal violence beyond law can be understood as the deadly state violence which manifested in the form of police violence. According to Sarat's argument above, this violence should be countered by legal violence to bring justice. In other words, following Sarat's argument, it is possible to consider legal processes of accountability as forms of legal counter-violence, which can be considered in relation to Felman's note on law's redemptive potential, as well as the People's Front's counter-violence. However, what I find striking in Sarat's quote is that, although this may not be his intention, the law appears as an interval between violence and justice, a waiting apparatus that promises justice that is 'not yet realised'. Sarat's unintentional exposure presents a lens to analyse the prolonged legal process of the Elvan case as an endless interval which holds the Elvan family in anticipation of justice. Indeed, the law's promise of justice is a troubled one, as it always comes by violence. Below, I begin by inquiring into this promise to comprehend how the law's promise of justice instead delivers violence, which provides the conceptual framework for the rest of the chapter. Then I turn my focus to the Elvan court case, starting from the indictment and then to the trial proceedings; I observe a constant *unseeing* of the violence and of the perpetrator. Although this appears as a collective effort, something I read through Felman's (2002) notion of *juridical blindness*, it takes various forms, such as distortion, disguise and silence. Despite the trial's blindness towards recognising the violence, the Elvan family continues to seek justice, and accountability, through legal means. As the time passes, the Elvan family gets more and more entangled with the law, which becomes a force, a performance that reconstructs their subjectivity while they are kept waiting before the law in anticipation of justice. In the final section, I unpack the Elvan family's wait with Franz Kafka's famous parable 'Before the Law' to expose the mechanism of waiting, or rather to be kept waiting, as a form of legal violence.

Law's Promise

Berkin's father, Sami Elvan, addresses the court at the first hearing with these words: 'Is there justice? I have been seeking an answer [to that question] for four years. I want all state officials to be prosecuted, from the lowest to the highest ranked'.[11] The Elvan family repeats this demand on every occasion. They wish to put the state and its violence on trial, to hold the state accountable. To do so, unlike the People's Front's extra-legal action, the Elvan family pursued legal means. In addition to the main trial in which one police officer, Fatih Dalgalı, was prosecuted, the family appeals to other higher legal authorities, to bring charges against other state officials for giving the orders and to other police officers who were present at the time of the event as accomplices. Before discussing the legal procedures, however, something catches my attention in Sami Elvan's words above: as he puts it, he is not only seeking justice for his son, but, through that search, he is seeking to discover whether there is such a thing as justice. In this section, I do not intend to inquire into this eternal question, but rather I inquire into the relationship between the law and justice to understand the dialectic between the family's anticipation of justice and its legal manifestation.

While tracing what justice meant for Walter Benjamin through his works and his life, Shoshana Felman (2002) notes, 'Benjamin seldom uses the word "justice," yet it is justice that is the point of departure for his critique' (10). In the context of a trial, Felman likens Benjamin's understanding of justice to Judgement Day:

> 'Judgement Day': the day on which historical injustice will be cancelled out precisely through the act of judgement; the day on which justice and memory will coincide (perhaps the day on which the court will be redeemed from its inherent political *forgetfulness*) [....] Judgement Day implies a necessary reference to history and of historical justice to a reawakening of the dead.
>
> (14–15)

As other scholars also point out (see Martel 2012; Derrida 1992a), Benjamin's understanding of justice is Messianic, which suggests bringing justice *to* the dead, not *for* the dead, through their reawakening. In reference to the discussion on Benjamin's notions of divine and mythical violence, which I discuss in Chapter 1, one can argue that the legal system is the mythical imitation of the divine. Thus, although trials imitate the final trial, Judgement Day, worldly trials do not have the divine power to bring justice to the dead by their reawakening. If so, we may as well conclude our investigation here, as justice in this world is impossible. However, the Elvan family, like many others who are subjected to state violence, carry on with their search with substantial demands and expectations from the law. Surely, this situation

11 See Beyza Kural, 'Berkin Elvan Davası: Mahkeme Sanık Polisin Tutuklanma Tablebini Reddetti.' *Bianet*, 6 April 2017. Accessed 16 July 2024. https://bianet.org/bianet/hukuk/185185-berkin-elvan-davasi-mahkeme-sanik-polisin-tutuklanma-talebini-reddetti.

indicates a dilemma, which, one can suggest, Derrida also finds himself in while elaborating on justice. In 'Force of Law', Derrida (1992a) first echoes a Benjaminian limitation on justice, stating that justice can neither be reduced to the calculations of law and legal systems nor to the calculations of the stately economy of punishment: 'Justice exceeds calculations, rules, programs, anticipations and so forth' (28). However, the law's possessive claim on justice presents a dilemma to the ones seeking justice: 'incalculable justice *requires* us to calculate' due to the urgency it bears (ibid.). As mentioned in the previous chapter, justice needs to be delivered, it bears an urgency; when it is needed, it needs to come right away. Justice does not wait (26). Derrida's elaboration on justice reveals a conundrum for those who seek justice after state violence, that in order to seek justice, it must be translated into legal language, it must be transferred, and hence reduced, to the calculations of legal conventions and procedures; to hold the ones accountable ... to account the violence ... to count .... How many police officers does it take to prosecute the state? How long of a prison sentence is enough to bring justice to Berkin Elvan? The notion of accountability has a significant entanglement with the dilemma of (in)calculability of justice. Derrida too finds himself torn by this dilemma. After addressing its impossibility, nonetheless, he suggests, 'one must always say perhaps for justice', and concludes that, although justice is something beyond legal calculations, we should not stop searching for it through legal means: 'That justice exceeds law and calculation, that the unpresentable exceeds the determinable cannot and should not serve as an alibi for staying out of juridico-political battles' (28). However, James Martel (2012) criticises Derrida's position on justice:

> For Derrida, we should rather hold to the immanence of justice, to its status as always being "perhaps" and "to-come". In this way justice remains transcendent, able to "haunt" and trouble our practices rather than being hijacked for the purposes of retroactively justifying them.
>
> (75)

As I disclose further in this chapter, justice as a transcendental possibility does indeed haunt the Elvan family's search for justice and holds them in an eternal state of waiting. In a Derridean vein, the Elvan family too 'say perhaps for justice' and, in return, find themselves in an exhausting, never-ending legal battle, which I present further throughout this chapter. Justice transforms into a substantial demand for accountability that is intelligible in legal terms. By accountability, the family means prosecution of all state officials, from those who gave orders to those who performed and collaborated. Thus the family reduces justice to legal accountability. It would be wrong to accuse the family of being naïve, for not knowing that they can never get true, historical, justice, as Benjamin calls it. Rather, it is possible to read this reduction in terms of the urgency of justice and the responsibility of the living towards the dead. Felman (2002) notes in reference to Benjamin that '[h]istory is thus, above and beyond official narratives, a haunting claim the dead have on the living, whose responsibility it is not only to remember but to protect the dead from being *misappropriated*' (15). Following Felman's remarks, as I discuss further in this chapter, the Elvan family's legal battle is also a battle against Berkin Elvan's misappropriation as the disobedient son who is responsible for his own death, which translates into the legal language in terms of Elvan's culpability. Furthermore, I suggest that the Elvan family's persistence allows us to register the trials' potential in recognising state violence during the Gezi protests, which manifested in the form of police violence. It has the potential to acknowledge, and bring to account, the historical injustice, even if it cannot undo the past. In that regard, each state violence trial bears the potential to rupture the vicious cycle between state violence and its unaccountability. At each state violence trial, courts have the historic opportunity to address, and refuse, their 'inherent political *forgetfulness*' (Felman 2002, 14–15). This is how I understand the Elvan family's persistent engagement with the law, their anticipation of justice and the significant demand for legal accountability.

However, so far, it appears that the Elvan trial court is dismissive of this historic opportunity and prefers to enact a repetition of unaccountability. *So far*, since, although the main criminal case has ended, its paradoxical ending suggests that the Elvan case is far from being concluded and that it will be ongoing at the national and international level ... ongoing without any prospect of its ending. Drucilla Cornell (1990) in reference to Derrida's 'Force of Law',[12] notes that 'the law just keeps coming' as she likens it to a childhood ghost story in which the ghost, in other words the law, 'draws closer to its victims' (1051).[13] Cornell makes this analogy in relation to the violence of criminal sanctions; however, I suggest her observations also relate to the Elvan family's juridical battle for justice. The more they demand justice, the more they are entangled with the law. Law keeps coming onto the subject with a promise to bring justice and hold the responsible accountable; in return, it binds the subject onto itself with the anticipation of this promise.

12 Derrida's 'Force of Law' was first published in 1990 in a special issue of *Cardozo Law Review*, which also contained a series of commentaries and reviews by other scholars; see: 'Deconstruction and the Possibility of Justice', *Cardozo Law Review* 11 (5–6), 1990: 919–1723.

13 Cornell's (1990) comment is a response to Stanley Fish, who, according to Cornell, insists on identifying law with justice (1050). 'The law is on the first step. The philosopher desperately tries to check the law – but to no avail – by appealing to "outside" norms of justice. The law is on the second step. Now the feminist critic tries to dismantle the law machine which is operating against her. Again, the law simply discards the criticism of its masquerade and here, heterosexual bias, as irreverent. The law is on the third step. It draws closer to its victims' (1051).

The more the Elvan family seeks justice, the more the law keeps coming, forcing itself onto the subjects. The victims of state violence transform into victims of the law who are caught within the endless spiral of legal procedures, which I analyse further in this chapter under the framework of *waiting*. To return to the law's promise, however: it promises justice and accountability, but the law does not guarantee their deliverance. What we rather witness regarding the Elvan case is a performance of its failure. This failure, Judith Butler (1990) suggests in their commentary on Derrida's 'Force of Law', is what keeps law operative:

> This transvaluation of values establishes the law (as the Good or as the force of law) as perpetually 'outside' existing law, but loses sight of the operation by which that 'outside' is established. This 'outside' and/or 'future' can be maintained only through a repetition of the performative, a repetition that in its perpetual necessity reveals itself as a failure, the constitutive and repeated failure that the law 'is', a failure that generates the law as a generative repetition.
>
> (1718)

Butler's comments above reveal that the law's foundational promise of justice is conditioned by the repetitive performance of its failure. To put it in Derridean terms, what makes the subjects to 'always *say perhaps* for justice' and seek it through legal means is its repetitive failure, which bears the potential of its success, one day. In a similar vein, what we witness in the Elvan case is the repetition of failure, which manifests in the form of repetition of unaccountability. As I disclose in the following section through an analysis of the indictment, the repetition of failure is performed through the self-referential legal process. Drucilla Cornell (1990) refers to this as 'self-conserving repetition', to emphasise the constituting function of this repetition through which law consolidates itself as a self-standing system, 'its own "positive" social reality in which the status of its own myth cannot be challenged' (1056–1057). Both Cornell and Butler understand legal repetition as something fundamental to the repetitive (re)construction of law and, hence, to its operation. Different to Butler, Cornell emphasises the aspect of violence rather than the aspect of failure, which coincides in the cases of legal (un) accountability, as the repetition of (legal) violence takes the form of failure to hold to account. In other words, although what is being performed is a failure, in a performative manner, through performing a repetition of self-referential legal conventions, the process nonetheless contributes to reconstructing the mythical force of the law. Thus, at state-violence trials, each failure consolidates the force of law and its promise of justice while delivering violence through its unaccountability.

While disclosing the law's *self-conserving repetition*, Cornell (1990) references a passage in Derrida's 'Force of Law', in which Derrida elaborates on the violence of legal interpretation and its repetition in reference to Benjamin's 'Critique of Violence':[14]

> For beyond Benjamin's explicit purpose, I shall propose the interpretation according to which the very violence of the foundation or position of law (Rechtsetzende Gewalt) must envelop the violence of conservation (Rechtserhaltende Gewalt) and cannot break it. It belongs to the structure of fundamental violence that it calls for the repetition of itself and founds what ought to be conserved, conservable, promised to heritage and tradition, to be shared. A foundation is a promise.
>
> (Derrida 1992a, 38)

What Derrida refers to above by the 'violence of conservation' (*Rechtserhaltende Gewalt*) is Benjamin's notion of law-preserving violence. To recall Chapter 1, *law-preserving* violence is 'the use of violence as a means for legal ends. For the subordination of citizens to laws' (Benjamin 2007, 284). Derrida's comment on legal violence reminds us of its origins; as Benjamin puts it, 'violence crowned by fate, is the origin of law' (286). It is this violence that is crowned by fate, that establishes the legal system and, hence, that is sustained by its repetition in the form of *law-preserving* violence. 'Justice is what is promised by law; its possibility is what keeps us obedient, patient and hopeful' (Martel 2012, 71). Justice is what is expected from a trial as this is the main, if not the only, motivation for appealing to the law. Furthermore, justice, or rather its promise, is what justifies law and its violence. Benjamin (2007) notes this relationship at the beginning of his 'Critique of Violence': 'If justice is the criterion of ends, legality is that of means' (278). However, regarding positive law, justice as an end quickly transforms into justified means, as Benjamin observes: 'positive law [...] "guarantee[s]" the justness of the ends through the justification of the means' (ibid.). In other words, the law becomes the means for its own ends and operates by preserving and repeating the violence that establishes the legal system. In legal systems, then, what is considered as justice is a just procedure. The correct performance of the legal repetition itself replaces justice with the claim of delivering justice through just means. However, prioritising the correctness of legal conventions and procedures, as I argue, only guarantees the legal repetition of the foundational violence. Thus, when state violence is on trial, what we witness, rather, is a repetition of failure. It is a failure, that is, the failure to hold the state and its violence accountable, which is a reperformance of its foundational violence in legal form. In that regard, the law's promise of justice is actually the law's promise of violence, which only suggests a possibility of justice but always guarantees violence.

14 Cornell references the 1990 edition of Derrida's 'Force of Law'. The quote is unchanged in the 1992 edition that I refer to in this book.

The conceptual discussion above on the law's promise presents a framework to demystify the violent repetition of unaccountability in the Elvan case. I suggest that the failure of the Elvan trial is related to the legal operation itself as it prioritises its own self-conserving repetition, which carries and repeats its foundational violence. As the legal process reduces justice to just procedures, it keeps repeating its foundational violence rather than delivering the promise of justice. Hence, it is possible to suggest that law and legal conventions turn a blind eye to state violence or that state violence is the law's blind spot.

In the *Juridical Unconscious,* Shoshana Felman (2002) suggests that trials, especially criminal trials, constitute a certain *blindness* due to their operating structure, which she observes in relation to trauma.[15] Felman's notion of *juridical blindness* stands for law's inability to recognise the historical importance of the case before them: 'law cannot and does not see that a juridical case becomes a legal trauma in its own right and is therefore bound to repeat itself through a traumatic legal repetition' (57). Certainly it is possible to address the problems within the Elvan trial from law's inability to register the family's trauma of losing Berkin Elvan and consider each hearing as a repetition of this trauma.[16] Furthermore, this trauma is not only a personal one but is a publicly shared trauma that passes on generation to generation and is voiced by the chant, 'The murderer state will be held to account'. Deadly state violence and its unaccountability is a collective trauma, a cultural wound in Turkey to which the trial turns a blind eye. 'Legal memory is constituted, in effect, not just by the "chain of law" and by the conscious repetition of precedents but also by a forgotten chain of cultural wounds and by compulsive or unconscious legal repetitions of traumatic, wounding legal cases' (ibid.). Thus, in the Elvan case, there is an aspect of trauma in terms of its legal repetition. However, rather than elaborating on the aspect of trauma, which is beyond the limits of my inquiry here, I borrow Felman's notion of *juridical blindness* to refer to the discussion above on the legal repetition of (state) violence through performing its failure, which I summarise as law's blindness towards acknowledging and registering state violence. In that regard, I understand *juridical blindness* towards state violence in relation to the law's self-conserving repetition. As I disclose in the following sections, what I observe through the Elvan case is that legal conventions prioritise their own repetition to be just, to conduct a just trial. This, I argue, not only reduces justice to legal procedures but also, either consciously or unconsciously, results in a legal mechanism that disguises state violence and

15 Felman first published an article on the matter in 1997. The book *Juridical Unconscious* appears to be a detailed version of the arguments presented in the article (see Felman 1997).

16 Especially when it is considered that the hearings are taking place in the courthouse which bears the name of the killed prosecutor Selim Kiraz.

hence repeats the violence in legal form. In the following sections, I unpack the mechanism of juridical blindness through presenting a detailed reading of the Elvan court case to expose its repetition of violence. To do so, I begin with the indictment to trace what is possible to see at the trial in the first place, in other words, what appeared and what is left out from appearing before the law.

The Indictment

Cornelia Vismann (2008), in her detailed study on the medium of files and their function within law, notes that 'the file contains its own progression [....] That is, they [files] allow access to that which came before the law' (8). Following Vismann's remarks, in this section I present an analysis of the Berkin Elvan indictment to disclose what came before the law. The significance, and the work, of the Berkin Elvan indictment are not limited to the charges it brings against the perpetrator but rather, it allows us to trace the legal reasoning and its process that led up to these charges, which, I suggest, expose the beginnings of *juridical blindness* in registering state violence. Generally speaking, indictments are curious legal documents which transform all types of objects into evidence and utterances into testimonies; in other words, they render life, everyday objects and speech into objects of law. As a result, the legal profession and scholarship alike treat indictments as records which guarantee 'the live transfer of an event' (ibid.). Furthermore, indictments translate a life event into a court case and to a punishable offence by providing a legal narrative to the courts. Although indictments claim to speak of facts, in other words, a true transfer of the event based on evidence, they (re)narrate life and the event according to the legal conventions. From the perspective of legal conventions, by which I refer to the accumulation of laws and procedures as well as legal culture, indictments tell a story, that is, the story of what happened from a legal perspective. Legal narration, however, consciously or unconsciously highlights some parts and dismisses others while translating life into law.

The indictment translates the legal interpretation of Elvan's death, which actually begins when Elvan encounters the police through his subjection as a disobedient subject, into a legal narrative. Thus, although the legal interpretation begins before the indictment, Elvan's subjection gains a legal seal, a claim of truth, through the indictment. In that regard, it is possible to note the crucial role that the indictment plays as the medium that transforms police violence into legal violence. As I disclose in this section through the Elvan indictment, the legal violence begins to materialise with the indictment's re-narration of his encounter with the police. Below, I present an analysis of Berkin Elvan's indictment to disclose how the law interprets Elvan and his killing and to trace what is left out of the records, what is overlooked and disappeared prior to appearing before the law.

The Berkin Elvan indictment begins with setting the scene, first by listing the names and identity information of the involved parties as if introducing the characters of a play, a tragedy perhaps. This listing of the names, and the roles they play within the court case, is followed by noting the date and the place of the event which leads to the accusation. The indictment lists the legal provisions upon which the accusation is based; in doing so, it reminds the reader of its self-referential, coercive force. The indictment refers to the articles of the Penal Code (art 82(1)(e), 21(2), 53(1), 54(1)) through which it brings the charge of probable intent to kill against the police officer Fatih Dalgalı. To briefly examine the articles referenced in the indictment, article 82(1) lists the conditions according to which the offender of the intentional killing should be sentenced to aggravated life imprisonment. The condition to which the indictment specifically refers is 'against a child or against somebody who cannot protect himself physically or mentally'. Article 21 describes intent, and section 2 reduces aggravated life imprisonment to life imprisonment in relation to probable intent charges: 'There is probable intent when the individual conducts an act while foreseeing that the elements in the legal definition of an offence may occur. Accordingly, for offences that require a penalty of aggravated life imprisonment, life imprisonment shall be imposed'. Article 53(1) lists deprivation of exercising certain rights when sentenced to imprisonment, and article 54(4) indicates confiscation of any property 'which has constituted an offence'. To sum up, according to the listed legal references, the indictment recognises Berkin Elvan as a child who was vulnerable at the time of the event and acknowledges that Fatih Dalgalı could have foreseen the consequences of his action. However, what is not possible to trace from the referenced articles is state violence, or, to put it in other words, the fact that Fatih Dalgalı was, and still is, a police officer who issued violence on behalf of the state. From the referenced articles, it appears as if Elvan died as a result of a foreseeable accident, a tragedy, while disregarding the fact that Officer Dalgalı was on duty at the time to suppress the Gezi protests according to the orders of his superiors. As such, the weapons subject to the event, the tear-gas pistol and canisters, were not his private property but instead were provided to him by the state to perform violence on behalf of the state.

The indictment continues by listing the evidence, which consists of objects, witness testimonies, CCTV footage and various expert reports. Based on the evidence, the indictment presents the legal narrative of the event resulting in the charges above. The legal narrative begins by telling the story of Elvan's killing from the legal perspective, which reveals something interesting. According to the indictment, what triggered the prosecutor's investigation was not Elvan's deadly injury but rather the four firecrackers which were allegedly found in Elvan's pockets when he was taken to the hospital. The indictment notes that the investigation began when these firecrackers were secured at the Juvenile Police Headquarters. It is necessary to reiterate the significance of firecrackers, marbles and slingshots in accusing Berkin Elvan of his own death, as they are items associated with non-peaceful protests in Turkey's politico-legal context. It is worth noting how everyday childhood objects translate as weapons of terrorism in the legal context and how they become evidence of Elvan's subjection as a disobedient child, if not a terrorist. Furthermore, when these childhood objects are registered as weapons of terrorism, they serve as evidence against Elvan's vulnerability as a child. In other words, the legal interpretation of childhood objects strips Elvan of his childhood.[17]

The indictment exposes that initially Elvan stood before the law as a suspect, as a legal extension of the police's hailing of Elvan as a suspect, which is discussed in Chapter 1. What is more striking is that the indictment advances by elaborating on this finding and its significance, as if the firecrackers are the main evidence of this case, as if the case is about an offence carried out by Elvan and his firecrackers. As the indictment notes that the firecrackers were tied in packs of threes and fours to cause a small-scaled bomb effect, it projects the image of a non-peaceful protestor onto Berkin Elvan. By doing so, Erdoğan's political subjection of Elvan as the disobedient son of the *father-state* receives a legal seal. Even though at the end the indictment concludes, 'although the deceased was among the protesting group, there is not any evidence on his usage of the slingshot, marbles and firecrackers at the time of the event', it nonetheless highlights this matter and shifts the focus of the case away from police violence, while establishing two *facts* regarding Elvan: first, that he was among the protestors and, secondly, that he had firecrackers, marbles and a slingshot on him.

This information may appear as a detail in the indictment's fact-finding mission; however, it re-narrates Elvan's encounter with the police. Indeed, the issue of firecrackers continues to be at the centre throughout the court case. The court hearings, too, begin with the witness testimonies from the

17 Turkey's legal system has a history of stripping children of the protection of their childhood status to punish them with harsher sentences. The most well-known example is Erdal Eren, who was seventeen years old when sentenced to capital punishment by the 1980 coup regime. Furthermore, between the years of 2006 and 2010 children were prosecuted as adults due to amendments made in the Counter-terror Law (no. 5532) and Penal Code (no.5237). The amendments allowed children above the age of fifteen to be prosecuted in high criminal courts like adults and prohibited punishments from being converted into other forms. The issue, commonly referred as *taş atan çocuklar*, which translates to 'children throwing stones', targeted Kurdish children on the basis of their participation in demonstrations. Within this period, children who were accused of counter-terror charges faced long pre-trial detention, and those convicted received long-term prison sentences. For more on this issue, see Justice for Children Initiative's 2009 shadow report to the UN Committee on the Rights of the Child: 'Children are not Terrorists', *Justice for Children Initiative in Turkey*. April 2009. Accessed 16 July 2024. http://ihop.org.tr/wp-content/uploads/2009/08/opaceng.pdf.

hospital personnel who filed the report on finding the firecrackers.[18] The indictment re-narrates Elvan's deadly encounter with the police while skipping the actual moment of the encounter. It presents the event starting from its aftermath, based on a filed report on firecrackers. I relate the indictments' selective timeline to the self-referential character of the law as the indictment builds its story on previous legal document(s), that is, the report on firecrackers, in which Elvan appears as a suspect. The indictment demonstrates to us that the *juridical blindness* towards state violence operates through its self-referential structure, which presents the events based on a selective, and partial, consideration of evidence. Although the indictment consists of witness testimonies which present an account of the systematic and organised police violence during the Gezi protests, the indictment does not elaborate further on this finding, which is undoubtedly more crucial to the case than the firecrackers. Despite being included in the indictment, the witness testimonies are dismissed as hearsay.

To present briefly the content of the testimonies, first of all, it is necessary to highlight that the majority of the witnesses are locals of Okmeydanı, and some were present at the scene as protestors; in other words, they too are disobedient sons of the *father-state*. Some appear to know Elvan personally due to the close-knit social relations of the neighbourhood. According to the testimonies, by the time of the event, only five or six protestors were left at the scene, chanting slogans while sheltering at the intersection of two roads. This is where Elvan attempted to cross the main road. The police were situated on the main road approximately 100–200 metres away from the protestors, and some officers were firing tear gas at the protestors from a close distance of approximately 20–35 metres. A number of witnesses cite their dialogue with Berkin Elvan, according to which Elvan said he was on his way to buy bread. Some witnessing protestors note that they had warned Elvan, that the police were 'aiming to shoot', in other words, firing gas canisters like bullets with aim at the protestors. The witness testimonies explain the moment of the incident in which Elvan was hit in the head as soon as he attempted to cross the street. They recall the aftermath, when the police kept firing tear-gas canisters after Elvan collapsed, which made it harder for them to seek help. The indictment, however, does not investigate the organised and systematic nature of the police violence that caused Berkin Elvan's deadly injury. On the contrary, it legitimises the presence of police violence by suggesting that the police were deployed to the area due to violent protests and looting.

In 'Critique of Violence', Benjamin (2007) explains that police violence occurs 'for security reasons' when the state is threatened, when it can no

18 It appears that the number of firecrackers written on the report has been changed multiple times. When the Elvan family lawyer questions the hospital police, he responds that he saw eleven firecrackers, but he was not responsible for filing the report.

longer attain its goals through the legal system (287). The indictment demonstrates to us that, in a cyclical fashion, police violence itself serves as evidence for the existence of such a threat. Despite the evidence – provided by the eyewitnesses and CCTV footage analysis reports – which suggests otherwise,[19] the presence of the police, and their violence, serves as affirming evidence that the protestors were, indeed, a security threat. At this point, the indictment revokes a stately fantasy, something recalling the phantasmatic enemy assemblages of Erdoğan, and paints a picture of heavy clashes between the police and the protestors at the time of the event. Blurring the line between fact and fiction, the indictment presents a distorted version of history in a bundle of so-called facts, which erases the systematic police violence and instead fabricates a sovereign fantasy in the form of violent protestors. In addition to the fantasies of a threat which re-narrates Elvan's encounter with the police officer, the forensics report on Elvan's cause of death provides an inconclusive finding, which states that Elvan's fatal head injury might well have been caused by a tear-gas canister or by a rubber bullet when aimed directly but also could have been caused by him hitting his head on a hard surface after his fall (3). The indictment presents the moment of Elvan's injury as his own tragic fate, if not his own making, which is caused either by being among the protestors or by hitting his own head. While some reports within the indictment note that firing gas canisters onto the protestors is deadly and against the protocol for using a tear-gas pistol, expert reports struggle to identify the police officer who fired the gas canister. After a chain of inconclusive expert reports on the CCTV footage, in 2016, facial-recognition analysis concludes that the police officer who fired the gas canister is Fatih Dalgalı, on a probability of 30.6%.[20] Dalgalı, in his testimony, denies the charges by stating that he was not deployed to that area but then also adding that he does not recall.

At the final stage, the indictment delivers Fatih Dalgalı as one bad cop, or 30.6% of him, who may have done wrong, who may have fired the tear-gas pistol against protocol in the heat of heavy clashes with protestors. The indictment presents a story, a distorted version of the reality. The indictment carries the claim of presenting the truth by relying on evidence; however, it instead presents a stately fiction, which even contradicts the evidence presented within the indictment. Legal interpretation, or re-narration, dismisses the systematic police violence and, hence, turns a blind eye to the origin of violence that killed Berkin Elvan. Elvan's fall appears as if it was an act of

19 The indictment presents a summary of three reports, in which it states that, at the time of the event, there were only a handful of protestors left and that none of the protestors used firecrackers or other explosive material. The police, however, were firing tear-gas capsules while intentionally aiming at the protestors.

20 The indictment mentions another suspect, Ayhan Pekgöz, who matches on a 28.9% probability with the perpetrator on the CCTV footage. However, considering other bodily features, the indictment concludes that the perpetrator is Fatih Dalgalı.

God. However, as argued in Chapter 1, what appears as fate is organised and systematic police violence. As the indictment singles out the event as the probable wrongdoing of one person, Fatih Dalgalı, it renders systematic police violence invisible before the law.

The Ghostly Perpetrator

Shoshana Felman (2002) elaborates on the significance of *seeing* in a trial. First, she relates the significance of seeing in relation to the theatricality of a trial, which, in historical cases, appears in the form of 'a show trial, a spectacularized case whose evolving courtroom drama was reproduced throughout the world, magnified and multiplied by millions of television screens' (81). Felman here refers to the O.J. Simpson trial, in which the theatricality of the trial is something reminiscent of a reality show, but also to the Rodney King trial, which is considered to be the first visually recorded account of racialised police violence in the US courts.[21] Although state-violence trials lack the entertainment aspect of a show trial, nonetheless they attract a specific audience. State-violence trials are public spectacles as they are observed, litigated, witnessed and reported; in other words, they are *seen*. Furthermore, state-violence trials can be understood as political trials (see Ertür 2022), exposing the state's working structure and its deadly manifestation to the public eye. In addition to the theatrical aspect, Felman (2002) adds that seeing is crucial to the operation of a trial, as evidence is something 'based on seeing', either in the form of eyewitness accounts, CCTV footage or in terms of recognising the meanings that an evidential document conveys: 'The strongest proof admitted by the court is proof corroborated by the eye' (81). Yet, as Felman observes, the trials often fail to see the issues that are central to the case. The *juridical blindness* that Felman observes in the cases she analyses is mainly related to the blindness of the jurors towards the visual signs of domestic abuse (battered face) and racialised police violence (filmed police beating of a black man).[22] In the Elvan case, however, what is *unseen* by the legal process so far is the systematic and organised nature of police violence. If the indictment makes the organised and systematic nature of police violence invisible before the law by re-narrating the event, the trial process renders the perpetrator invisible before the law.

21 A recent BBC News article recalls the Rodney King trial before the George Floyd trial as 'one of the first instances such brutality had been filmed' and publishes the courtroom sketches from the King trial with the title 'Rodney King Trial: Sketches Reveal Drama from Court'. See: 'Rodney King Trial: Sketches Reveal Drama from Court', *BBC News*, 5 March 2021. Accessed 28 September 2021. www.bbc.co.uk/news/world-us-canada-56297810.

22 In the cases Felman (2002) analyses, what the trials fail, or rather refuse, to see are two beatings, one indicating domestic violence in the O.J. Simpson case and the other to police violence based on race in the Rodney King case (81).

From the very beginning of the court hearings, the accused officer Fatih Dalgalı had been absent from the courtroom; instead, Dalgalı attended virtually via video communication. The Elvan family's lawyers opposed this, as the video image was never clear enough to *see* him and to identify him. Hence, they contended that he must testify before the law in person. Indeed, the trial judge passed on the Elvan family lawyer's request to Officer Dalgalı at the first hearing by asking, 'would you like to give your testimony in here?'. Dalgalı refused on the grounds of concerns over his security, and the court accepted his reasons for not appearing before the court in person. At each hearing, the Elvan family's lawyers demanded his arrest, and the court declined. Rather than bringing him before the law, which would have resolved the conundrum of verifying the perpetrator's identity, instead the trial occupied itself with a never-ending cycle of re-collecting evidence to match Fatih Dalgalı with the perpetrator seen on the CCTV footage. However, there is something interesting in that exchange between the trial judge and the police officer, which, I suggest, resembles Erdoğan's *father-state* performance. In a similar manner to Erdoğan's comparison of the two sons, which is discussed in Chapter 2, the trial judge is benevolent towards the accused police officer while dismissing the violence inflicted upon Berkin Elvan and the family's demand of accountability. The trial judge turns a blind eye to the violence that killed Berkin Elvan and *unsees* it; by turning a blind eye, he is performing its repetition in the courtroom. His legal performance of the *father-state* repeats the police violence and exposes law's 'blind spot' (Felman 2002, 83). Furthermore, there is something common between Karamanoğlu, the favoured son of Erdoğan's father-state performance, and the perpetrator Fatih Dalgalı. As the former was a military veteran and the latter is a police officer, they both issue violence on behalf of the state towards the disobedient ones. Thus, I suggest Dalgalı's excusal from appearing before the law is a stately pardon towards the violence inflicted on its behalf, which takes the form of *unseeing* or *juridical blindness*.

Felman suggests that '[e]very trial [...] by its very nature as a trial, is contingent on the act of seeing' (81). However, as the Elvan trial demonstrates, the (over)emphasis on *seeing* itself may present challenges to the legal process. In 'Law and the Evidential Image', Piyel Haldar (2008) reminds us that visual evidence can be manipulated, 'torn apart and rendered unstable' to obtain a meaning, although it is often favoured due to its 'potential to tell an objective truth' (140). The evidential image promises accuracy, an accurate representation of the truth; however, on the other hand, especially when digital images are concerned, it is easily manipulated (142). In Berkin Elvan's trial, distortion of visual evidence, *seeing*, takes place in two forms. The first one is Officer Dalgalı's distorted appearance through video conference, which disguises his bodily features from the courtroom, and the second is the distortion of the CCTV footage by the Scientific and Technological Research Council of Turkey (TÜBITAK), which renders the perpetrator unidentifiable.[23] The more the officer in the CCTV footage and the accused officer Dalgalı become unseen, unidentifiable, faceless figures, the more they separate from one another. This gap of uncertainty constitutes the possibility of Dalgalı's acquittal. Indeed, other police officers who testify as witnesses rely on this gap between the two faceless figures. They state that they can neither identify the officer on the CCTV footage nor identify Fatih Dalgalı from the video conference. A collective performance of amnesia follows their unseeing, regarding the moment of the event as how they all respond: *I do not know, I do not recall.*[24] This reveals an interesting paradox which runs throughout the trial process: although the trial prosecutes Fatih Dalgalı on the one hand, on the other the trial occupies itself with identifying the perpetrator on the CCTV footage. The importance of *seeing* and of visual evidence as a privileged form of evidence obstruct the legal process. The legal conventions of verifying the perpetrator's identity prevent the trial from progressing towards a decision. In that regard, the Elvan trial exposes how the legal convention of identifying, *seeing*, the perpetrator could transform into a mechanism of delay which prevents its own progression. At that point, the hearings perform a repetition, a repetition of *unseeing*, which, to put it in Felman's (2002) terms, repeats the violence and trauma. The trial becomes violent and traumatic as it refuses to see the violence and trauma 'that the trial was supposed to remedy' (81–82).

The *juridical blindness* of the Elvan trial operates through rendering the perpetrator into a faceless, ghostly figure, which recalls Benjamin's (2007) and, later on, Derrida's (1992a) comments on the ghostliness of police violence that is presented in Chapter 1. To reintroduce these briefly, both Benjamin and Derrida read the police as a faceless figure whose 'power is formless, like its nowhere tangible, all-pervasive, ghostly presence in the life of civilized states' (Benjamin 2007, 287). Furthermore, the Elvan trial demonstrates that the ghostliness of the police extends to the legal process, rendering the perpetrator police intangible and unaccountable. Regarding the Elvan trial, it is possible to argue that the court consciously hid the perpetrator from sight: from the sight of the Elvan family, from the sight of the public and also from the sight of the law. To understand the reasons behind this reflex, it is necessary to discuss the relationship between the police and the law.

Michel Foucault, in his lectures published under the title of *Security, Territory, Population* (2009), elaborates on the police in relation to the law;

23 At the end of the second hearing the court decides to send the CCTV footage to TÜBITAK and to Turkish Radio and Television Corporation (TRT), the national public broadcaster, for its enhancement. While TRT responds negatively to the court's orders by stating that they lack expertise, according to Elvan family lawyers, TÜBITAK distorts the already unclear CCTV footage.

24 Police witness testimonies were taken on the ninth hearing on 28 November 2018.

he writes, 'Of course, from the beginning of the seventeenth century the idea of a police power will be clearly distinguished from a type of exercise of royal power, which is the power of justice, juridical power. Police is not justice' (339). And he continues:

> Of course, like justice it derives from royal power, but it remains clearly separated from justice. At this time, police is in no way thought of as a sort of instrument in the hands of juridical power, as a sort of way of really applying regular justice. It is not an extension of justice, it is not the king acting through his apparatus of justice; it is the king acting directly on his subjects, but in a non-juridical form.
>
> (ibid.)

Thus, Foucault understands the police as 'a permanent *coup d'État* coming directly from the royal power' (340). I cross-read Foucault's remarks on police power with Benjamin's comments on police violence, which, according to Benjamin, performs both *lawmaking* and *law-preserving* functions of violence. In other words, police violence performs violence that establishes the legal system and sustains or preserves it through its repetition. In that regard, to put it in Foucault's terminology, the combination of the two functions is what makes police violence non-juridical, or rather beyond juridical, a permanent coup, and hence, I argue, unaccountable. Following Benjamin, Butler (2020) exposes this association between police violence and the law:

> Although law-instating [lawmaking] and law-preserving *Gewalt* are described by Benjamin as distinct, the police operate both forms, which implies that the law is "preserved" only by being asserted, again and again, as binding. The law thus depends on the police or the military to assert and preserve the law.
>
> (125)

If the indictment's re-narration of the event presents an obscured version of Elvan's encounter with the police, hence preventing the systematic and organised police violence from appearing before the law, the trial visually disguises the police officer, who enacted violence on behalf of the state. As the law depends on the police, and its violence, for its preservation, the Elvan trial turns a blind eye to the police and its violence by rendering him unidentifiable and faceless. Nonetheless, it is still possible to hear him talk when called by the court, as if he is communicating behind the shadows. Thus, the perpetrator, as a material human figure, transforms into a ghostly figure. However, his absence is very present within the courtroom; his invisibility renders him visible: '*I see you are not there*' (Gordon 2008, 16). His absence has a haunting presence. In *Ghostly Matters*, Avery F. Gordon (2008) notes that 'the ghost is primarily a symptom of what is missing. It gives notice not only to itself but also to what it represents' (63). Through the ghostly presence of the perpetrator Dalgalı, the mythical omnipotent and omnipresent state enters the courtroom.

Yet, all of a sudden something unexpected, or what is expected from the legal process, happens that ruptures the repetition of *unseeing*. On 4 April 2018, the Istanbul Gendarme Criminal Lab report exposed the identity of the perpetrator and confirmed, this time with a higher percentage (75% and above), that the perpetrator seen in the CCTV footage is 'highly likely' Fatih Dalgalı.[25] Although Dalgalı was still absent in the courtroom, his ghostly presence gradually came into existence on the case file. The witnessing protestor's vague, ghostly descriptions of the perpetrator gain materiality: a name, a body and even humanly mortal traits, such as hair loss, which becomes one of the main signifiers of his identification as the perpetrator.

Although the court received an evidential verification of the perpetrator's identity, Officer Dalgalı's exposure launched yet another endless cycle of evidence collection. The court continued with more police testimonies, ordered a crime-scene investigation in 2019 (six years after the incident) and ordered further expert reports. After Dalgalı's exposure, the so-called fact-finding mission of the trial accelerated, this time to disassociate Officer Dalgalı from the charges. I read this period, between Dalgalı's exposure and the verdict in June 2021, as Kafkaesque, as the trial resembles a Kafka parable that is choked in procedures, forms and reports from various institutions and experts, all pretending to be doing their part in this mundane but yet mystical operation. James R. Martel (2011) uses the term 'Kafkaesque' as something indicating 'the inevitability of defeat' (62). However, at the same time, Martel suggests, in reference to *The Trial* and *Before the Law*, that Kafka's parables illuminate the ordinary operation of the arbitrariness of justice (67–71). What I observe as Kafkaesque regarding the Berkin Elvan trial is the ordinary, mundane operation of its cover up of the police officer through an endless repetition of legal convention. What is interesting is that it is this mundane repetition that, at the same time, seems mystical, almost conspiratorial. The myth of the almighty state continues to haunt the trial.

A Failed Verdict

On 24 January 2020, the court received another Gendarme expert report upon request.[26] The report mentions that the court was not satisfied with relying only on the CCTV footage to decide on the accused officer's culpability and hence ordered the expert report to consider all the evidence to deter-

25 Istanbul Gendarme Criminal Lab Report 2018: 'Uzmanlık Raporu', Istanbul Jandarma Kriminal Laboratuvar Amirliği, 4 April 2018. Document no: 2018/585025.

26 Expert Report 2020: 'Ek Bilirkişi Raporu', Jandarma Genel Komutanlığı, 24 January 2020. Document no: 2016.325.

mine the perpetrator's culpability. Considering all the evidence, the report states that the police officer's use of force did not violate the regulations despite finding him responsible for the incident. While determining the intent, the report notes that it is not possible to aim to shoot with a tear-gas gun, and hence concludes that the incident must have been 'involuntary and momentary', which indicates lack of intent. What is remarkable about this report, however, is that, in addition to the police officer, it finds Berkin Elvan culpable for his own death. The report presents a legal version of Erdoğan's comments on Elvan's death by finding Elvan culpable for being among the non-peaceful protestors, for acting recklessly. The report finds Officer Dalgalı as culpable in the first degree (asli kusurlu) and Elvan as culpable in the second degree (tali kusurlu).[27] What is also worth noting here is that the report does not address the perpetrator by name but rather describes him as 'the police officer in the CCTV footage who appears with a bandage on his arm'. On the one hand, the report distances the police officer from the act by finding Elvan responsible for acting recklessly, while, on the other hand, disassociating his identity again from the act by finding an unknown, unidentified, officer partially responsible for Elvan's death. Between the first Gendarme report of 2018, which exposed the police officer, and the most recent one in January 2020, which finds Elvan responsible for his own death, the evidence provided by the institutions and experts poked holes in the case file to *unsee* the police violence and the perpetrator Fatih Dalgalı.

The findings of the final report reflect on the prolonged verdict, which comes at the final hearing on 18 June 2021. The court sentences Fatih Dalgalı to sixteen years and eight months in prison with the charge of probable intent to kill despite the family lawyers' demand for him to be sentenced with direct intent to kill. The court explains the reduction of the sentence from life imprisonment, which is the highest sentence for probable intent to kill, in relation to weakness of intent and consideration of the impact of the sentence on the accused. Despite the sentence, the court did not order his arrest, and Officer Dalgalı remains on duty as a police officer. In that regard, even when uttering the verdict, the court performed its failure. The court's failing verdict is rather interesting as it challenges the common understanding of law and the operation of legal violence. Furthermore, the Elvan trial verdict poses a challenge to J.L. Austin's (1975) elaboration of legal performatives. To briefly mention Austin's interest in legal performatives, which he refers to as 'acts in the law'

27 I understand the report's findings as an attempt to reduce Dalgalı's sentence from probable intent to kill to recklessness; as article 22(6) of the Turkish Penal Code states, 'A penalty shall not be imposed if, as the result of a reckless act, the offender becomes a victim to such a degree (by reference to his personal and family circumstances only) that imposing a penalty becomes unnecessary. Where the offence is committed with conscious recklessness then penalty to be imposed may be reduced by one-sixth to one-half'.

(19), and their privileged position in the Austinian notion of performativity, he notes: 'Examples are more easily seen in law; they are naturally not so definite in ordinary life, where allowances are made' (36). Following this, the most obvious example of the legal performative is the moment of uttering a verdict, which Austin refers to as *verdictives*: 'verdictives, are typified by the giving of a verdict, as the name implies, by a jury, arbitrator, or umpire' (151). However, I argue that what we observe instead in the Elvan trial is a failed legal performative in which the utterance does not deliver the action it utters. In other words, the court actually nullifies its verdict. It concludes the trial without a conclusion rather and keeps the decision in suspense.

In *Spectacles and Specters*, Başak Ertür (2022) develops the conceptual framework of legal performatives while offering a reading of political trials. For Ertür, focusing on the legal performative 'allows us to account for how sovereign schemes can misfire, how trials can come to have unintended political lives and afterlives, and how law entangles with and perpetuates certain histories of violence, rather than every simply mastering these or providing closure' (3). In her work, Ertür discloses how legal failures are a part of the legal performatives despite Austin's attempts to exemplify legal performatives as the ideal form of performative utterances (57–64). Although Ertür emphasises their significance, noting that 'Many of the key utterances in the course of a trial are performative utterances', she extends 'the performative operation of law' beyond such utterances (69). In relation to the previous discussion on the law's promise of justice and its failure, legal performatives operate through the repetition of legal convention.

What interests me in Ertür's analysis of legal performativity are her remarks on criminal trials, which provide a lens to understand the failures in the Elvan trial. Ertür explains that 'a criminal trial is the amalgamation of a number of essential performative operations, such as the establishing of facts, the interpretation of the law, and the application of substantive law to the facts of the case' (69). In that regard, the indictment's function of establishing facts, the trial's fact-finding mission, and the court's interpretation of the law, which in the end delivers an inconclusive verdict, could all be considered within the repertoire of legal performatives. What is more striking, however, is Ertür's observation that this performative operation of a criminal trial is disguised as constative due to its hyper-conventional performance. To briefly recall from the discussion on performative utterances in Chapter 2, for Austin (1975) constatives are statements that are either true or false, and Austin distinguishes performative utterances from constatives (1–4). As I argued in Chapter 2, through the end of Austin's lectures, this distinction does not hold, which I read as Austin's own failure while performing the performatives and thus argued that despite Austin's attempt to clarify its borders, performative utterances include its failures, among other exclusions. Ertür, however, picks up a brief but critical remark from Austin's lectures which cautions against the performatives' disguise; she explains:

> Thus the performative is said to often *masquerade* as a descriptive or constative statement, seeming to display a relation of externality to its reference, and thereby deceiving us into ascribing it a "truth value" in such disguise.
>
> (65)

The performative operation in a criminal trial disguises itself as constative and thus claims to be stating the facts, the truth, as the Elvan trial also claims to be doing. Thereby, Ertür suggests, the trial appears as 'if it were fate' (69–70). Ertür's observations allow us to register the connection between Elvan's deadly fate and the fate of the trial. While the *stately performative* of Erdoğan renders Elvan's killing as a deadly fate of a disobedient child, the trial's performative operation disguises the *stately performative* as a factual statement (constative) and finds Elvan culpable for acting recklessly, and thus diminishes the criminal responsibility of the perpetrator Dalgalı. However, the fate of the Elvan trial and its inconclusive ending do not come as a surprise. The repetitive failures of legal processes of accountability in state-violence trials in Turkey, expose the performative operation in state-violence trials. Ertür, also, observes this exposure in relation to political trials;

> the exposure of the performativity of a trial is usually due to a crisis of masquerade, that is, a failure in one of the several ways in which performatives ordinarily disguise themselves as constatives in the course of a trial. That the question of trial performance comes under scrutiny in political trials and accusations of theatricality ("show trial," "circus," "kangaroo court," etc.) begin to fly around can be understood as closely connected to this exposure of performativity.
>
> (70)

Despite the well-known fate of state-violence trials, and the performative exposure of the Elvan trial that performs its own failure and delivers a null verdict, rather than holding the perpetrator accountable, the Elvan family persistently demand accountability and justice from the law. Not only had the perpetrator been excused from appearing before the court throughout the four-year-long trial process, but he was also excused from his sentence. This generates another issue regarding the fact that who awaits before the law is not the accused perpetrator. Rather, it is the Elvan family and their lawyers, the initiators of the legal proceedings, who have to wait for it to function to deliver accountability. While the Elvan family was present at every single hearing, waiting before the law, waiting for justice and accountability, the accused officer, Fatih Dalgalı, was exempt, excused from standing before the law. This dichotomy reveals a fundamental question regarding the state-violence trials: *Who is on trial?*

Waiting before the Law

Contrary to the perpetrator's ghostly presence/absence, the Elvan family has always been present at the hearings, waiting for the prosecution to proceed, waiting for a verdict, for accountability, waiting for justice. Since 2013 the family has been waiting for the law to operate. The act of waiting dominates and defines their experience. Their waiting is not only a reflection of the historical waiting for (divine) justice, but also reflects the experience of many others who are kept waiting by the legal processes of accountability in the aftermath of state violence in Turkey. 'A trial and a literary test do not aim at the same kind of conclusion. Nor do they strive toward the same kind of effect', writes Felman (1997), continuing, 'A trial is presumed to be a search for truth, but technically, it is a search for a decision, and this in essence, it seeks not simply truth but a finality: a force of resolution' (738). At the Elvan trial, however, what we witness is, rather, the absence of a resolution, despite a verdict. The court's verdict fails to conclude, which I read in terms of the legal repetition of failure that fails to *see* the violence. Hence, the absence of a resolution is a form of legal performance that fails to hold state violence accountable.

At first glance, such practices of failure may appear contradictory to the law and to its working principles as they indicate its impotence rather than its authoritative force. In the scholarship, the force, and hence the violence, of law is often considered in relation to its decision-making powers, either in terms of its 'naming practices' – as Butler (2020) points out, '"This will be law," or "This is now the law"' (124) – which is then followed by its defining powers, or, in terms of deciding on someone's fate, by uttering a verdict (see Cover 1986). However, what we witness in the Elvan trial is the suspension of a decision, a departure from naming and defining the powers of the law, which is common in state-violence trials. This suspension could also be understood as a decision itself, one that is not uttered but rather practiced through its failure. In that regard, I suggest that the Elvan trial exposes a form of legal violence that is specific to state-violence trials, which is yet to be explored in the scholarship and that operates in the form of legal action through inaction. Its violence manifests itself in the form of waiting, or rather through keeping the subject waiting. This violence emerges from the grey area of the possibility of justice, in Derridean (1992a) terms, when justice is always a possibility that is yet to come. If so, how to approach the law's silent violence, how to understand its static doings, how to see it and register it as a form of legal violence? Felman (1997) notes that, contrary to a trial's search for a decision, the occupation of 'a literary text is [...] a search for meaning, for expression, for heightened significance and for symbolic understanding', and she suggests that we 'make use of this difference [...] by reading them *across* each other and against each other' (738). To unpack the legal mechanism of waiting, I follow Felman's suggestion, and below I present an analysis of the Elvan family's waiting before the law through Franz Kafka's rich parable 'Before the Law' (2007, 171–172).

To begin with, a brief presentation of Kafka's parable: A countryman waits for his lifetime in front of a door to be admitted before the law. The door is guarded by a doorkeeper. When the countryman comes before the law and asks to be admitted, the doorkeeper does not reject the countryman's wish but leaves it open as a future possibility: '"That's possible," says the doorkeeper, "but not now"' (171). Although the door is never closed, the doorkeeper intimidates the countryman by stating, '"From room to room there are doorkeepers, each one mightier than the one before"' (ibid.). Thus, the countryman decides to wait for the doorkeeper's permission while thinking, 'the law is supposed to be open to anyone at any time' (ibid.). The doorkeeper interrogates him at times; however, the interrogations do not lead to his admission. As the countryman tries various ways to gain admission, he becomes fixated on the doorkeeper, forgetting the existence of others following the one in front of him. At the end of his life, the countryman wonders, 'Everyone wants to go to law, how is it then that over so many years no one but me has tried to gain admission?' (172). The parable ends with the doorkeeper's answer: '"No one else could gain admission here, because this entrance was intended for you alone. Now I am going to shut it"' (ibid.).

Indeed, as a literary text, the parable describes an exaggerated version of the Elvan family's experience of waiting before the law. However, its exaggerated account makes the legal mechanism of waiting intelligible. James R. Martel (2011) comments on what I note as an exaggerated account in Kafka's parable in relation to the *stuckness* of his characters: 'Rather than try to save his characters from their delusions, Kafka gives them over to them, but in such a way as to subvert and distort their object' (63). Indeed, Kafka's parable presents the mechanism of waiting through the subject's – the countryman's – experience, exposing the relationality between the law and the subject. In that regard, Kafka's parable corresponds with the Elvan family's experience of the law, in terms of their waiting in anticipation to reach the law, which attributes power to the law and, in a cyclical manner, transforms the subject. However, the parable's subversive potential is limited to its exposure of the law's waiting game in terms of its powers and violence. By destining his protagonist to wait unto death before the law, Kafka does not only close the door of the law but also closes the door to his subject's subversive potential. I elaborate on this potential further in reference to the Turkey-specific context. Before doing so, however, first I would like to expand the discussion on the legal mechanism of waiting and its violence to present a conceptual framework for the family's waiting before the law.

Derrida (1992b), in his reading of Kafka's parable, which was originally presented as a lecture in 1982,[28] refers to the parable as 'the story (of what never happens)' (206). This inaction, however, does not indicate a lack of legal violence: 'In fact, here is a situation where it is never a question of trial or judgement, nor of verdict or sentence, which is all the more terrifying. There is some law, some law which is not there but which exists. The judgement, however, does not arrive' (205). Derrida's quote is relevant to the violence that comes with the failure of the verdict in the Elvan case. Resembling the ghostly perpetrator, the law also gains phantom-like qualities due to its lack of materialisation. This phantom-like law haunts the family, as it haunts the countryman: 'The man from the country has not expected such trouble; the law is supposed to be open to anyone at any time, he thinks' (171). However, Derrida highlights the labyrinths of the law when he writes that 'one never accedes directly either to the law or to persons, one is never immediately before any of these authorities; as for the detour, it may be infinite: the very universality of the law exceeds all finite boundaries and thus carries this risk' (196). Derrida's comments on the law's infinite detours resonate with the Elvan case's long path from High Criminal Court to Supreme Court, from national jurisdiction to international jurisdiction. Indeed, the trial judge signals the endless detour at the end of the hearing on 5 February 2020, almost three years after the first hearing, which may be considered as a foreshadowing of what awaits the Elvan family. First, the trial judge made a *promising* statement stating that 'despite the obstacles, we have now completed 90% of the case file'. Although his statement anticipates an ending, a resolution, he continued by reminding the courtroom of its infiniteness: 'There are contesting issues on the case file which would be discussed among the high courts. The decision of this court is not final'. Reminiscent of the many doors, and doorkeepers, in Kafka's parable, the legal process in the Elvan case appears *as if* it is progressing from one stage to the other since 2013, while holding the Elvan family in suspense with its promise. Derrida (1992b) elaborates further on this matter:

> He [the countryman] wants to see or touch the law, he wants to approach and "enter" it, because perhaps he does not know that the law is not to be seen or touched but deciphered. This is perhaps the first sign of the law's inaccessibility, or of the delay it imposes upon the man from the country. The gate is not shut, it is "open as usual" (says the text), but the law remains inaccessible.
>
> (197)

28 Part of the French text was then published under the title 'Devant la loi' as a part of the *Royal Institute of Philosophy Lecture Series* (see Derrida 1983). In this work, I use the completed version that is published under the title 'Before the Law' in *Acts of Literature* (see Derrida 1992b).

Many questions arise from the juxtaposition of the open door of the law and its inaccessibility. Why does the countryman continue to wait in agony to be admitted rather than entering through the door? Why does the countryman not just leave? Interestingly, Derrida reads the countryman's act of waiting in anticipation as something related to his naivety, or even his ignorance,[29] rather than relating it to the legal operation itself. In a similar vein, Martel (2011) mentions the failures of Kafka's characters: 'Kafka's characters desperately try to conform to the various powers that they see as organizing their life, but they fail, usually miserably, in their attempt' (63). On the contrary, in reference to the discussion above, I read this failure as the failure of the law itself, which fails to account for the violence inflicted upon Berkin Elvan, which fails to see the perpetrator, which delivers an ineffective verdict ... etc. In other words, it is the law that fails to perform the powers it is set to perform. However, while I oppose projecting the law's failure to the family, I do recognise that the family's expectation of the law attributes power to the law. In a similar vein to the countryman's position, waiting before the law generates suspense in the sense of expectation and anticipation while holding the subjects in suspense. Furthermore, keeping the subjects waiting is not only a demonstration of legal power, but in a performative manner, it also attributes power to the law. As Butler (1999) observes, in reference to Derrida's reading of the parable:

> There the one who waits for the law, sits before the door of the law, attributes a certain force to the law for which one waits. The anticipation of an authoritative discourse of meaning is the means by which the authority is attributed and installed: the anticipation conjures its object.
>
> (xv)

Thus, as an awaiting apparatus, the law derives its power from the performance of waiting. To put it in terms of Kafka's parable, what establishes the law and what renders the countryman's waiting as an act of waiting before the law is the co-performance of the countryman and the doorkeeper. Their collective performance of waiting establishes the law, or rather, manifests the law.[30] In return, the act of waiting subjectifies and dominates the countryman and his life. In his reading of Kafka's parable, James R. Martel (2012) highlights how the act of waiting before the law transforms the subject by

29 Derrida (1992b) speculates on the countryman's literacy: 'Perhaps man is the man from the country as long as he cannot read; or, if knowing how to read, he is still bound up in unreadability within that very thing which appears to yield itself to be read' (197).

30 Derrida (1992b) also recognises that the doorkeeper, too, is waiting before the law with the countryman. The difference is, however, while the doorkeeper has his back to the door, in other words to the law, the countryman faces towards the law. Derrida reads this as the countryman's respect for the law (200).

rendering him 'an obedient subject, subordinate to and reflective of an absolute, sovereign authority in whose name he continues to wait' (71). However, if the subject's own waiting attributes power to law, then there must be a potential for its subversion. I argue that Martel fails to recognise this potential as he, like Derrida, considers the act of waiting before the law only as a passive act, something indicating the failure of the subject. At this point, I reiterate Butler's (2011) comments on Althusser's notion of *interpellation*, which is discussed in Chapter 1. Butler argues that compliance with the law also bears the potential of its 'rearticulation of the law against the authority of the one who delivers it' (82). Indeed, although I agree with Martel on the law's subjection through the mechanism of waiting, I observe both active and passive forms of waiting in the Elvan family's waiting before the law. On the one hand, they are kept waiting, pacified and subjectified by the waiting powers of the never-ending legal process; but, on the other hand, they actively engage with the law, through which the family transform their agency against the state, the law and its waiting powers. I read the passive and active forms of waiting in relation to two modalities of waiting that Peter D. Dwyer observes (2009): 'Situational waiting is an experience fully embedded in time. Existential waiting is seemingly removed from time or rather, from the meanings – linear and repetitive, yet endlessly consuming, consumed and irreversible' (21). In that regard, regarding the Elvan family's act of waiting, I understand situational waiting as active waiting and existential waiting as passive waiting, which corresponds to the passive waiting for justice to come. In the Elvan family's experience, both forms of waiting coexist; indeed, this significant pattern can be observed as a common trait in Turkey's state-violence trials.

Zerrin Özlem Biner and Özge Biner (2019), in their co-edited book on waiting, discuss different forms and practices of waiting in Turkey's particular socio-legal and political context.[31] In their interview with prominent philosophy professor Nilgün Toker, Toker elaborates on the powers of waiting and its use in authoritarian regimes (25–44). Although Toker suggests that, in Turkey, sovereign power over time functions through creating a regime of uncertainty, rather than a regime of waiting (29), nonetheless, she reads waiting as a sovereign tool that aims to diminish the agency of the waiting subject (27). Regarding the waiting subject, Toker highlights a separation between will and agency. According to Toker, waiting or being kept waiting, creates a gap between the will of the subject and their agency, as a result of which the subject cannot actualise their own will (ibid.). Thus far, Toker elaborates

31 Later, Biner and Biner (2021) in their editorial piece for the special issue of 'On the Politics of Waiting' in *Social Anthropology/Anthropologie Sociale*, elaborate in a similar manner. The special issue provides analysis on waiting in relation to different facets of war (Biner and Biner 2021).

her analysis in a similar vein to Derrida and Martel regarding the suppressive function of waiting on the agency of the waiting subject. However, according to Toker, and Zerrin and Özge Biner, the waiting subjects can transform themselves through action and reconstruct their agency (34). In that regard, contrary to Derrida and Martel, they not only recognise the active form of waiting but also provide a framework to register the transformation of the subject, which can resist its subordination.

Never-ending or inconclusive state-violence trials are common practices in Turkey's politico-legal culture. Surely, due to the statute of limitations, there is a tactical element in overstretching the time taken: the legal process becomes a never-ending, Kafkaesque spiral until the time bar expires. As discussed in the previous section, the legal process in the meantime ties itself in knots, making the event and the association between the event and the perpetrator(s) even more unintelligible. In doing so, the Kafkaesque legal procedure triggers *conspiratorial imagination*, as Ertür (2016) calls it, closing the gap between fact and fiction. When the law fails to see the violence, it repeats the past failures; as it does so, the case loses its singularity and becomes a piece in the history of state violence and its unaccountability. When the law turns a blind eye to the violence, the ghostly, almighty perpetrator, *the State* with the capital 'S' emerges, and waiting for justice gains a rather transcendental, existential, and hence impossible, meaning. Moreover, the subjects get stuck in this suspense: 'The law is transcendent and theological, and so always to come, always promised, because it is immanent, finite and so already past. Every "subject" is caught up in this aporetic structure in advance' (Derrida 1992a, 36).

It is possible to observe this passive and impossible form of waiting in the Elvan family's waiting. Moreover, the more they try to rupture this suspense – by appealing to various other legal means, such as the Constitutional Court – the more they are entangled with the law. Furthermore, not only does the process subjectify the Elvan family in terms of dominating their agency, but their persistent engagement, in juxtaposition with the absence of the perpetrator, causes a shift in roles. Berkin's sister Özge Elvan verbalised this shift during the press statement after the seventeenth hearing: 'It is us being prosecuted in that courtroom'.[32] Indeed, in 2021, Erdoğan opened a defamation case against Berkin Elvan's mother Gülsüm Elvan and father Sami Elvan for stating Erdoğan's responsibility in the killing of their son in a press statement following one of the hearings.[33] Elvan's sister's words and the case against the

32 See: 'Gülsüm Elvan: Yeter Artık Biz Kardeşçe Yaşamak İstiyoruz', *Bianet*, 23 September 2020. Accessed 28 September 2021. http://bianet.org/bianet/insan-haklari/231422-gulsum-elvan-yeter-artik-biz-kardesce-yasamak-istiyoruz.

33 See: Elvan Family Indictment: Republic of Turkey, Istanbul Office of the Chief Public Prosecutor, Investigation no: 2020/132869, Case no: 2021/36095, Indictment no: 2021/23370.

family echo Derrida's observations on Kafka's parable: 'but since he is *before* it because he cannot enter it, he is also *outside the law* (an outlaw)' (1992b, 204). However, if the law always subjectifies the subject as a suspect, can it be otherwise? In that regard, I consider the Elvan family's waiting before the law as an act that demystifies the law in terms of its authority and promise of justice.

Özgür Sevgi Göral (2019) elaborates on the act of 'waiting for justice' in relation to the cases of enforced disappearances in Turkey in the 1990s (45–85). Göral suggests that the relatives of the forcibly disappeared endure different modes of waiting as time passes, from waiting for their relatives to come back alive to waiting for their bones (55–60). Throughout this time, Göral observes a change in the meaning of the perpetrator. She suggests that while, in the first stages of waiting, the perpetrator refers to those who actively carried out the act of kidnapping and killing, at the final stages of the waiting, however, the perpetrator stands for the whole state (58–59). I interpret this expansion in the meaning of 'perpetrator' in relation to unaccountability; as the law fails to account for and register the violence inflicted on their relatives, the meaning of the perpetrator expands to cover all state structures. As more and more state institutions and officers contribute to *juridical blindness*, it becomes harder to distinguish the juridical repetition of violence from the initial act of violence. Göral's observation on the expansion of the meaning of the perpetrator presents a lens for us to comprehend the Elvan family's wish to prosecute the state. The more they are kept waiting before the law, the more meanings are attached to the figure of the perpetrator. As time passes, the perpetrator becomes a ghostly haunting figure and becomes synonymous with the omnipotent and omnipresent state. *How many officers does it take to prosecute the state?* Moreover, interestingly, Göral refers to the relatives' waiting for justice as an impossible demand while adding that the relatives would never stop their search for justice despite recognising the impossibility of their action. Göral reads their persistent search for justice as a form of resistance against the state's erasure of the disappeared subject (79).[34] In another article, Göral (2021) expands on the transformation of the waiting subject; she writes:

> The subjectivities of the relatives of the disappeared are shaped, maintained and changed through the temporality of enforced waiting imposed by the state. Yet the temporal subjectivity of the close relatives of the disappeared is also shaped by their determination to wait, which is conceived as an act of loyalty, hope and persistence.
>
> (805)

34 Göral (2019) raises this point in reference to Banu Bargu's work on the matter. See Bargu 2015.

I suggest that what Göral observes is not a dilemma that indicates the *stuckness* of the subject, but, rather, it is an act of disobedience which bears the potential to rupture the mystical authority of the law and the state. Surely, on the one hand, as Toker raises, the relatives of the enforced disappearances need an official recognition (Biner and Biner 2019, 35). They need the bones of their relatives almost as a gesture of a confession from the state, which would serve as a recognition and acceptance of the fact that their relatives were forcibly disappeared. In relation to the both passive and active forms of waiting that I observe in the Elvan family's waiting, Göral too observes similar temporal modalities of waiting, and she suggests that '[w]aiting, thus, is a dynamic process, including different degrees of hope, expectation and anxiety as well as different degrees of passivity and activity' (805). On the other hand, however, as both Toker (Biner and Biner 2019) and Göral (2019, 2021) highlight, the relatives of the forcibly disappeared have transformed and reconstructed their agency against the subordination of waiting under the name of the *Saturday Mothers* (Cumartesi Anneleri).[35] I observe such a transformation of subjectivity in the Elvan family's waiting. On the one hand, they engage with the law to gain an official recognition of the violence that is inflicted upon their son; on the other hand, their persistent presence threatens the mythical powers of the law and the state. Their wait, although impossible, does not pacify or subordinate their agency, but rather, their persistent wait holds the law accountable.

Although, as Göral (2021) also identifies, waiting, or rather keeping the justice-seeking subject waiting, appears as a specific form of legal violence in state-violence cases (811), the family's exhausting and most probably lifelong struggle exposes the failures of the law: its mundane *juridical blindness*. This exposure liberates the facts and the truth from being held hostage under the legal narrative. Surely, the law and legal processes of accountability may serve as an official validation of the truth. Perhaps this is the only potential of justice that the law and legal procedures of accountability bear in state-violence cases. Law, as the storyteller, has the potential to narrate history from the perspective of the dead and to resist violent forces which aim to erase the dead from history. Law could borrow its authority from the dead: 'Death is the sanction of everything that the storyteller can tell. He has borrowed his authority from death' (Benjamin 2015, 93). However, we, as the witnesses of violence, do not need the law to account for the violence. Thus, in the Berkin Elvan trial, the law prosecutes itself, and it is Elvan family who holds the law to account.

35 Relatives of the forcibly disappeared have been gathering in Istanbul at Galatasaray Square every Saturday since 27 March 1995, hence being known by the name Saturday Mothers. For more on the Saturday Mothers, see Ahiska 2014.

References

Ahiska, Meltem. 2014. 'Counter-Movement, Space and Politics: How the Saturday Mothers of Turkey Make Enforced Disappearances Visible'. In *Space and the Memories of Violence,* edited by Estela Schindel and Pamela Colombo. London: Palgrave Macmillan. 162–175.

Austin, J. L. 1975. *How to Do Things with Words.* Oxford: Oxford University Press.

Bargu, Banu. 2015. 'Sovereignty as Erasure: Rethinking Enforced Disappearances'. *Qui Parle* 23(1): 35–75.

Benjamin, Walter. 2007. 'Critique of Violence'. In *Reflections: Essays, Aphorisms, Autobiographical Writings.* New York: Harcourt Inc. 277–300.

Benjamin, Walter. 2015. 'The Storyteller'. *Illuminations.* London: Penguin. 83–107.

Biner, Zerrin Özlem, and Özge Biner. 2019. 'Nilgün Toker'le Beklemeye Dair....' In *Beklerken: Zamanın Bilgisi ve Öznenin Dönüşümü.* Istanbul: İletişim. 25–44.

Biner and Biner 2021. 'Introduction: On the Politics of Waiting'. *Social Anthropology/ Anthropologie Sociale* 29(3): 787–799.

Butler, Judith. 1990. 'Deconstruction and the Possibility of Justice: Comments on Bernasconi, Cornell Miller, Weber'. *Cardozo Law Review* 11(5–6): 1715–1718.

Butler, Judith. 1999. *Gender Trouble: Feminism and the Subversion of Identity.* New York and Oxford: Routledge.

Butler, Judith. 2011. *Bodies That Matter: On the Discursive Limits of 'Sex'.* Oxford: Routledge.

Butler, Judith. 2020. *The Force of Non-Violence: An Ethico-Political Bind.* London: Verso.

Cornell, Drucilla. 1990. 'The Violence of the Masquerade: Law Dressed Up as Justice'. *Cardozo Law Review* 11(5–6): 1047–1064.

Cover, R. M. 1986. 'Violence and the Word'. *The Yale Law Journal* 95: 1601–1629.

Derrida, Jacques. 1983. 'Devant la Loi' *Royal Institute of Philosophy Lectures* 16: 173–188.

Derrida, Jacques. 1992a. 'Force of Law: The "Mystical Foundation of Authority". In *Deconstruction and the Possibility of Justice,* edited by David Gray Carlson, Drucilla Cornell and Michel Rosenfeld. New York and London: Routledge. 3–67.

Derrida, Jacques. 1992b. 'Before the Law'. In *Acts of Literature,* edited by Derek Attridge. New York: Routledge. 181–220.

Dwyer, Peter D. 2009. 'Worlds of Waiting'. In *Waiting,* edited by Ghassan Hage. Victoria: Melbourne University Press. 15–26.

Ertür, Başak. 2016. 'The Conspiracy Archive: Turkey's "Deep State" on Trial'. In *Law, Memory, Violence,* edited by Stewart Motha and Honni van Rijswijk Oxford: Routledge. 177–194.

Ertür, Başak. 2022. *Spectacles and Spectres: A Performative Theory of Political Trials.* New York: Fordham University Press.

Felman, Shoshana. 1997. 'Forms of Juridical Blindness, or the Evidence of What Cannot Be Seen: Traumatic Narratives and Legal Repetitions in the O.J. Simpson Case and in Tolstoy's "The Kreutzer Sonata"'. *Critical Inquiry* 23(4): 738–788.

Felman, Shoshana. 2002. *The Juridical Unconscious: Trials and Traumas in the Twentieth Century.* London: Harvard University Press.

Foucault, Michel. 2009. *Security, Territory, Population: Lectures at the Collége de France, 1977–78.* Edited by Michel Senellart. Translated by Graham Burchell. Hampshire and New York: Palgrave Macmillan.

Gordon, Avery F. 2008. *Ghostly Matters: Haunting and the Sociological Imagination.* Minneapolis and London: University of Minnesota Press.

Göral, Özgür Sevgi. 2019. '"İmkansız Bir Talep" Olarak Adaleti Beklemek: Kaybedilenler ve Yakınları'. In *Beklerken: Zamanın Bilgisi ve Öznenin Dönüşümü,* edited by Zerrin Özlem Biner and Özge Biner. Istanbul: İletişim. 45–85.

Göral, Özgür Sevgi. 2021. 'Waiting for the Disappeared: Waiting as a Form of Resilience and the Limits of Legal Space in Turkey'. *Social Anthropology/Anthropologie Sociale* 29(3): 800–815.

Haldar, Piyel. 2008. 'Law and the Evidential Image' *Law, Culture and the Humanities* 4: 139–155.

Kafka, Franz. 2007. 'Before the Law'. In *Metamorphosis and Other Stories,* translated by Michael Hofmann. Great Britain: Penguin Books. 171–172.

Martel, James R. 2011. *Textual Conspiracies: Walter Benjamin, Idolatry, and Political Theory.* Ann Arbor, MI: University of Michigan Press.

Martel, James R. 2012. *Divine Violence: Walter Benjamin and the Eschatology of Sovereignty.* Oxon: Routledge.

Sarat, Austin. 2001. 'Situating Law Between the Realities of Violence and the Claims of Justice'. In *Law, Violence, and the Possibilities of Justice.* Princeton, NJ: Princeton University Press.

Vismann, Cornelia. 2008. *Files: Law and Media Technology.* Stanford, CA: Stanford University Press.

Conclusion

Awaiting

The chant 'The murderer state will be held to account' captured the sentiments that were expressed during Elvan's funeral ceremony. Although I have chanted this slogan countless times before within large crowds of protestors, perhaps being in an observer position this time allowed me to reflect on its meanings. The familiarity of the chant was a painful reminder of the repetitive nature of state violence and its unaccountability. In reference to the global and Turkey-specific political and legal history of state violence and its legal address, we knew very well the trajectory of the legal process before it began to unfold. *What is the reason behind this familiar repetition?*

I wondered whether something else is repeated here, something which manifests in the form of violence and unaccountability. The chant not only communicated the demand for accountability but also referred to the state as the murderer. Although I do not dispute this conclusion that the state was responsible for Elvan's death, I wondered, when an act of violence is associated with the state, hence recognised as state violence, what assumptions are made about the state and its violence that make this association possible? Furthermore, I wondered whether the repetition of state violence and its unaccountability have something to do with the meanings and assumptions attributed to the state. I wondered whether the historic murderer signifies the assumption of an omnipotent and omnipresent, all-powerful entity, 'the State', which hides the ones who enact violence on its behalf, hence resulting in unaccountability. If so, how come the state appears in such a form, and how does it materialise through violence, and specifically through police violence? Thus, I have posed the question: *How do the meanings and assumptions concerning state violence impact the political demands and legal processes of accountability?*

By focusing on the myths and assumptions that encircle the state and its violence, I have aimed to discover connections between the state, law and violence which produce a repetition of unaccountability that escapes from institution-orientated analyses. Instead of tracing the ontological roots of the state to explain its violent manifestations and legal unaccountability, this book followed the ghosts of state violence and their hauntings. In *Specters of*

DOI: 10.4324/9781032690070-6

Marx, Derrida (2006) writes, '[t]o haunt does not mean to be present, and it is necessary to introduce haunting into the very construction of a concept. Of every concept, beginning with the concepts of being and time. That is what we would be calling here a hauntology' (202). Following ghosts, myths and assumptions allow us to register the ghostly, mythical character of the state while registering the material impact of its violent manifestations, and the challenges this juxtaposition imposes on the legal processes of accountability.

In my efforts to answer the issue of the unaccountability of state violence, I traced the case of Berkin Elvan, the fourteen-year-old boy who was killed by the police during the nationwide protests of the summer of 2013 in Turkey. By offering a detailed study of one case, I proposed to shift the focus from institutions to subjects. In so doing, I not only aim to stress the central role of the subject — as the ones who acclaim the state and its killing powers, and the ones subjected to it — but also to highlight the subject's central role in the social and political lives of the institutions. Conducting a detailed analysis of one particular case, from the moment of the emergence of state violence to the legal process, allowed me to unearth many meanings attributed to the state and our expectations of the law. I could register how these meanings and expectations are formed in relation to the different subject positions, which exposed a mutual (re)construction of the state and the subject. From this perspective, it was also possible to trace the role of the mythical state on the public demands for accountability and on political and legal responses to such demands. I argued that the mythical imaginary of the state exposes a particular challenge not because there is no one to hold to account but rather because it hides the ones who must be held accountable. Thus, I also aimed to unveil the subject from the disguise of the mythical constellation of the state and its institutions. By placing the subject at the centre, I have carried out a three-dimensional analysis, which accounts for the many meanings attributed to the state, their impact on the demands and legal processes of accountability and the transformation of the subject in relation to the state and law.

Drawing from critical literature on the state and its powers (Taussig 1992; Navaro-Yashin 2002; Aretxaga 2005, Rose 1996), I argued that the state is not a fixed reality, but rather a political, legal and social imaginary construct that is animated through the subject and the subjects' performances. Certainly, the police officer is not an ordinary subject. The disproportional power dynamic between the police and other subjects is caused by the separation between sanctioned and unsanctioned violence. The police officer, as the subject who holds the legal right to issue violence, in turn demands and expects obedience from those whose violence is illegal. In that regard, any encounter with the police serves as a reminder of the possibility of sanctioned, unaccounted, state violence. The police officer is the embodiment of this reminder, which is often visible through the gear and uniforms of the police forces. Hence it is, through this reminder of legitimate violence, that the state materialises on the body of the police officer. This book argues, however, that this grim scenario does not affirm the absoluteness of the state and its killing powers but rather indicates a political and legal imaginary of such an absolute power. Thus, the book approaches police violence from a fresh perspective and argues that the police operate through a fantasy of such a power while expecting obedience from the subjects and performing violence on behalf of an imaginary higher subject, *the State*.

The task of analysing state/police violence and its unaccountability, then, requires us to consider the mythical construction of the state, rather than adopting it as a fixed reality. The state, as a modern political and legal construct, has a mythical bodily imaginary that is often expressed by the term *body politic*. The bodily imaginary of the state suggests a unified, omnipotent and omnipresent power that is situated between the godly and the worldly. It is human-like, but also all of its organs work in a machine-like harmony which stands for an analogy for state institutions and bureaucracy. This mythical construction of the state establishes the foundation of our modern political and legal systems. Furthermore, the state's monopoly on violence is legitimised and repeatedly performed to sustain the political and legal systems founded on this assumption. It is possible to argue that the issue of unaccountability begins here, as the law grants killing powers to this ambiguous higher subject called the state but does not address the question of how it could be held accountable. Moreover, the figure of the body appears to play a significant role in establishing the association between police violence and state violence. When the police perform violence on behalf of the state, the police derive their killing powers from an assumed higher subject of the state. The police embody the state through the bodily overlap between the imaginary body of the state and the material body of the police officer. When a police officer enacts violence on behalf of the state, the mythical body of the state manifests through the material body of the police officer, which, in return, renders the police officer invisible.

The police and their violence have become a part of life as they operate within the everyday life of a state. Rather than an outside enemy, police violence is directed towards the lives of the subjects within the territorial bounds of a state. The constant threat of police violence is camouflaged within the cities. Police are faceless figures, and the uniformity of their uniforms brings anonymity. Thus, as Walter Benjamin (2007) and Jacques Derrida (1992a) highlight, police violence has a ghostly presence. Walter Benjamin's analysis of police violence allows us to comprehend the significant character and operation of police violence through registering its double function; one that establishes the law and the other that sustains it, or to put it in Benjaminian terms, *law-making* and *law-preserving* functions of violence. This significant combination makes police violence even more arbitrary, and, when combined with its ghostliness, I argued, police violence disguises itself as fate.

Indeed, the then-Prime Minister, now-President, R.T. Erdoğan, interpreted Elvan's killing by the police precisely as his deadly fate. In his response to the death of Elvan, Erdoğan evoked Turkey's state imaginary, the *father-state*, which initially materialised in the figure of modern Turkey's founding father M.K. Atatürk. The theoretical framework on performative utterances (Austin 1975; Butler 1990, 1999, 2003; Cavell 2005; Constable 2015; Sedwick 2003) revealed to us how Erdoğan's rally speech reconstructed the state as he performed his rally speech, which I referred to as a *stately performative*. It is possible to observe a double construction in his *stately performative*. By evoking the mythical imaginary of the *father-state*, on the one hand, Erdoğan aimed to (re)construct the damaged authority of the state after the Gezi protests and the subsequent corruption scandals, while, on the other hand, to consolidate his own authority through embodying the figure of the *father-state* himself. His paternalistic address exposed a meaning of the state specific to Turkey, which is situated in between the sovereign right to kill and the paternal right to punish. According to Erdoğan's *stately performative*, Elvan was a disobedient son of the *father-state* whose death was a fateful outcome of his own disobedience and, thus, did not require accountability.

Thus, at first glance there appears to be an irreconcilable difference in meanings attributed to the state and to its violence, which results in a dispute over the need for accountability between the ones who claim to speak and act on behalf of the state and the others who are excluded from this imaginary and, thus, subjected to the violent manifestations of the state. This difference bears the potential to transform into a violent contestation. This is how I understand the People's Front's hostage-taking of the prosecutor Selim Kiraz, who was the head prosecutor of the Elvan case at the time. Through their violent action, the People's Front militants claimed to bring justice to Berkin Elvan. Indeed, there is an element of revenge in their counter-violence; however, I argued the action challenges the mythical imaginary of the state and exposes the limits of its legally constructed monopoly on violence and law. The sardonic tone of the hostage-takers could be understood in this regard, that their action itself was a mockery of the state and of its ostensibly omnipotent, omnipresent powers. The People's Front's hostage-taking action served as a reminder that, although the state claims to hold the monopoly on law, and hence, legal accountability, the notion of accountability exceeds those institutional limits. Accountability is a social concept; recalling the chant, the state and its institutions are not the only actors or enactors of accountability.

This is also why the book grounds its inquiry in the notion of accountability and not in that of impunity. I understand the demands for accountability after the death of Elvan as a social demand which is related to social demands of peace and justice. Beyond the issue of punishing the perpetrators, accountability refers to a process that consists of facing the past, accepting wrongdoing and setting up systems to avoid its repetition. Thus, when the institutions fail to satisfy the social and public demands of accountability, the institutions and their authorities would be challenged. This challenge may come in different forms, whether in the form of public protests or riots, as we have witnessed globally, or in the form of directed actions such as in the case of the People's Front's hostage-taking. Nonetheless, they are always violent events as they respond, *counter*, the initial (state) violence. This violence can be directed towards one's own self, as in self-sacrificial actions, or towards the other. I have read the hostage-taking as a combination of the two, that it was a self-sacrificial action which was directed towards the other, or to put it in other words, it was an action directed towards the other which was only made possible by the militants' self-sacrifice. Within this constellation, the book discloses an intimate association of the subject to the collective demands of accountability: *What makes someone sacrifice their life to bring justice for the dead?*

What caught my attention in the hostage-taking action was the transformation of the subject, which I unpacked through Sophocles's figure of Antigone. The hostage-takers were tied to Elvan through a non-traditional kinship bond, which transformed the militants into *militant-martyrs*. The kinship between the militants and Elvan was not based upon their membership of the People's Front, as state officials argued, but, rather, was founded upon their vulnerable position against the state. As working-class young males who are Alevi and/or Kurdish, they were registered as potential disobedient subjects of the *father-state*. The militants' demand to be addressed as Berkin (Elvan) during the negotiations could be understood in that regard: that the militants' embodiment of Elvan was possible due to their shared subjectivity. Indeed, their insistence in referring to Elvan by his forename, Berkin, is an expression of this kinship, claiming Elvan's subjectivity through familiarity. I argued that their self-sacrificial action was both a re-enactment of Elvan's deadly fate but also, similar to Antigone taking her own life, the militants attained agency over their own fate. In the economy of Turkey's nation-state, their fate was already a deadly one. The militants opposed their subjection and performed their agency by deciding on their own deadly fate while transforming their bodies into *human weapons* (Bargu 2014). Although their hostage-taking was an act of disobedience, it nonetheless appropriated the deadly fate that was attributed to them by the *father-state*. My criticism here is of the subject's acceptance of its own subjection. Although the hostage-takers exposed the mythical construction of the state's monopoly on violence and law through their parodic repetition, nonetheless, their action failed to break off from the chains of the state's (deadly) subjection.

It is possible to recognise this double move of rejection and appropriation in the militants' demand and act of justice as well. On the one hand, the militants opposed the unified imaginary of the state by challenging its monopoly on violence and law; on the other hand, they appropriated the state's monopoly on violence and law for their own cause. This double movement can be understood in terms of a parodic repetition of the state which contains the potential of its subversion; however, this also runs the danger of reconstructing it as a bad fetish, *maleficium* (Taussig 1992). Thus, reinstating the mythical imaginary of the omnipotent and omnipresent state.

Moreover, the action was a direct violence towards the prosecutor and a direct threat to his life. This was not a misdirection, but rather, a manoeuvre which exposed the associations between police violence and legal violence. Police violence, when left unaccounted for by the law, continues in the form of legal violence. For the militants, the prosecutor was an accomplice. The hostage-takers demanded the identities of the police officers who were involved in Elvan's killing while threatening the life of the prosecutor. In so doing, the militants were asking for the state to choose between the police and the law. The hostage-takers' mocking tone was noticeable here: *who is more valuable? Your murderer police, and the ones who gave the orders, or your precious prosecutor? It's yours to decide.* Perhaps the mocking tone bears a tragic insight that the law's function is to protect the state's monopoly on violence, which the prosecutor performs with his life. The disposability of the prosecutor has a glorified position within the *father-state* through the discourses of martyrdom. As both the prosecutor's father and Erdoğan praised the prosecutor, and glorified his death, I argued the *father-state's* love is also deadly in that it demands sacrifice from the devoted sons of the *father-state*; the ones who acclaim the state and who claim to act on behalf of the state.

The legal process in the aftermath of Elvan's killing allows us to discover how the mythical imaginary of the state and its violent performance associate with law. The mythical construction of the state brings a particular challenge to the legal process, not because there is no one to hold to account but rather the mythical imaginary of the state hides the ones who must be held accountable. The public demands for accountability and the Elvan family were not satisfied with the prosecution of one police officer, Fatih Dalgalı, who enacted violence, and instead they have been demanding for the state to be held accountable. However, the legal process fails to recognise the responsibility of the state. As the perpetrator-subjects hide behind the imaginary subject of the state, their violent acts are left unrecognised and unaccounted. Thus, the legal processes of accountability often result in unaccountability and are experienced as a form of legal violence by those who appeal to the law while seeking justice.

What requires our attention as legal scholars is the common operational pattern of waiting and suspense. While the mythical imaginary of the state keeps the law in suspense, the law, or rather the legal process, keeps those waiting in anticipation of justice and accountability. Law's waiting game has also been observed by Özgür Sevgi Göral (2019, 2021) in relation to the trials concerning enforced disappearances in Turkey; however, the legal operations of waiting and suspense are yet to be developed further within legal scholarship as a part of the repertoire of legal performance. In the literature, legal performance is understood in terms of law's authoritative norm-making and decision-making powers. Thus, legal violence is commonly understood in terms of law's authoritative performance of sentencing: in other words, uttering a verdict. What, rather, we observe in legal processes of accountability after police violence, or state violence in general, is the silent operation of legal violence through the suspension of legal performative: when the law decides not to speak, not to utter a verdict, not to deliver its violence to the accused, in other words not to account for the violence that was inflicted on the victims of police (state) violence. As a result, what we globally observe in state-violence trials is a prolonged legal process which cripples itself; the law performs its own failure.

This book has argued that the legal process in state-violence trials exposes a function of the law which I refer to as the *waiting apparatus*, as it keeps the ones who demand justice waiting in anticipation. Waiting before the law, (trans)forms the subject as it is observed through the Elvan family's waiting. As I explored through the critical literature on Kafka's 'Before the Law' parable (Derrida 1992b; Martel 2011, 2012), waiting may indicate a passive form, in which the law acquires its power through subordinating the subject in an eternal wait. However, as I argued through the Elvan family's engagement with the law, in reference to the many others before them, the subject's waiting is not only pacifying. It would be wrong to claim that the ones who seek justice, or accountability, after state violence via legal means are not aware of the law's false promise of justice. Especially when certain groups of people who have been systematically targeted by state violence are considered, such as in the case of Berkin Elvan's killing, I find such an argument patronising. Everywhere, people who are disproportionately targeted by the fatal politics of the state do have a collective memory of how the law operates in the aftermath of such violence. Their anticipation of justice is not an outcome of naivety or ignorance, but rather, it is an outcome of a necessity, an urgency for change, for breaking the cycle, for justice. That is precisely why their waiting practices are not only passive but consist of active resistance against the pacifying subjection of the law's waiting game. The Elvan family's active waiting practices have been transforming their subjectivity and resisting their subordination. The Elvan family's persistent engagement with the law has been challenging the legal repetition of unaccountability, as their actions do not allow the law to close the case in silence. Thus, the Elvan family's legal battle for holding the state into account also holds the law to account. The Elvan family, together with others who have lost their loved ones to state violence, has been performing their resistance and persistence. They turn to the public and generate a public discussion on police/state violence and its unaccountability. I argue their active engagement with the law bears the potential of rethinking and reconstructing accountability from a subject-oriented perspective.

Thus this book offered an analysis of state violence and its unaccountability by repositioning the subject at its centre. Through the Elvan case, I aimed to demonstrate that the subject is situated at the centre of the matter; as it is the subject who performs state violence, who is affected by state violence and who objects to state violence and demands accountability, and it is the subject who acknowledges and accounts for state violence. The book exposes the necessity of pursuing a subject-orientated approach, which enables us to consider the mythical foundations of the political and legal institutions through the subjects' performances. It is argued that, in so doing, it is possible to address the contradictions within the legal and political mechanisms of accountability, which result in the repetitive cycle of state violence and unaccountability. This work, on the one hand, exposes the limits of political and legal institutions in delivering accountability, but, on the other hand, opens up a path to new possibilities for understanding and performing accountability which would not exclude the subject from the process.

Echoing the Elvan family's wish to prosecute Erdoğan and other state officials, I argue that the subject-orientated perspective does not mean that we, the witnesses of state violence, should stop demanding that the law recognises and holds to account the organised nature of state violence. Legal recognition is necessary for personal and public healing, peacebuilding and social justice. Current demands of abolishing or defunding the police could be considered as an outcome of such a search for measures which would break the repetition of police violence. Indeed, the abolitionist project has been a significant source of exposing how law subjectifies certain groups of people while disclosing the continuities between colonial practices and contemporary policing and incarceration practices in today's criminal justice system. Although it was beyond the scope of this book, I consider the questions raised in this book regarding state violence and unaccountability as part of the current debates led by the abolitionist project. This is something I briefly touched upon in relation to the deadly fate of Berkin Elvan and the People's Front militants. Indeed, the fact that all Gezi martyrs were young men with working-class, Alevi or Kurdish backgrounds displays a continuity which resembles the continuum that the abolitionist project brings to our attention. Turkey's politico-legal history is full of examples of unchecked, unaccounted-for systematic violence inflicted upon excluded groups. While the ghosts of the ones who forcibly disappeared in the 1990s still linger among us, addressing the issue of accountability for the dead, for those who were killed by the ones who acclaim state and perform violence on behalf of the state, appears to be more and more urgent each day to enable public healing, peacebuilding and social justice. Justice does not wait ... yet we are awaiting. As we wait in defiance, the mythical imaginary of the state and its institutions unravel before our eyes. To end with Avery F. Gordon's (2008) words: 'The task then remains to follow the ghosts and spells of power in order to tame this sorcerer and conjure otherwise' (28).

References

Aretxaga, Begoña. 2005. *States of Terror: Begoña Aretxaga's Essays*. Edited by Joseba Zulaika. Nevada: Center for Basque Studies.

Austin, J. L. 1975. *How to Do Things with Words*. Oxford: Oxford University Press.

Bargu, Banu. 2014. *Starve and Immolate: The Politics of Human Weapon*. New York: Columbia University Press.

Benjamin, Walter. 2007. 'Critique of Violence'. In *Reflections: Essays, Aphorisms, Autobiographical Writings*. New York: Harcourt Inc. 277–300.

Butler, Judith. 1990. 'Performative Acts and Gender Construction: An Essay in Phenomenology and Feminist Theory'. In *Performing Feminisms: Feminist Critical Theory and Theatre,* edited by Sue-Ellen Case. Baltimore: The John Hopkins University Press. 270–282.

Butler, Judith 1999. *Gender Trouble: Feminism and the Subversion of Identity*. New York and Oxford: Routledge.

Butler, Judith. 2003. 'Afterword'. In Shoshana Felman. *The Scandal of the Speaking Body: Don Juan with J.L Austin, or Seduction in Two Languages*. Stanford, CA: Stanford University Press. 113–123.

Cavell, Stanley. 2005. 'Performative and Passionate Utterance'. In *Philosophy the Day After Tomorrow*. Cambridge, MA: Harvard University Press. 155–191.

Constable, Marianne. 2015. *Our Word Is Our Bond: How Legal Speech Acts*. Stanford, CA: Stanford University Press.

Derrida, Jacques. 1992a. 'Force of Law: The "Mystical Foundation of Authority"'. In *Deconstruction and the Possibility of Justice,* edited by David Gray Carlson, Drucilla Cornell and Michel Rosenfeld. New York and London: Routledge. 3–67.

Derrida, Jacques. 1992b. 'Before the Law'. In *Acts of Literature,* edited by Derek Attridge. New York: Routledge. 181–220.

Derrida, Jacques. 2006. *Specters of Marx: The State of Debt, the Work of Mourning and the New International*. New York and London: Routledge.

Gordon, Avery, F. 2008. *Ghostly Matters Haunting and the Sociological Imagination*. Minneapolis: University of Minnesota Press.

Göral, Özgür Sevgi. 2019. '"İmkansız Bir Talep" Olarak Adaleti Beklemek: Kaybedilenler ve Yakınları'. In *Beklerken: Zamanın Bilgisi ve Öznenin Dönüşümü,* edited by Zerrin Özlem Biner and Özge Biner. Istanbul: İletişim. 45–85.

Göral, Özgür Sevgi. 2021. 'Waiting for the Disappeared: Waiting as a Form of Resilience and the Limits of Legal Space in Turkey'. *Social Anthropology/ Anthropologie Sociale* 29(3): 800–815.

Martel, James R. 2011. *Textual Conspiracies: Walter Benjamin, Idolatry, and Political Theory*. Ann Arbor, MI: University of Michigan Press.

Martel, James R. 2012. *Divine Violence: Walter Benjamin and the Eschatology of Sovereignty*. Oxon: Routledge.

Navaro-Yashin, Yael. 2002. *Faces of the State: Secularism and Public Life in Turkey*. Princeton, NJ: Princeton University Press.

Rose, Jacqueline. 1996. *States of Fantasy*. New York: Oxford University Press.

Sedwick, Eve Kosofsky. 2003. *Touching Feeling: Affect, Pedagogy, Performativity*. Durham: Duke University Press.

Taussig, Michael. 1992. *The Nervous System*. New York and London: Routledge.

Index

FSC
www.fsc.org
MIX
Papier | Fördert
gute Waldnutzung
FSC® C083411

Kolibri 360 GmbH
Ferdinand-Jühlke-Straße 7
99095 Erfurt, Deutschland
produktsicherheit@kolibri360.de